THE TEXTILE MUSEUM JOURNAL 1999-2000

VOLUMES 38 AND 39

CONTENTS

75th
1925 2000
ANNIVERSARY
THE TEXTILE MUSEUM

2320 S STREET NW WASHINGTON DC 20008-4088
www.textilemuseum.org

Marion Stirling in 1939 at
the camp of Tres Zapotes,
Veracruz where the Stirlings
found the first of the great
Olmec heads. Photo by
Richard Hewitt Stewart.

Marion Stirling Pugh (1911-2001)

The Textile Museum has lost a Trustee who shaped the direction of the Museum for over thirty years and who was the last direct link to the Museum's founder, George Hewitt Myers. Profoundly interested in the art and history of weaving, Marion Pugh was a Trustee of The Textile Museum from 1968, serving as Secretary, Treasurer, Vice President, and President.

Marion was just shy of her 90th birthday when she died in Tucson after an extraordinarily productive life that saw continuing accomplishment in a variety of scholarly disciplines ranging from archaeology to geography.

She was born Marion Illig on May 12, 1911, in Middletown, New York, the daughter of Louis and Lena Randall Illig. In 1930, Marion received her BS degree from Rider College, and afterward moved to Washington, DC, where she attended George Washington University from 1931 to 1933. During this time Marion also worked at the Smithsonian Institution's Bureau of American Ethnology as secretary to Matthew W. Stirling, Director of the Bureau. On December 11, 1933, Marion and Matthew were married.

Together the Stirlings shared a career of archaeological adventure and discovery, beginning with a series of joint National Geographic Society-Smithsonian Institution expeditions to explore the little-known ruins of Mexico's Gulf Coast regions between 1938 and 1946. These journeys by Marion, Matthew, and National Geographic photographer Richard Hewitt Stewart took place mainly by boat and horseback through the humid rain forests of Veracruz and Tabasco states. Despite the physical difficulties, the expeditions proved successful beyond all expectations, for they revealed and recorded a truly lost civilization—the Olmec, producers of the famed colossal heads of stone and other remains, dated to around the beginning of the first millennium B.C., that proved it to be one of the earliest high cultures in all of the Americas.

From the Mexican work the Stirlings and Stewart moved on to other areas of the hemisphere, including Ecuador, Panama, and Costa Rica. The results of these expeditions appeared regularly as articles by Marion, Matthew, or both in the *National Geographic Magazine, Américas,* and other journals. In 1941, Marion shared with Matthew the prestigious Franklin L. Burr Award of the National Geographic Society.

Marion's ever-broadening interests are reflected in her memberships in the Association of American Geographers and the Society of Woman Geographers, where she served on the Executive Council in 1954, and as President, 1960-63 and 1969-72.

Matthew Stirling died in 1975. One of Marion's prized possessions was a silver pendant that Matthew had made for her in Mexico, embossed with a jaguar mask on the obverse and the date of a stele whose date she decoded on the reverse.

In 1979 Marion married Major General John Ramsey Pugh, the son-in-law of George Hewitt Myers, who was active himself in the work of The Textile Museum. Together they made their home at Little Fiddlers Green, General Pugh's family estate in Round Hill, Virginia. They updated this stone house dating from 1770 to pursue their interests, building a library for their books and memorabilia, and a lap swimming pool.

Marion's interest in Mexican textiles led her to establish the Mexican Research Fund at The Textile Museum for the purchase of textiles for the collection. She both contributed to this fund and also asked that gifts in expression of sympathy on the death of Matthew Stirling be made to it. In 1979, General and Mrs. Pugh broadened the scope of the fund and it was accordingly renamed the Latin American Research Fund. Marion endowed this fund in December 1993. The fund has been the Museum's only source of purchase funds for textiles in this area, making possible many significant additions to the collections from Guatemala, Ecuador, Peru, and Bolivia as well as Mexico. Purchases have been made of material collected in the field in the course of textile research in each of these countries and outstanding examples offered by dealers. Marion also supported other Western Hemisphere Department projects such as fieldwork by curator Ann Rowe in Ecuador, and a forthcoming publication on Q'ero textiles from the Cuzco area of Peru.

Art and adventure were Marion's pursuits. We do well to follow in her footsteps.

Ursula E. McCracken
Director, The Textile Museum

George E. Stuart
Center for Maya Research

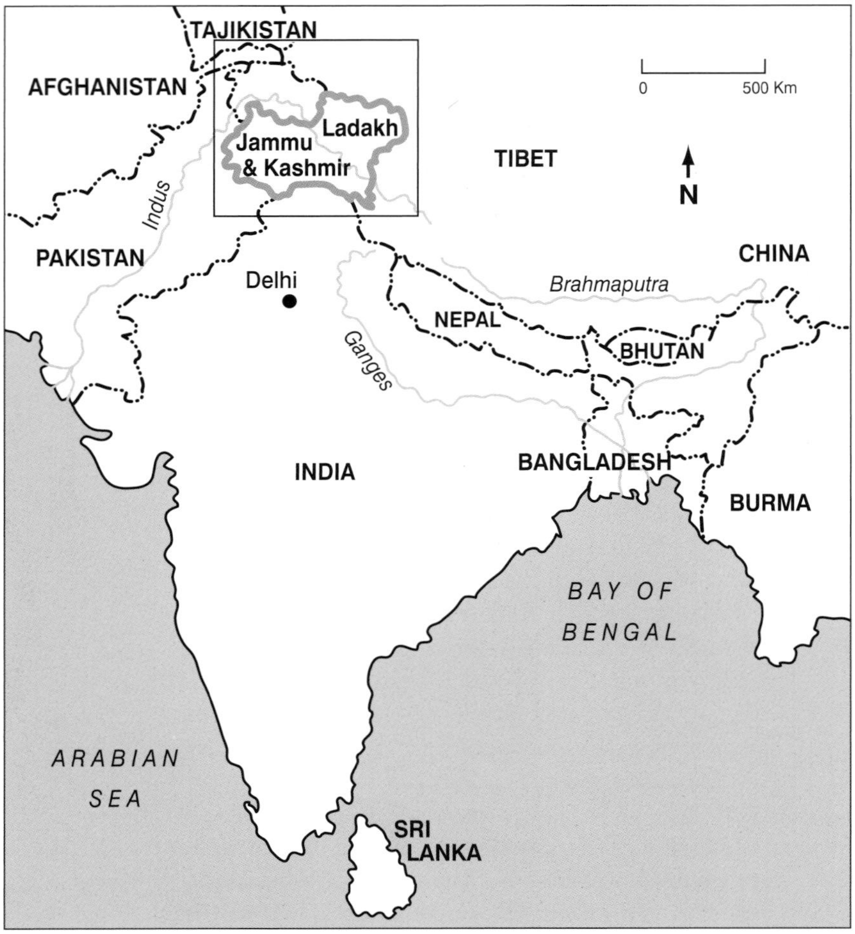

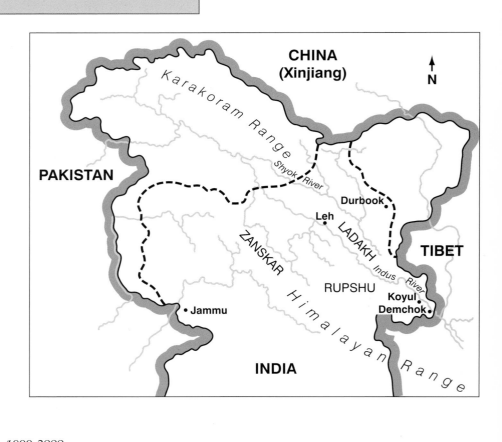

Fig. 1. South Asia

Fig. 2. Ladakh and neighboring areas

Subduing Demons: Women and Weaving in Rupshu

Monisha Ahmed

In the beginning the world was populated by gigantic, humanlike beings known as *bdud-po* (demon) and *bdud-mo* (demoness).[1] They destroyed everything in sight and ate their own children. Some even say that the *bdud-mo* ate the *bdud-po*. They were very strong and powerful, and no one could get any work out of them. One day a big lama came and told these demons that they must stop their bad ways and live peacefully with all living creatures.[2] He then taught religion to them. The *bdud-po*, who were wiser, listened to the lama. But the *bdud-mo* did not. They still went around doing bad things. So the lama taught the *bdud-mo* how to weave. Then the *bdud-mo* became women, but in order to stop them from becoming *bdud-mo* again and going back to their wicked ways, they had to keep weaving. That is why, even today, women are kept busy weaving the whole day so that they do not stray back to their bad ways.

This is what Abi Yangzom said and chuckled to herself, "There are still some *bdud-mo* among the women here, but I won't tell you who they are."

Despite her 77 years, failing eyesight, and arthritis, Abi Yangzom faithfully unrolls her loom each morning, emphasizing the importance of a woman's weaving: "There is always the danger that women who don't weave will become the *bdud-mo* again," she explained, "that is why we women must keep weaving." Abi Yangzom realizes that the risk of not weaving may mean her transformation back to the *bdud-mo*, thereby imperiling the order of the everyday world. Though men also originated from the demon, there is no similar assumption about having to control them, perhaps because they listened to the lama and learned religion.

This narrative, first heard in Rupshu when I started fieldwork there in 1992, made me realize that the study of textiles reveals much more than their artistic and functional values; textiles contain a vast repository of symbolic interpretations and cultural potentialities.[3] The narrative exposes how the belief system underlying weaving in Rupshu is linked to the gods, to ancestors, and to the advent of religion. Further, weaving is not conceived merely as a technical activity and the loom a piece of equipment; each holds dense symbols of gender which express notions and beliefs regarding procreation, birth, nurturance, and spirituality. In addition, textile production relates to the creation and sustenance of social structures within Rupshu. This paper attempts to look beyond design and cloth-making in Rupshu to the role of textiles in articulating themes such as gender, kinship, and social constructions. These themes are discussed first with respect to the types of looms used in Rupshu and the weaving process. Then, taking examples of particular pieces woven there, I examine the gender, spatial, and hierarchical relations that they express and perpetuate.

Rupshu is located on the edge of the Changthang (*byang-thang*)[4], or northern plateau, in the eastern part of Ladakh, in north India (figs. 1, 2). The region covers nearly 6,436 square kilometers, one of the highest inhabited areas in Ladakh; its altitude ranges from 12,000 to 16,000 feet. The Rupshupa are pastoral nomads who herd goats, sheep, and yak.[5] They are Mahayana Buddhists who belong to the Kargupa sect.

Weaving Practices

Traditionally Ladakh has been a land of high altitude farmers, cultivating fields along the Indus, and herders roaming the Changthang or 'northern plain.' Animal husbandry was wide-spread since yak, goat and sheep wool were needed for ropes, tents, clothing and other textiles. Spinning and weaving are done in virtually every household (Myers 1983, p. 42).

Though weaving is widely found throughout Ladakh, the practice is not uniform and differences are recognized. The contrast lies essentially between villages in the regions of lower and

Fig. 3. Woman weaving a *snam-bu* (woolen cloth) on the *sked-'thags* (backstrap loom), using sheep's wool.

Fig. 4. Man weaving a tent strip on the *sa-'thags* (fixed-heddle loom), with goat and yak hair.

central Ladakh, on the one hand, and those in Changthang, on the other. In the former, weaving is exclusively men's work and a foot loom (treadle loom, *'thags-cha*) is used. In fact, in these same areas women are not permitted to weave.[6] This is unlike Changthang, where both men and women weave.

In other parts of the Himalayas, where weaving is also commonly practiced, differences with respect to the tradition may be observed. In Tibet, women are the main weavers (Denwood 1974; Kuløy 1982); the same is true in Nepal (Diemberger 1993; Dunsmore 1993). In Bhutan, too, although men cut already-woven cloth and sew it into finished forms, as a rule they do not weave (Myers ms., p. 3).

Picton and Mack (1989, pp. 20–21) observe that in areas where men weave, they are usually full-time specialists; if a woman weaves, it is because weaving is among the various skills expected of her in that culture. Furthermore, there are few areas where both men and women weave; in such places they each use a different loom. Rupshu happens to be one such place.

In Rupshu both women and men weave on portable looms on which the warp lies parallel to the ground and the cloth stretches out in front of the weaver. Women weave using a *sked-'thags*, which is a backstrap, or body-tensioned, loom (fig. 3), and men work on a *sa-'thags*, or fixed-heddle loom (fig. 4). While looms are commonly referred to as *'thags*, the Rupshupa differentiate between the looms used by women and men by calling them *bo-mo 'thags* (female loom) and *bu-tsha 'thags* (male loom), respectively.

While it is mandatory that all women, including nuns, weave, it is not essential for a man to weave, and monks are not permitted to do so. From a very young age, girls in Rupshu start helping their mothers clean and spin wool, and by the age of thirteen they begin learning to weave. In contrast, men learn at a much later age than women, generally around twenty or even as late as thirty.

Women weavers create a number of textiles for a wide variety of uses: clothes, containers for foodstuffs and valuable possessions, coverings for floors, tent walls, blankets, and saddlecloths (figs. 5–7). Men weave saddlebags, blankets, and tents (fig. 8). While men weave using only the technique of plain weave, women do plain, twill, and pile weaves. Men in Rupshu informed me that although they cannot do a woman's weaving, a woman could do a man's weaving if it were absolutely necessary.

The main source of fiber for weaving in Rupshu is from the local herds of livestock. Wool comes from both sheep and yak, and hair from goats and yak. It is interesting to observe that women primarily weave with wool, while men weave mainly with hair.[7]

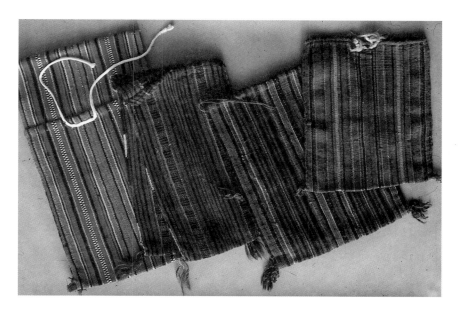

Fig. 5. Women weave these bright, warp-striped containers for keeping dry food items such as salt, tea, sugar, and rice. Left to right: 25.5 x 93 cm; 20 x 74 cm; 28 x 36 cm; 25.5 x 30.5 cm.

Fig. 6. This blanket (*tsug-dul*), woven with natural-colored brown yak wool (*ku-lu*) and stripes of red-dyed sheep wool (*bal*), is made from several narrow strips, stitched side by side along their length. The number of strips, which may range from six to twelve, depends on an individual's preference. 114 x 165 cm.

Fig. 7. This saddlecloth is the piece that is placed below the wooden saddle. Its ground color is natural-colored yak wool, and the designs have been woven with acrylic yarn. Women weave saddlecloths in matching pairs.

Fig. 8. The black tent (*re-bo*) is woven by men. It consists of long narrow strips of goat and yak hair, which are placed side by side and then stitched. Yak hair (*rtsid-pa*) is preferred because it is warmer, but goat hair (*ral*) is also used because the Rupshupa keep fewer yaks these days.

In addition, machine-spun acrylic yarn, known in Rupshu as *pham*, has been gaining popularity for the last ten to fifteen years (fig. 9). It is used with discretion and a great deal of restraint. While men continue to weave with local hair, women use this acrylic yarn in weaving their textiles. The women say it allows them to introduce a greater variety of colors into the articles they weave. They do not use it to weave fabric for their clothes, but only for designs in their rugs (fig. 10), blankets, bags, and saddlecloths. It is almost always used in textiles in combination with local wool.

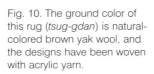

Fig. 9. For the last fifteen years, women have been using machine-spun acrylic yarn (*pham*) for their weaving. Before this yarn is used for weaving, however, it is twisted to make it thinner and finer.

Fig. 10. The ground color of this rug (*tsug-gdan*) is natural-colored brown yak wool, and the designs have been woven with acrylic yarn.

The Loom and the Weaving Process

Looms are usually inherited, and one loom can last for generations. Loom parts are made primarily from wood, rope, wool, and metal. Trees do not grow in Rupshu because the region lies above the tree line; therefore, gifts of wood from relatives or friends in other villages in Ladakh, where trees do grow, are much appreciated. At other times the Rupshupa exchange wool for small pieces of wood from visiting traders. Men make looms for both men and women. It is claimed that there is little difference between the structure of the looms in use now and those used in the past.[8] One change may be that the newer looms have more metallic parts that are now more easily procured from shops in Leh. Although metal is stronger and lasts longer than other materials, its use is restricted to a few sticks or the edge of the beater because it adds to the weight of the loom, which then becomes difficult to transport during moves of the camp.

The loom as nurturance

Looms in Rupshu are described with reference to the popular expression "*Mi rgyu la rtsam-pa spun*" (The warp is like a person, the weft is like barley flour). "We say that this warp (*rgyu*), it is like an empty body or a person (*mi*) without food," Nawang Tharchen explained. "It is only when we fill the warp with the weft (*spun*), or the body with food (in this case barley flour, *rtsam-pa*), that we get form and life." The saying is that just as the weft gives the warp form and only then is it cloth, so food gives the body life and only then can a person work—the one without the other is not possible. The term "work" (*le-ka*) is generally also associated with a man offering or delivering sexual services to a woman; other interpretations of the female and male looms affirm this connection (see below).[9]

In Rupshu, both women and men weavers have significantly different experiences and explanations of their weaving. It is said that a woman's loom and a man's loom are not the same and that this difference is expressed in the same way as the contrast between a woman and a man. Abi Yangzom relates:

A woman's loom is like a woman giving birth. We say that this warp is like the mother, and these balls of wool, the weft she inserts to make her cloth, is like the child conceived within her womb. As her cloth is made so the child inside her grows. Women are the creators of life we say.

The female loom represents "giving birth," where the warp is like the mother and the weft is the child growing within her womb. At one level, then, and corresponding to the proverb given above, the weft which is seen as "food" is analogous to a mother feeding the growing child within her womb. The more the mother feeds the child, the faster it will grow. Thus, a woman's weaving symbolizes birth as well as nurturance.

Apart from the warp and weft, the various parts of a female loom are also associated with the analogy of a mother and her child. The beater (sdag) is referred to as the mother and the other parts of the loom, apart from the belt (sked), as her children.[10] At times, it is also said that the front and back rollers (tshig-pa and thal-shing), as well as the large shed stick ('u-lu), are identified with the mother.

Distinctions are drawn between female and male looms, and one of the most immediate and common responses given by the Rupshupa when asked about the difference between female and male weaving is: "Men do not sit and weave, they kneel. Women sit on their backsides and weave." "It's because men can't have children," Tashi Zangmo stated. Though women give birth lying down, the analogy of the weft to the growing child within her womb is the reason for noting this difference in sitting postures.[11] Men sit on their knees and weave so as not to associate themselves with the weaving of women and with childbirth. A man who sits and weaves will be ridiculed.[12]

Sexual metaphors

Nevertheless, life-giving capabilities are not associated with females alone: the metaphors associated with the male loom embody the sexual union between man and woman.[13] Here the warp, which is strong and tightly twisted, is said to represent the man. The weft, which is weak and loose in comparison, is the woman. However, the two are said to support each other and work together toward a common goal. That goal, similar to that of the female loom, is the eventual birth of a "child."

Discourses on the loom as a metaphor for reproduction and birth are not unusual. Among Kodi women weavers of eastern Indonesia, the metaphoric parallel begins right from the stage of dyeing and extends to the production of cloth (Hoskins 1989, pp. 151–54). In Bhutan, beliefs about weaving suggest that a woman's reproductive nature, as well as her artistry, is expressed through the activity of making cloth, and that any interference with activity at the loom has dire implications for marriage, fertility, and even life itself. For instance, the Bhutanese say that if a woman steps over the warp of a pattern-shed rod for picking out designs, either she will never marry or she will have a mute child (Myers 1994, p. 85).

Though the final result of male and female weaving may be the same in Rupshu, the discourse on identification with weaving is stronger for women than for men. The importance of weaving in a woman's life is thought to be a measure of her maturity and character. Weaving, therefore, becomes a significant indicator in the general growth of a girl. A skillful weaver is always highly commended by others; those who do not weave are considered useless and unproductive. In Rupshu, as in many parts of the world, a woman is seen first and foremost as a potential mother, and a woman who will not or cannot fulfill her reproductive functions is looked upon as bad or pitiful. Thus, it might be said that a gifted weaver will be blessed with several healthy children, while a poor weaver may remain barren and is therefore unwanted as a bride.

It is interesting at this point to emphasize the weaving done by nuns. Nuns are said to be inferior to lamas and to married women, who owe their value to their birth-giving ability. At one level, then, a nun's weaving may be one way through which she can bridge this gap and accommodate to this disparity in her values. One might say that a nun weaves "threads of life," thereby playing out the act of reproduction in which she is forbidden to participate. When nuns leave for the nunnery, they or their mothers weave the same large saddlebags (tshang-'dur) that are woven for a bride at the time of her marriage (fig. 11). On the other hand, lamas are not permitted to weave. Thus, while Buddhism does not condemn nuns who weave, lamas are dissuaded from doing so. A reason for this may be that a nun is thought of as being less pure than a lama because she goes through a period of impurity each time she menstruates.

Thus, the significance of all women learning to weave becomes apparent in the perceived relationship between weaving and reproduction. In addition to this important connection, women's weaving is thought to preserve the order of the world.

Weaving: The Need to Keep Women Working

Viewed as dangerous and marginal to Buddhism because they originated from the demoness, women in Rupshu are controlled through weaving. It is said that a woman who is preoccupied and absorbed with her weaving will have little time to think wicked thoughts or commit sinful actions.[14] The making of cloth is therefore also linked to notions about feminine virtue and morality. While men do weave, their weaving is not associated with these beliefs because they are said to be more spiritually advanced than women. Thus, it is important for a woman to be kept weaving the whole day, but a man may weave only occasionally.

This important connection is reinforced by the story of Duguma, wife of King Gesar of Ling, the legendary hero-god in the Buddhist world of the Himalayas. Duguma is often said to be the archetype for all women weavers in Rupshu. There is a popular saying that Duguma "weaves only one row a year" (*lo 'thags lo gcig la sked gcig*) and that when she completes her fabric, the world will come to an end. Abi Yangzom related:

> Everything will go upside-down and there will be nothing left here. In fact, it is said that she has only another fifteen rows or so left to weave, so there really isn't very long left before the world ends. Anyway, I'm old now so at least I know I won't be around when it happens!

Thus, Duguma's weaving also illustrates the pressure on women to weave: as long as she weaves, preservation of the world order is ensured.

That women spend more time than men on their weaving is also determined by the structure of their loom and the fabric being woven on it. The male loom has only one heddle rod in it; women weave with one, two, or three heddle rods depending on the cloth being made. The number of heddle rods present in the loom correlates with the fineness of the textile being woven. Textiles woven with one heddle rod are relatively thicker than those woven with three. While the greater number of warp yarns present also determines the fineness of a fabric, this is usually not commented on by the Rupshupa, who tend to say it is on account of the number of heddle rods present.

Thus, thicker fabrics such as those woven by men can be finished in a day. In contrast, the finer fabrics woven by women require several days to finish. Men are prohibited from weaving with more than one heddle rod. This restriction, men say, prevents them from weaving the cloth that women do. However, since there is no similar stipulation for women, they can weave men's fabric.

Perhaps in a bid to keep women weaving and bring them into the sphere of religious activities, the technology of the female loom is associated with Buddhist teachings and the world of spirituality. This is not the case with the male loom. Women sing a song that draws analogies between weaving and religion:[15]

> See the loom as precious,
> That is good.
> See the loom as a lama's shrine room,
> That is good.
> See the loom as Buddha's shrine room,
> And you will grow.[16]
> The parts of the loom are like a mother with her twelve children,[17]
> Only twelve.
> See the raising of the heddle while weaving as ascending in this world after death,
> That is good.
> See the lowering of the heddle while weaving as pushing all sin down with your feet,
> That is good.
> Hear the clap of the beater as the voice of a lama,
> That is good.
> Hear the clap of the beater as the voice of Buddha reciting prayers,

That is good.

See the balls of weft passing from right to left as the lama's kettle that serves tea up and down the monastery hall,

That is good.

See the two pieces of the front roller as the wooden covers of a lama's religious books,

And you will grow,

That is good.

The spiritual metaphors of the loom are clearly evident. The whole process of weaving becomes a continuing reminder of fundamental spiritual concepts, demonstrating the constant movement by Buddhism to penetrate and absorb every aspect of life (Aris 1994, p. 43). In a sense, this song makes claims about the spiritual merits of women's weaving. Religious beliefs are recognized and reinforced only through women's weaving, not through men's. This is because Buddhism is obliged to hold down and suppress whatever is uncontrolled and threatening—including the feminine form (Gyatso 1987, p. 47).

The Tamang of Nepal make a similar analogy between weaving and writing in a song called "Story of the Loom," where writing essentially refers to Buddhist scriptures. In her analysis, March (1983, pp. 733–35) juxtaposes weaving with women and writing with men, and she suggests that the tension between the two demonstrates women's spiritual subordination to men. The same attitude prevails in Bhutan, where the higher value accorded to a male weaver's work manifests the tension between women's esteemed role as weavers and their spiritual inferiority to men (Myers 1994, p. 86). The common term for woman in Tibet is *skye-dman*, literally meaning "low birth" (Jaeschke 1987, p. 28). According to Buddhist principles, men are superior to women in the hierarchy of life forms: "They are born in this life as males because of good deeds in previous lives; they have more 'spiritual merit' than women" (Myers and Pommaret 1994, p. 143).

The superior merit of men is made explicit at several occasions and events in Rupshu. At birth, a male child is offered a *kha-btags* (ceremonial white scarf), a baby girl is not. Women are not permitted to make offerings at the village shrine to the gods (*lha-tho*); divinities are said to be more dangerous to women because the gods are sooner infuriated by a woman than by a man (Reis 1983, p. 225). In the monastic order itself, nuns are inferior to monks, and this applies even to comparisons between a senior nun and the

youngest or lowest male novice. Havnevick (1989, p. 29) writes that although women are granted the possibility of becoming a Bodhisattva or a Buddha, it is only on the condition that they change their sex.

In short, legends and spiritual beliefs explain the reasons why women must keep weaving and reveal that the Rupshupa are bound by their fear of the *bdud-mo*. Despite their weaving, however, women are identified with the *bdud-mo*. The *pad-rag* (turquoise-studded headdress) and other jewelry worn by women are said to have been fashioned along the lines of jewelry once worn by the *bdud-mo* (fig. 12).[18]

Fig. 12. A woman wearing her *pad-rag* (turquoise-studded headdress). The headdress is said to be the same as that worn by the *bdud-mo* (demoness), from whom women are said to have originated. The red cape (*sbog*) she is wearing over her back is made of felt and lined with fleece. This type of cape, called a *yo-sgar*, is generally worn in winter.

Fig. 13. Wrapping the weft thread around the gauge rod (*tsug-lcags*) to knot the pile for a blanket made of yak and sheep wool.

Fig. 14. The base color for this blanket (*tsug-dul*) is white sheep wool, and the designs are of brown yak wool. 193 x 140 cm. Wool blankets are generally used exclusively by women.

Making *Snam-bu*: Cloth of the Female Loom

The weaving of the *snam-bu* (woolen cloth), the main fabric used for clothing in Rupshu (fig. 3), typically occupies most of a woman's time. During the course of a year she must weave a new *snam-bu* for each member of her family.

Snam-bu is woven using a simple twill weave, and the warp consists of approximately 160 warp yarns of 2-ply yarn. While the breadth of the fabric is determined by the width of the loom, which is 25–35 centimeters, the length of the warp usually depends on the size and height of the person for whom the *snam-bu* is being woven. Narrow widths of fabric do not restrict the Rupshupa's style of weaving or the form of their finished pieces. Chemit Tsering remarked:

> On the contrary, they are superior to broad ones because the small widths are easier to wash in the water after weaving, and washing the cloth makes it stronger. In a narrow strip it is also easier to hit the weft down with the beater and to really push it in, with the result that the cloth is much tougher.[19]

Clothes worn in Rupshu are made from several pieces of narrow fabric lengths. This is an essential part of the design. The reasons for this are discussed below.

Color and design

Snam-bu is always woven in a single color, and no designs are incorporated into the fabric. It is mainly when women do pile weaving that they can incorporate patterns and a variety of colors into the fabric. Pile weaving is used for making rugs and blankets (figs. 13, 14), which are usually woven from a combination of sheep and yak wool and acrylic yarn. The designs that women use are often taken from what they see around them, mainly flowers or religious images (figs. 15, 16); Buddhist symbols, such as the eight lucky signs, are common. Designs are seldom drawn and kept for later use but are improvised while women weave.

Fig. 15. The design outlines the thunderbolt (*rdo-rje*), the Buddhist symbol of wisdom.

Gender differences

To understand the role of dress in a given society, an analysis of the creative act of making clothes is essential, and usually the production of objects that are to be worn is itself gender specific (Barnes and Eicher 1992, p. 4). Clothes are essentially gender specific in Rupshu, and apart from stylistic differences in their design, distinctions are made right from the time of processing the wool and weaving the *snam-bu*.

No differentiation is made in the sex of the "child" developing on the female or male loom except when women weave the *snam-bu*. Before beginning to weave the *snam-bu* they must decide whether the cloth is being made for a female or a male as the choice of wool and techniques employed in its processing and weaving will vary. The resulting cloth is referred to as "that meant for a *bo-mo gos* (female robe)," or "that meant for a *bu-tsha gos* (male robe)." Thus, by controlling the process of weaving, a woman metaphorically shows that she mediates not only in the birth and shape of her future "child," but also in its sex.

Preference for particular types of wool is demonstrated at the time of weaving the *snam-bu*. Women prefer the warp to be of wool that is long and straight, and the weft to be made from wool that is short and curly. They maintain that wool from a ram is generally longer and rougher and, therefore, more suitable for the warp, while that from an ewe is shorter and softer and more appropriate for the weft. Lamb's wool, which is even softer than ewe's wool, is also preferred for the weft. Thus, the separation of male and female and the opposition of their qualities—and the confrontation of male and female—are enunciated early on, before weaving even begins.

Furthermore, softer and finer wool will always be used for weaving the *snam-bu* meant for a man, and the wool will be carded (fig. 17). This is not the case for the female *snam-bu*. For a male *snam-bu*, one row will contain two weft threads: the weaver sits with one ball of wool on either side of her, and at each row both balls of wool are passed through the warp. Thus, the fabric will be thicker and warmer. Again this is not the practice for *snam-bu* made for a woman, where only one ball of wool passes through each shed. Further napping and shearing of the excess fibers must be done for all male *snam-bu*, but these are optional for the female *snam-bu*.[20]

Women in Rupshu explained that these differences in weaving a *snam-bu* exist because

Fig. 16. This dark shape represents the *bum-ba*, the receptacle for holding holy water.

men's clothes have to be well made, and men must look good in them. This principle does not apply to women; they can wear anything and it would not matter. "We say a woman is born in this world to work," Tharchen reported in explanation of this disparity, and "a man to do good things and to travel here and there."[21] Women's clothes are essentially considered to be bad (*btsog-po*) or polluting (*'bag-pa*), especially women's trousers, because they have a lot of blood in them. This is an articulation of the idea of women's bodies as "dirty" when they are menstruating and of the concept of *khrel-ba*, or "shame" (Aggarwal ms., p. 232). Women's bodies are also "polluted" at the time of childbirth and purified only after they have bathed and prayers have been recited. For this reason, a woman's clothes, especially those worn below the waist, cannot be placed on yak that are dedicated to the gods;[22] nor can they carry her loom because of its strong metaphoric relationship to reproduction.

Fig. 17. A woman cards wool using a pair of wooden wool cards (*bal-shed*).

Clothes Made from *Snam-bu*: The Female Robe and the Male Robe

The *snam-bu*, the main product of a woman's loom, is primarily used to make garments in Rupshu. These include the *sul-ma* for women and the *gos* for men. While all weaving is done by women, all cutting and stitching is done by men. Most men in Rupshu know how to sew, and they generally make the everyday clothes their families wear. For festive occasions and more expensive fabrics, such as silk and velvet, they request the more specialized tailors (*'tshem-po pa* or *'tshem-mkhan*) to sew for them. These professional tailors receive orders to make velvet and brocade robes, capes, and hats. Some of them also make patchwork and appliqué felt saddlecloths and bands for carrying a bell which encircle the neck of a horse (fig. 18).

The woman's *sul-ma*

The *sul-ma* is a woman's main garment (fig. 19). It has probably been structurally the same for many generations, as older women emphatically stated that this has been the style for many, many years. The *sul-ma* is a round-necked, long-sleeved dress with gathers (*sul*) around the waist and knee-length slits. It is an ankle-length garment, though often it falls midway between the knee and ankle. Ankle-length garments are generally worn on special occasions, while the shorter ones are kept for daily use when there is work to be done. The *sul-ma* is secured by a belt (*sked-rags*) around the waist, and this is generally a length of *snam-bu* about 10 to 15 centimeters in width. At times corduroy, cotton cloth, or even rope may be used. Silk belts are worn at festivals, weddings, and religious ceremonies.

Under the *sul-ma* women wear a loose, long-sleeved blouse (*gres-len*) made from polyester, cotton, or silk. The blouse reaches to the waist and has a soft collar that rolls over the neck of the *sul-ma*. The blouse sleeves are rolled over the sleeves of the *sul-ma* into a wide cuff. These blouses are rarely sewn in Rupshu, and it is more common for the women to purchase ready-made ones from the shops in Leh.

On top of the *sul-ma*, women often wear a short sleeveless jacket (*khan-mjar*) with a Chinese collar and two round brass buttons (*tub-ci*) along the left side (fig. 20). The jacket is generally made from velvet; black, dark green, maroon, and navy blue are the most usual colors. The jacket is edged around the collar and down the side of the buttons with white nylon piping.

Fig. 19. Abi Yangzom in her *sul-ma*. This is made from *snam-bu* that has been dyed a reddish brown.

Fig. 18. These appliqué and patchwork felt bands (*thing-thing*) are made to hold a bell around a horse's neck. top to bottom: 11.5 x 66 cm; 12 x 91.5 cm; 12 x 88 cm.

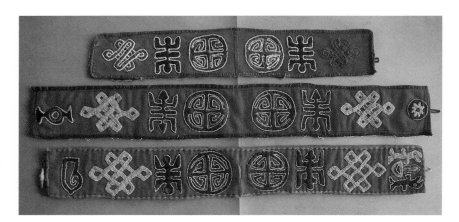

Over the *sul-ma* women wear a knee-length, rectangular cape (*sbog*). The cape wraps around a woman's back and shoulders, and it is secured in the front with woolen ties (fig. 21). A variety of capes are worn in Rupshu, depending on the occasion and the season (fig. 22). While capes made from *snam-bu* are mainly worn in summer, capes made from brocaded silk are worn at marriages and other ceremonies (fig. 23). The cape made from *snam-bu* consists of four equal-sized panels cut along the weft of a loom length and stitched together lengthwise with tassels at the lower end (fig. 24). In winter a cape made from felt and lined with white-colored fleece is worn; it is called a *yo-sgar* (fig. 12). The purpose of all capes, apart from shielding women from the cold, is to protect their clothes when they carry loads on their backs or their babies papoose-style.

After she has had her first child, a married woman wears a *rked-slog* (fig. 25) over her *sul-ma*. This is a rectangular garment that wraps around her lower back and hips, and ties in the front at her waist. It is made from *snam-bu* that has been woven from lamb's wool and is lined with lamb-skin—nowadays it is also made from other fabrics, such as corduroy. Women say that they wear the *rked-slog* to protect their reproductive organs and to keep them warm.

Fig. 21. A woman poses in her cape (*sbog*), which wraps around her back and shoulders, tying in the front. Her husband turns a prayer wheel in his right hand.

Fig. 20. The short sleeveless jacket (*khan-mjar*) is made from black felt and edged with white piping. 58.5 x 53 cm. Women wear this over their robes.

Fig. 22. Women wearing their capes: the woman on the left is wearing one made from red *snam-bu*, the one in the middle wears one made from red felt, and the woman on the right has a green embroidered cape.

Fig. 23. On the occasion of a horse race in Rupshu, a woman wears her brocaded cape.

Fig. 24. Capes made from *snam-bu* are generally worn in summer. They consist of four equal-sized panels cut along the weft of a loom length. These are stitched together lengthwise with tassels, and sometimes a design, at the lower end. 105.5 x 86 cm.

Fig. 25. Abi Yangzom wearing her *rked-slog*. This is a rectangular garment worn around the lower back and tied in the front. Instead of making one out of *snam-bu*, she has fashioned a shawl into the required shape by folding it several times.

The man's *gos*

The man's *gos* is a full-length robe that overlaps on the right side (fig. 26). It is buttoned from the left shoulder down its length and has a Chinese collar and slits along the sides. The robe is secured by a belt around the waist from which men hang an assortment of things, such as a spoon, knife, purse, and needle-case. Before tying the belt, a man folds the robe into two wide pleats from his hip toward his back. He then winds the belt tightly around his waist and twists it through at the center of his back, where both ends are left hanging down. The front part of the robe then blouses over the belt and acts as a pocket in which he can keep such things as a bowl or cup, dried apricots, and sweets. In the past, it was not customary for men to wear anything under their robes, but today many wear T-shirts, shirts, or sweaters. It is common to see a man going around with one arm out of his sleeve (usually the right) and the sleeve hanging down or tucked into the waist. The men say this increases their mobility. Women claim they do this to show off, especially on cold days.

Young children's clothing

The clothing of a newborn child is essentially gender neutral. Newborns are kept wrapped in the skin of a young goat and placed in a bag (*tsha-'u*) made of felt or *snam-bu*. The preferred color for the bag is white; black is also used. In the bottom of the bag, and away from the child's skin, heated sheep or goat dung is used to keep the infant warm. Children are kept like this for the first few months, and then they wear a short top. When they start walking, a robe from *snam-bu* is made for them, and it is the same for both girls and boys (fig. 27). The pattern follows that of the male robe. Girls can wear this until they get married, although some girls change over earlier to the female robe or interchange between the two types of dress. Once married, a woman may no longer wear the male robe.

Clothing structure, design, and meaning

Structurally, the *sul-ma* and the *gos* are made from rectangular pieces of *snam-bu* that are either used in their entirety or cut into smaller lengths. The skirt of the *sul-ma* is made from as many as twenty pieces, some being rectangular, others triangular. All these pieces are joined at the waist, and the flare of the skirt is fairly wide and loose.

Fig. 26. Dressed in his woolen robe (*gos*) and with a *kha-btags* (ceremonial white scarf) around his head, this man is ready to participate in the horse race.

Fig. 27. A young boy in his *gos* (male robe). Both boys and girls wear this type of robe from a young age, though once girls get married they are no longer permitted to do so.

It is said that this design facilitates a woman's movements, especially while she is working. It can also spread out to cover her legs while she is sitting.

The design of garments is based on the use of narrow strips of cloth. The Rupshpa say that when several narrow strips of cloth are stitched together, the resulting garment is stronger and more durable than a garment made from a piece of wide cloth, and therefore will last longer. The other reason given is that the greater number of seams there are in a garment (where the strips are joined), the thicker the cloth and the longer it takes to wear out.

Both female and male robes also express the relationship of a mother to her child. Here, the main body of the garment is referred to as the "mother" (a-ma) and the sleeves (phu-dung) as her "child." In fact, the large rectangular pieces in both garments are also called a-ma. Aba Palle explained:

> The mother is the body of all clothes. Without the mother, what will the sleeves do on their own, and without the sleeves, how will we wear our clothes properly? They are joined together in the same way a child is always stuck to the mother, especially when drinking milk.

Color Proscriptions

Colors in clothing are not mere personal preferences, but are determined by specific customs, changes in fashion trends, and the availability of dyes and fabrics. Dark colors such as black, gray, and navy blue are the most popular colors for women's robes, while men prefer maroon.

All dyes used in Rupshu are commercial, and the snam-bu is always dyed before it is cut and sewn. Applying dye is specifically women's work; each woman dyes her own family's cloth. This differs from dyeing practices in lower and central Ladakh, where dyeing is a specialized male occupation and the dyers are known as tshos-mkhan.

The tradition in Rupshu is that women must never wear white, but men may. However, very few men wear white today, white being a color usually associated with the older generation. Men nowadays prefer to wear red or maroon. Until around 1950, when dyes were not so easily available, women wove their woolen cloth with black-or brown-colored wool. This continues to be the practice for women from families who find it expensive to buy dye. When dye is available, men's clothes are always given first priority. Thus, most present-day Rupshupa take great pride in wearing dyed garments, and even the wearing of white by old men is derided and looked down upon as a practice from the past.

It is difficult to ascertain why women were, and still are, prevented from wearing white. One possibility is that white is the color of the gods, and women are prohibited from wearing it because they are deemed less pure than men. Some of the elders in Rupshu mentioned that it was only married women who were prohibited from wearing white and the unmarried could wear white, but not everyone was clear on this point.

The earlier practice of men wearing white snam-bu and women wearing natural-colored ones of black or brown was common throughout Ladakh, where color was primarily a sign of status. In the old days, wearing dyed or colored garments seems to have been the prerogative of the nobility and the clergy, while the rest of the population was dissuaded from wearing dyed cloth. Through the 1940s, color was synonymous with costliness because the process of dyeing was expensive and lengthy, one that few could afford. Only later, when commercial dyes that required little effort to process became easily and cheaply available, did color proscriptions begin to change in Ladakh.

Cloth: The Connector

In addition to reinforcing religious beliefs and spiritual values, weaving also expresses and strengthens ties between people. Kinship and descent are for a community the "flow of life;" cloth can be the essential mediator (Barnes 1989, p. 51).

In Rupshu, woven cloth is used as a metaphor to express a family network, the linking of men to women and mothers to their children. As Abi Yangzom stated:

> Warp and weft is always there in the talk between husband and wife, or a mother and her children. It is there amongst relatives. After all, we are all warp and weft (nga-zha rgyu spun yin).

It is said in Rupshu that men and women weave threads that reflect kinship: patrilineal descent is defined in terms of pha-rgyu (father's warp) and matrilineal descent as ma-rgyu (mother's warp). One's progeny is generally seen as spun (weft), the endless lengths of threads stretching out before the weaver.[23] Thus, to be warp and weft is to know your family, to understand your lineage, and to recognize your relatives on both sides. Even in Ladakh villages where women do not weave, it is said that "women spin threads that hold together the social fabric of society" (Aggarwal ms., p. 229–30).

Although the tradition of women's weaving is stronger than men's in Rupshu, it is nevertheless male weaving that illustrates the continuity and imperishable nature of the male line. Among Buddhist Ladakhis, descent is recognized primarily through the father's lineage: members of the same family are said to belong to a patrifraternal group (*pha-spun*, literally "father's brothers").

The Black Tent

The tent (*re-bo*) is square in shape, with a flat roof (fig. 8). It is woven from goat or yak hair, or a combination of the two fibers. Yak hair is preferred because it is both warmer and stronger. Its high grease content also makes it relatively waterproof. Men who do not own many yak generally use a combination of the two fibers, which are kept in their natural shades of brown and black. The warp for a tent consists of 34 to 40 warp lengths of 2-ply yarns. At the time of weaving, the warp is laid to weave one long strip, and it may be used in its entirety or cut into smaller strips, depending on the position within the tent. The breadth of all the strips is a standard 30.5 centimeters. Once woven, the strips are placed alongside one another and sewn together.

Kinship links

Separation and formation of new tents in Rupshu express some of the strongest kinship links. The eldest son inherits the tent from his father at a ceremony known as *phog-srod* (literally "to take charge"). Tents in Rupshu are referred to as "big" (*reb-chen*) and "small" (*reb-chung*), depending on who is currently residing in them. When a man's eldest son marries and starts a family of his own, his father gives him his "big" tent and moves with his wife and their remaining unmarried children into what is known as the "small" tent.[24] Though separate, the two tents continue to be related to each other since they are pitched close together and the eldest son continues to look after his elderly parents.[25]

The *Yud*

Along with the "big" tent, the eldest son also inherits the specific pattern of identification his father weaves into his fabric for saddlebags (*lug-sgal*) and blankets (*chal-li*) (figs. 28, 29). This is known as the *yud*. These patterns always consist of stripes woven in various combinations from natural-colored wool.[26] They are referred to by name and are read vertically from right to left. There are four basic patterns; generally, the *yud* is a combination of one or more of these. The most typical is the sheep's eye (*lug-mig*), which is represented by two black or brown stripes with a

Fig. 28. A saddlebag (*lug-sgal*) made from goat and yak hair. The vertical stripes on the saddlebag are a pattern of identification (known as *yud*) that men weave into their saddlebags and blankets. The *yud* is read from right to left. The one on this saddlebag reads: "one sheep's eye, one straight line."

Fig. 29. This blanket (*chal-li*) is woven by men from goat and yak hair. The *yud* reads: "one straight line, one sheep's eye." Blankets such as these are used mainly by men.

Fig. 30. The pattern of the sheep's eye is always made from a color that contrasts with the ground color.
From right to left, the *yud* of this saddlebag reads: "two straight lines, one sheep's eye, one straight line".

white stripe in the middle (figs. 30, 31). Then there is a single straight line (*jar-kang*), or a group of three stripes (*yud-leb*), each a warp yarn apart (fig. 32). The stripes for both patterns will be woven in a color that contrasts with the base color of the saddlebag. The fourth pattern consists of alternating rectangular blocks known as *re-so*, woven from natural-colored black-and-white or brown-and-white hair (fig. 33).

Modifications to these basic patterns result in the variety of *yud* encountered in Rupshu, a diversity that arises from the way these patterns are used, separately or in combination with each other, and the thickness or thinness of the stripe width. Some *yud* may consist of two or three sheep's eyes, or there may be two sheep's eyes with a *jar-kang* or a *yud-leb* in the middle (fig. 30).

As long as sons live in their father's tent,

they use his *yud*. But when a father hands over his tent to his eldest son, he also relinquishes the use of his pattern because no two men can have the same *yud*. Having now moved to a new tent, the father must make himself a new *yud*. The general pattern followed by men who are related is to make a few alterations to the original *yud*.

Apart from determining descent, these specific patterns that men weave are also present so that they can recognize their own saddlebags and blankets. In the past, when men went on long trading journeys to Tibet, Zanskar, and Himachal, there would be hundreds of saddlebags strewn around the campsite when they stopped for the night. Their individual patterns enabled them to easily identify their possessions. Thus, the *yud* ensures that saddlebags and their contents do not get mixed up (fig. 34).

Fig. 32. The *yud* in this saddlebag consists of three lines, each the width of a warp yarn length apart, and is called *yud-leb*.

Fig. 33. The *yud* in this blanket consists of one sheep's eye and one line of rectangular blocks (*re-so*) in alternating colors of brown and white.

Fig. 31. The motif of the sheep's eye is also shown as round circles made with brown wool outlined by a ring of white wool, as depicted in this band made to hold a bell around a horse's neck; but this motif is not known as *yud*.

Spatial organization within the tent

Spatial organization within the tent is a crucial element to express gender separation and relationships among individuals. If one stands at the tent door facing inward, the left-hand side of the tent is referred to as the *bo-mo 'do* (female side) and the right-hand side as the *bu-tsha 'do* (male side). This gender division extends outside the tent as well and is accentuated further by the articles kept and the work performed on each side of the tent. The women of the house, including those who visit, inhabit the left side. It is here that women give birth and babies are nursed. All cooking is done on this side, and food and cooking utensils are stored here. The right side of the tent is the male sphere, and all male family members and visitors sit here. The male domain is also where religious items, such as prayer books and incense, are stored—it is also where saddles and other horse gear are kept.

Arrangement of space within a tent is often a reflection of social organization and elaborate systems of hierarchy. There is a well-ordered and ritually-defined ranked seating arrangement, known as *gral*, observed around the hearth; the order takes into account a man's importance and status. It is customary for those highest in rank to sit near the altar. Those lowest in rank sit closer to the door of the tent. In the tent, the altar and door are always positioned opposite one another. The uppermost seat (*gral-mgo*) is usually inhabited by the head of the household, and the best carpets will always be kept here; all other adult male members of paternal descent seat themselves in order of seniority after him, ending at the lowest seat (*gral-zug*). The head of the household would give up his seat to a man higher in rank than he, or to a lama. The same order is practiced by the women on the left side of the tent. Children sit in a semicircle around the bottom of the hearth, close to the entrance.

Conclusions

The tent and the *yud* are tangible woven objects that men pass down to their kin to define the linear immortality of their male line. Women have no such inheritance. Thus, while the male line continues through the tent and *yud*, female textiles, in contrast, are the more elusive social thread. Nonetheless, a woman does try, through her weaving, to link a number of households and to symbolically tie people together. One way she achieves this is by making gifts of cloth at the time of a wedding in her family, or on the occasion of her nephew's hair-cutting ceremony. She also forms new links through the progeny to whom she gives birth. But, like cloth, there is always the danger of these links becoming frayed.

As part of an income-generating scheme, a local nongovernmental organization has been trying to introduce the women in Rupshu to foot looms so that they can weave faster and increase the width of their fabric. Women are the main targets because it is believed that if they weave faster they can make many more textiles, some of which they can then sell. Though the idea of having their own income appeals to the women, the idea of weaving on a foot loom does not, and so they have approached the scheme with some trepidation.

Since weaving and the loom are sacred, women argue that cloth cannot be made with the "feet," the lowest part of one's body, but must be made with the "hands." "Cloth is pure," they say, "connected to the gods and the ancestors, so how can we make it with our feet?"[27] In addition, the design and use of the loom relate to more than just the breadth of the cloth being woven; they bear on other notions and beliefs regarding nurturance, spirituality, procreation, and birth. At the same time, the ritual and discourse that surround women's weaving are more intimidating because of the ominous fear of the demons.

The local nongovernmental organization has probably not recognized, or has disregarded, these underlying symbolic beliefs that prevent changes to the tradition of weaving in Rupshu. It is not that tradition does not allow for transformation; the women are open to weaving with new fibers and colors, and eager to learn new designs. But, so far, they have resisted efforts to change the structure of their looms or to introduce foot looms, as either would undermine the basic premise on which weaving originated in Rupshu.

Fig. 34. Once a year the Rupshupa journey to the lake called Tso Kar to collect salt. Often their saddlebags lie strewn around the bank of the lake, and the *yud* prevents them from getting mixed up. Here the saddle-bags, filled with salt, are ready to be loaded onto the sheep's backs.

Acknowledgments

I am grateful to Jasleen Dhamija, who first drew my attention to the subject of weaving and gender, and to my supervisors at Oxford University, Nicholas J. Allen and Ruth Barnes, for their guidance. The late Aba Palle, from Leh, was most helpful in providing historical background for weaving traditions in Ladakh. But the people to whom I am most indebted are the men and women in Rupshu who let me into their lives and shared their knowledge. I would especially like to acknowledge the support and encouragement of Nawang Tharchen and his family members, especially his mother, Abi Yangzom, without whom my stay and work in Rupshu would not have been possible.

Textiles illustrated are from the author's collection, photographed by Prakash Rao. Field photographs were taken by the author between 1992 and 1998.

About the Author

Monisha Ahmed received her doctorate in social anthropology from Oxford University in 1996. The subject of her dissertation, weaving traditions among the nomadic pastoralists of Rupshu in eastern Ladakh (north India), is being published as *Living Fabric: Weaving in Ladakh Himalaya.* Her current project, funded by a fellowship from the Cambridge University Museum of Archaeology and Anthropology, is to document the textile arts of Ladakh. She is also co-founder of the Ladakh Arts and Multicultural Outreach Trust that works with local performance artists and women's weaving organizations in Ladakh.

Notes

1. All Ladakhi terms appear in italics and have been transcribed according to the system prescribed by Wylie (1959); the orthography is based on the work of Jaeschke (1987). Place names and personal names have been spelled in a manner closest to their pronunciation in English. The words *bdud-po* and *bdud-mo* literally mean "enemy" (Michael Aris, personal communication, Oxford, 1995). The suffix *po* and *mo* refer to male and female, respectively.

2. I was told that the "big lama" was actually a god in disguise, but opinions regarding his identity vary. Some people in Rupshu told me that the lama was Guru Rinpoche (also known as Padmasambhava). This is the Indian yogi who brought Buddhism to Tibet and is quite well known for his demon-quelling rituals (Snellgrove and Richardson 1968, pp. 96–7). Others said he was Pulon Rigpachen, a figure who is associated with the origin of almost everything in Rupshu. In some versions of the story Pulon Rigpachen is supposed to have accompanied the lama, and they say that it was he who taught the *bdud-mo* how to weave.

3. Between the years 1992 and 1996, I did fieldwork in Rupshu for my doctorate in social anthropology from Oxford University (Ahmed ms.).

4. The Changthang is situated in Ladakh's easternmost portion, extending from Durbook in the north, Demchok and Koyul in the center, to Rupshu in the east.

5. The suffix *pa* is added to the end of place names to indicate people who come from that place. Thus, Rupshupa refers to a person from Rupshu.

6. Male weavers from these areas claim that if a woman were to weave, her hands would burst into flames. Kim Gutschow, who has done fieldwork in Zanskar, mentioned that it was said that if a woman were to weave, the mountains would collapse (personal communication, Leh, August 1993).

7. No one in Rupshu could give me a reason for this disparity. Myers (1983, pp. 43–4) mentions that in lower and central Ladakh, goat hair is spun only by men, while women spin wool.

8. Little is known about the historical development of weaving in Ladakh, and few, if any, early sources and records exist on the subject. Archaeological excavations have not yielded much information. The origin of weaving in Ladakh is closely linked to that in Tibet, since the looms used in the two places closely resemble one another; thus leads can be drawn from the research done there. According to Myers (1984, p. 21), weaving of some sort on the Tibetan plateau probably extends as far back as one can chart human habitation, since it is common to find clay spindle whorls at Neolithic sites in Tibet.

9. Diemberger (1993, p. 108) mentions a similar analogy among the Khumbo of northeast Nepal where weaving is primarily a female activity.

10. The beater is literally known as *sdag-mo* (female beater).

11. Jasleen Dhamija, who has worked with nomadic weavers in Iran, suggests that in a back-strap loom the warp "looks like" it is coming out of the woman's genitals, where the warp resembles an extension of her pubic hair. Therefore, the whole act of weaving is closely tied in with a woman's reproductive nature (personal communication, New Delhi, November 1994).

12. This is not to say that men do not ever sit and weave; I saw several who did.

13. These metaphors are also spoken about by male weavers, from lower and central Ladakh, who work on the foot loom (from interview with Aba Palle, Leh, August 1995).

14. The Rupshupa make the same analogy with women in agricultural societies, saying that they work in the fields the whole day and so have little time to stray.

15. Abi Yangzom first sang this song for me but added that this was not the full version as she could not remember all the words. Unfortunately, there were few elderly women in Rupshu who remembered all the words and so this is not the full text. A similar song on the spiritual metaphors of the loom is included in a Tibetan text on the biography of Ashi Nangsa; a Dzongkha version is used in all schools in Bhutan (Aris 1994, p. 42).

16. This refers to spiritual growth.

17. The parts of the loom add up to twelve only when a *snam-bu* (woolen cloth) is being woven. At this time the beater is referred to as the "mother," and the other parts of the loom are said to be her "children." Buddhist culture reflects the image of women as "nurturers" of Buddhism through routine merit-making activities, and the provision of sons as potential monks (Kirsch 1985, p. 311). Thus, this line could be encouraging women to have more children in order to perpetuate Buddhism.

18. It is the same in Nepal, where divinities central to Tamang shamanic practice, the *tsen*, are transmitted from one woman to another (typically from mother to daughter), along with the inheritance of silver jewelry or fine cloth (March 1983, p. 732).

19. From interview with Chemit Tsering, Rupshu, October 1992.

20. Napping refers to the manual raising of fibers on the face of a fabric to give a pile-like surface (Burnham 1980, p. 92). It is done to raise superfluous fibers, which are then cut, and to remove any dirt that might be lodged in the fabric.

21. From an interview with Nawang Tharchen, Rupshu.

22. Yak dedicated to the gods are known as *mgon-po*, and their female counterparts, the *'bri-mo*, as *mgon-mo*. They are said to be sacred animals, conferred upon Rupshu by the gods, and are a means through which the people receive divine blessings.

23. Jaeschke (1987, p. 330) states that in addition to the word *spun* meaning "weft," it also refers to children of the same parents, brothers and sisters, and in a wider sense refers to cousins, brothers-in-law, and sisters-in-law.

24. This practice is followed throughout Ladakh, where houses are known as *khang-chen* (big house) and *khang-chung* (small house).

25. When a man has no sons, a husband is brought into the tent for his eldest daughter. He stands in as a surrogate son and the tent is left to him.

26. Parallels to the *yud* are not widely found in other areas of the Himalayas. Amongst the Sherpa of eastern Nepal, Dunsmore (1993, pp. 151–52) identifies a feature on their sacks and bags used on trading expeditions which she refers to as a "luggage label;" this she describes as the line of white yak hair twining on one of the panels near the bag opening which helps the owner identify his bag.

27. A parallel situation exists among the Dolpo in Nepal, where women also weave on backstrap looms. Recently the Tibetan frame-treadle loom was introduced there. Dunsmore (1993, p. 161) reports that use of this loom was opposed on religious grounds: the women believed that weaving on this *khri 'thags* (literally "seat loom," the seat being part of the frame) would be a grave religious error because only a lama has the right to use the raised seat, or *khri*.

References

Aggarwal, Ravina

ms.   From Mixed Strains of Barley Grain: Person and Place in a Ladakhi Village. Ph.D. diss., University of Indiana, Bloomington, 1994.

Ahmed, Monisha

ms.   "We are Warp and Weft": Nomadic Pastoralism and the Tradition of Weaving in Rupshu (Eastern Ladakh). D.Phil. diss., University of Oxford, Oxford, 1996.

Aris, Michael

1994   Textiles, Text, and Context: The Cloth and Clothing of Bhutan in Historical Perspective, *From the Land of the Thunder Dragon: Textile Arts of Bhutan*, pp. 23–45. Edited by D. K. Myers and S. S. Bean. Peabody Essex Museum, Salem and Serindia Publications, London.

Barnes, Ruth

1989   The Bridewealth Cloth of Lamalera, Lembata, *To Speak with Cloth: Studies in Indonesian Textiles*, pp. 43–55. Edited by Mattiebelle Gittinger. Museum of Cultural History, Los Angeles.

Barnes, Ruth, and Joanne B. Eicher, editors

1992   *Dress and Gender: Making and Meaning*. Berg Publishers, Providence and Oxford.

Burnham, Dorothy K.

1980   *Warp and Weft: A Textile Terminology*. Royal Ontario Museum, Toronto.

Denwood, Philip

1974   *The Tibetan Carpet*. Aris and Phillips, Warminster.

Diemberger, Hildegard

1993   Blood, Sperm, Soul and the Mountain-Gender Relations, Kinship and Cosmovision among the Khumbo (N. E. Nepal), *Gendered Anthropology*, pp. 88–127. Edited by T. del Valle. Routledge, London and New York.

Dunsmore, Susi

1993   *Nepalese Textiles*. British Museum Press, London.

Gittinger, Mattiebelle, editor

1989   *To Speak with Cloth: Studies in Indonesian Textiles*. Museum of Cultural History, Los Angeles.

Gyatso, Janet

1987   Down with the Demoness: Reflections on a Feminine Ground in Tibet, *Feminine Ground—Essays on Women and Tibet*, pp. 33–51. Edited by J. D. Willis. Snow Lion Publications, Ithaca.

Havnevick, Hanna

1989   *Tibetan Buddhist Nuns: History, Cultural Norms, and Social Reality*. Institute for Comparative Research in Human Culture, Oslo.

Hoskins, Janet

1989   Why do Ladies Sing the Blues? Indigo Dyeing, Cloth Production, and Gender Symbolism in Kodi, *Cloth and Human Experience*, pp. 141–73. Edited by A. B. Weiner and J. Schneider. Smithsonian Institution Press, Washington and London.

Jaeschke, H. A.

1987   *A Tibetan-English Dictionary*. Motilal Banarsidass, Delhi. Originally published in 1881.

Kantowsky, Detlef, and Reinhard Sander, editors

1983   *Recent Research on Ladakh: History, Culture, Society, Ecology*. Weltforum Verlag, Munich.

Kirsch, Thomas A.

1985   Text and Context: Buddhist Sex Roles/ Culture of Gender Revisited, *American Ethnologist*, vol. 12, no. 2, pp. 302–20. American Ethnological Society, Washington.

Kuløy, Hallvard K.

1982   *Tibetan Rugs*. White Orchid Press, Bangkok.

March, Kathryn

1983   Weaving, Writing, and Gender, *Man*, vol. 18, pp. 729–44.

Miller, Beatrice D.

1980   Views of Women's Roles in Buddhist Tibet, *Studies in History of Buddhism*, pp. 155–66. Edited by A. K. Narain. B. R. Publishing Company, Delhi.

Myers, Diana K.

1983   Traditional Weaving and Dyeing in Ladakh, *HALI*, vol. 6, no. 1, pp. 42–45. HALI Publications, London.

1984   *Temple, Household, Horseback: Rugs of the Tibetan Plateau*. The Textile Museum, Washington.

ms.   Textiles, Gender and Society: A New Way of Exploring Bhutan. Paper presented at Csoma de Körös Conference, School of Oriental and African Studies, London, 1993.

1994   Women and Weaving, *From the Land of the Thunder Dragon: Textile Art of Bhutan*, pp. 83–89. Edited by D. K. Myers and S. S. Bean. Peabody Essex Museum, Salem, and Timeless Books, London.

Myers, Diana K., and Susan S. Bean, editors

1994   *From the Land of the Thunder Dragon: Textile Arts of Bhutan*. Peabody Essex Museum, Salem and Serindia Publications, London.

Myers, Diana K., and Françoise Pommaret

1994   Cut and Stitched: Textiles Made by Men, *From the Land of the Thunder Dragon: Textile Art of Bhutan*, pp. 143–66. Edited by D. K. Myers and S. S. Bean. Peabody Essex Museum, Salem and Serindia Publications, London.

Narain, A. K., editor

1980   *Studies in History of Buddhism*. B. R. Publishing Company, Delhi.

Picton, John, and John Mack

1989   *African Textiles*. The British Museum Press, London.

Reis, Ria

1983   Reproduction or Retreat: The Position of Buddhist Women in Ladakh, *Recent Research on Ladakh*, pp. 217–29. Edited by D. Kantowsky and R. Sander. Weltforum Verlag, Munich.

Snellgrove, David, and Hugh Richardson

1968   *A Cultural History of Tibet*. Shambala Publications, Boston.

Valle, Teresa del, editor

1993   *Gendered Anthropology*. Routledge, London and New York.

Weiner, Annette B., and Jane Schneider, editors

1989   *Cloth and Human Experience*. Smithsonian Institution Press, Washington and London.

Willis, Janice D., editor

1987   *Feminine Ground: Essays on Women and Tibet*. Snow Lion Publications, Ithaca.

Wylie, Turrel V.

1959   A Standard System of Tibetan Transcription, *Harvard Journal of Asiatic Studies*, vol. 22, pp. 261–67. Harvard-Yenching Institute, Cambridge.

Fig. 1. Map of Burma. Chin State stretches from the Indian border of Manipur in the north and Mizoram to the west, and from the Bangladesh, Chittagong Hill Tracts border in the southwest to the junction of Magwe Division and Arakan (Rakhine) State in the south. The Sagaing and Magwe Divisions comprise the eastern border. The Chin/Zo groups can be found in all the surrounding areas, from as far north as the Naga Hills in India to as far south as Paukkaung, which is east of the city of Prome.

Notes from the Field:
On the Trail of Khumi, Khami, and Mro Textiles

Deborah Lindsay Garner
and Jay Bommer

In recent years, various intricately woven textiles have surfaced on the Southeast Asian art markets of Bangkok, Chiang Mai, and Mae Sai/Thachilek. Visually dynamic and technically superb, these "mystery" weavings appeared without provenance or accompanying documentation. When asked, the more knowledgeable Thai dealers could only shrug their shoulders and answer with a simple "Burma;" some offered "Chin" as a possibility.

The dimensions of the objects and their structure led us, and most scholars we consulted, to conclude that they were garments. The elaborate embellishments of silk single-faced, supplementary-weft patterning, complex beading, and cowrie-shell decoration testified to the many hours that must have been needed to produce them. Surely these garments were intended to be worn at important junctures in the owner's life. Similarities in design motifs and technique led to speculation that they may have been produced by the same group.[1]

As dealers and collectors of textiles and traditional costume, we had been in Burma collecting in the field for years and had not come across the talented weavers who produced these intriguing textiles. Nor could any of our Chin/Zo[2] friends (who are mostly central and northern Chin/Zo) identify the examples we brought along, although each of them, male and female, expressed appreciation of the quality of the workmanship displayed.

In the United States, research in British colonial publications and more modern anthropological studies, followed up with many interviews via telephone, letters, and e-mail with Chin/Zo contacts here and abroad, turned our attention to southern Chin State in Burma.

Our speculation is that these textiles were produced by the Khumi, Khami, and Mro.[3]

These groups live in villages in the lush, tropical environs of the Kaladan River valley and the surrounding hills in northern Arakan State and southwestern Chin State in Burma (figs. 1, 2). The focus of this article is on the weavings that comprise the traditional costumes of the Khumi, Khami, and Mro and, to a lesser extent, those of the Laytu and Zantu people,[4] all of whom are members of the larger Chin/Zo ethnic group.

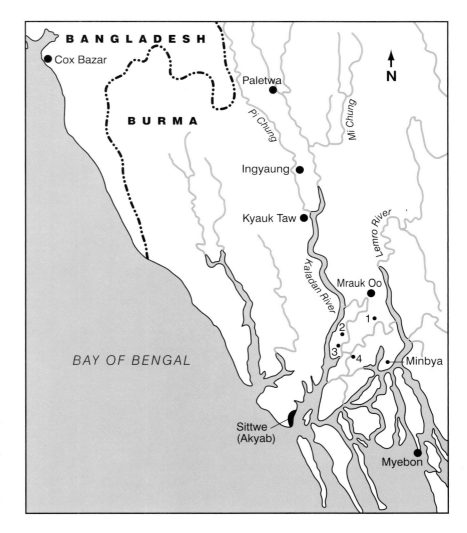

Fig. 2. Kaladan River valley and vicinity. 1. Pan Be Dan village, 2. Maung Hna Ma village, 3. Laung Shi Chaung village, 4. Agi Daw Ma village.

The Khumi

The Khumi are mostly hill people who inhabit settlements along streams and rivers in the vicinity of the Kaladan River and its tributaries (Mi Chaung, Pi Chaung, Sami Chaung) north, northeast, and northwest of the town of Kyauk Taw, with a major concentration in the Paletwa area.[5]

Khumi dress

The Khumi women still wear traditional dress for festival days. Besides their richly woven skirts, elaborately edged with multicolored beads, they wear a breastcloth, a small scarf of black or darkly colored cotton measuring about 10–13 cm in width.[6] The Khumi name for this garment is *ne kouk*[7] (figs. 3, 4), it is worn across the back of the neck and draped across the breasts. At the bottom on both ends are usually several rows of fine weaving consisting of simple geometric designs. Further embellishment is provided by rows of tiny glass beads that are sometimes capped with halves of small brown seeds. The edges of the *ne kouk* are literally studded with clusters of beads. Occasionally, brightly colored tufts of acrylic or cotton fibers are also added. In traditional dress this would be the only upper-body covering, but nowadays a woman usually wears the *ne kouk* over a blouse purchased in the market.

Women also wear a short, tubular skirt called *nay na*, which falls just above the knee (figs. 5, 6). These skirts display tightly controlled single-faced weaving with elegant geometric patterns. The top and bottom edges are ornamented with rows of beaded fringes. This skirt is secured by a metal or glass beaded belt that is tied in front and sometimes draped gradually down in the back to behind the knee.

On her head, a woman is adorned with a plain white fillet (*sa bong* or *sam bang*), commonly woven of cotton, occasionally of silk. Into this, she places a long, rectangular bamboo comb (*pahti*) that is positioned at the back of the head (fig. 7). The *pahti* is sometimes covered with copper for decoration and is then called *patoe*. The Khumi woman's outfit is completed by heavy metal bracelets (*kascee*) and large disk earrings (*dai roung*).

U Pri Kwin, a Khumi man, told us that men wear a long loincloth, *samtu nay na*, made of plain white cotton with a section of blue indigo, about 77 cm, richly patterned on both ends (figs. 8, 9).[8] This is traditionally worn without any type of upper-body covering, but today it would be worn with a modern-style shirt and only on important ceremonial occasions. The man's head scarf is called *lu paung*.

Fig. 3. Khumi women wear a strip of woven cloth over their shoulders; called *ne kouk*, it drapes down the front, covering the breasts. 94 x 12.7 cm.

Fig. 4. Detail of Khumi *ne kouk* shown in figure 3.

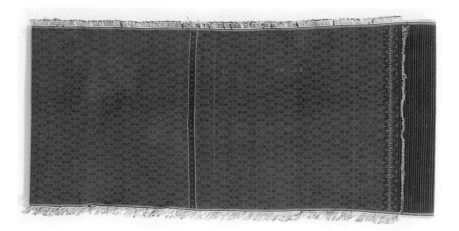

Fig. 5. Khumi woman's lower-body wrapper (*nay na*).
96.5 x 44.5 cm.

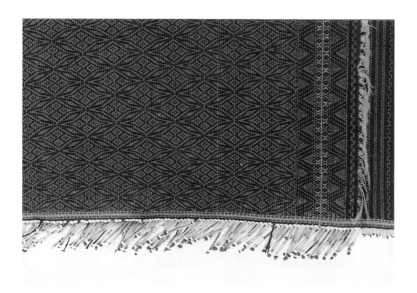

Fig. 6. Detail of Khumi *nay na* shown in figure 5.

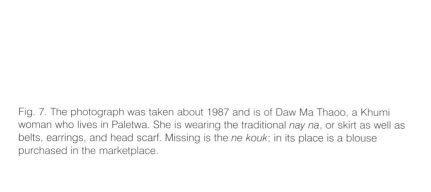

Fig. 7. The photograph was taken about 1987 and is of Daw Ma Thaoo, a Khumi woman who lives in Paletwa. She is wearing the traditional *nay na*, or skirt as well as belts, earrings, and head scarf. Missing is the *ne kouk*; in its place is a blouse purchased in the marketplace.

Fig. 9. Detail of Khumi *samtu nay na* shown in figure 8.

Fig. 8. Khumi man's loincloth (*samtu nay na*). This style of loincloth is shared by the people of the Paletwa, Matupi, and Haka areas, and possibly other Chin/Zo people as well. 589 x 43 cm.

Fig. 10. Mro- or Kyauk Taw-style breastcloth (*marankite*). 68.5 x 35.5 cm.

The Mro

The Khumi and the Mro seem to live in close proximity to each other. U Sar Khaung, a Mro man, told us of several Mro villages along the Mi Chaung, northwest of Kyauk Taw, that are inhabited by both Khumi and Mro. Current political restrictions on traveling outside of Mrauk Oo precluded a visit to these villages. Individuals interviewed agreed that the Mro and the Khumi have slightly different dialects and different dress styles for men and women, but apart from these, few differences exist between them.[9]

We met with Mro weavers from the village of Ingyaung, which is situated on the Pi Chaung, a tributary of the Kaladan River. This village is about 12 miles north of Kyauk Taw. The Mro women interviewed said that women in their village continue to weave their traditional costume, which they wear for traditional celebrations and ritual observances such as the building of a new house, a wedding, the birth of a baby, and harvest time. All the Mro women we spoke with began to weave as young girls and learned the skill from their mothers. The Mro weavers continue to use a backstrap loom called *po paung*.

Mro dress

The Mro women's traditional dress is more similar to the outfit worn by the Khami than to that worn by the Khumi. They wear a breast-cloth, but not in the style of the Khumi. Called a *marankite* (figs. 10, 11), it is a small textile that measures about 76 x 35 cm. Each woman makes her own, and dimensions vary according to the weaver's size. The *marankite*, passing under one arm, covers the front and back of a woman; two corners are tied together above the opposite shoulder, leaving one shoulder exposed. Sometimes it is tied again under the arm near the waist. This would be the only upper-body garment in traditional costume, but now the Mro women, like the Khumi, prefer to wear the *marankite* over a modern blouse. Complementing the *marankite* is a shoulder scarf, or *naga pong*; it is intricately patterned and edged with colorful glass beads and small metal bells (figs. 12, 13).

Instead of the short tubular garment worn by the Khumi, the Mro women wear a flat lower-body garment (*wantalite*), which wraps around the body and is secured by a belt. The belt (*srkra baung*) is composed of many strands of glass beads that tie in front. An older style of

Fig. 11. Detail of Mro *marankite* shown in figure 10.

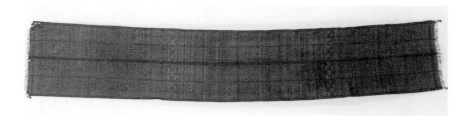

Fig. 12. Mro- or Kyauk Taw-style woman's shoulder scarf (*naga pong*). 185.5 x 38 cm.

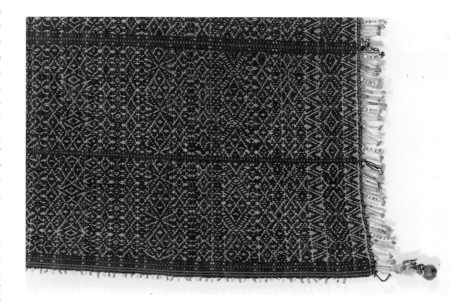

Fig. 13. Detail of Mro *naga pong* shown in figure 12.

lower-body wrapper has beads along the edges and is more like the Khumi-style skirt. The costume is further accessorized with strands of carnelian beads, white metal bracelets (*khit sei*), and cylindrical earplugs of white metal (*deroung*).

Traditional dress for Mro men would be a long loincloth, or *daun* (figs. 14, 15). The *daun* differs from the Khumi *samtu nay na* (figs. 8, 9). It is about 10 cm wide compared to the much wider Khumi piece.[10] The men with whom we spoke, who ranged in age from 39 to 50, have never worn the traditional *daun*; they prefer the Burmese *lon-gyi*, a tubular lower-body wrapper. A white head scarf (*lu pong*) and earrings (*na haung*) also used to be worn. Like the loincloth, the earrings are rarely worn today.

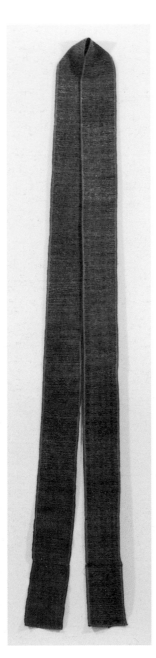

Fig. 14. Mro man's loincloth (*daun*). 10 x 325 cm.

Fig. 15. Detail of Mro *daun* shown in figure 14.

The Khami

The Khami live in a large area south of the Khumi and Mro. The area forms a roughly triangular shape that lies between the Kaladan and Lemro Rivers: with its apex at the town of Kyauk Taw, one side runs south down to Minbya, and the bottom stretches west to southwest as far as Sittwe. There are some Mro villages that lie along the Kaladan River within this triangle, but most of the population is Khami.[11] This area is a flat river valley of rice fields and numerous meandering creeks and streams. The Khami are primarily rice farmers and fishermen, traveling by small dugout and framed canoes to the many islands that surround their villages. The Khami villages we visited (Laung Shi Chaung, Maung Hna Ma, Agi Daw Ma, and Pan Be Dan) are located approximately 90 meters away from the edge of the Kaladan River's tributaries and are protected from tidal-surge flooding by earthen mounds or dikes that stand 1–1.5 meters in height. These mounds also serve as corrals for livestock, to enclose rice fields, and for elevated footpaths. In 1996 many fields, bridges, and homes were destroyed by floods that ravaged the whole area.

Inside a village, the grounds are very spacious: there are wide footpaths, many palm trees, and wood and bamboo houses that are built about 1.5 meters above ground level (fig. 16). On the first floor of the house is a large sitting platform used for entertaining guests. Upstairs, the house is sectioned into two or three rooms for sleeping and storage. The compound for each house comprises about 28 square meters of land enclosed by a bamboo fence. Here a family has its own vegetable garden for personal consumption: any excess is brought to the nearest market, in this case Mrauk Oo. Holding ponds for shrimp and fish, and household water for communal use are usually set back deep into the village. The religion of all the villages we visited was Buddhist; each has its own open-sided temple with one or more Buddha images and an adjacent monastery.

Khami ceremonial life and other customs

Traditional Khami (and Khumi) life was animistic and revolved around propitiating spirits to ensure successful crops. Sacrifices of fowl or pigs were performed at the time of sowing seed and again just before harvesting crops.

Ancestor spirits were honored in the old days with a ceremony known as *Hplaw*. The Khami ritual executed after the harvest was called *Ta-proung pa oung*, which means "opening of the dead house." Traditionally, small spirit houses were built outside a Khami village to house the ashes of deceased relatives. At *Ta-proung pa oung*, relatives of the deceased prepared food and rice liquor to be taken to spirit houses where the doors would be ritually opened and small amounts of food and drink would be offered to each spirit. Then the doors would be ritually closed, and the family members, openly weeping for their loved ones, would sit down to consume the remaining food and liquor. They would return to their homes in the village in the evening.[12]

The younger Khami women continue to dress for ceremony at least once a year. Ceremonies that require traditional dress are weddings, the building of new homes, the birth of babies, and Union Day (see below). It seems that as a woman gets older, she wears traditional dress less and

Fig. 16. U Kyaw Zan, headman of Maung Hna Ma village, with young Khami girls in full dress.

Fig. 17. Khami elders of Laung Shi Chaung village in full dress. The older Khami women wear a skirt, called *inok*, different from the type worn by younger women (see figure 22). Missing also is the *htip paum*, or shoulder scarf, reserved for young girls.

less often. Most of the women with whom we spoke were past the age of fifty and had not dressed traditionally for at least ten years. Some of these women have kept one set of traditional garments in their homes even though they had not dressed traditionally since before they were married (fig. 17). None of the older men interviewed had worn a loincloth for at least forty years, and most men interviewed had never worn one.

All the women had learned to weave from their mothers, and they in turn have taught their daughters. Many of the older weavers said that styles have not changed from those worn when they were young girls. Every woman weaves her own clothes on a backstrap loom, called *tapaur* or *tapet* by the Khami (fig. 18). The Khami also weave a large cotton blanket (*kane*), richly patterned with brightly colored warp stripes (fig. 19). Older people say that the younger girls weave less today than in the past. Expense and lack of availability of cotton may be contributing factors in decreased production of woven products. British records of 1879 show that the Khami villages on the Kaladan River grew large yields of cotton, which was much sought after by the Arkanese. The British Secretary of Commerce in Bombay, India, described the quality of the cotton as being "somewhat superior to ordinary Bengal cotton but inferior in staple, fiber and texture to Egyptian cotton."[13] Native cotton is still

Fig. 18. A Khami weaver from Maung Hna Ma village weaving a *kane*, or large cotton blanket (see figure 19). She is using a typical backstrap loom (*tapaur*).

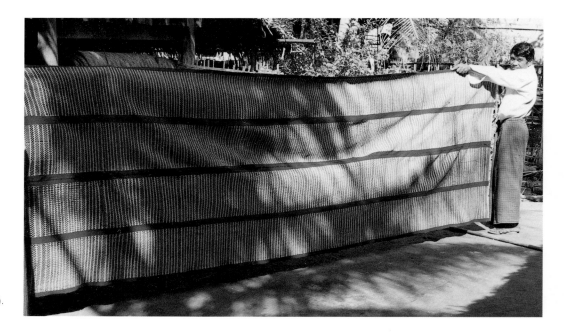

Fig. 19. Large cotton blanket (*kane*). Approximately 548.5 x 100 cm.

grown in the upper Lemro River valley and in the upper Kaladan River valley, starting just north of Kyauk Taw. But the extensive fields in the lower Kaladan region, recorded in British journals as cotton fields, now grow mostly rice.

In recent field interviews conducted in many small villages of Khami and other tribal affinities that inhabit tributaries of the Kaladan, women talked of the difficulty of obtaining cotton today. Some weavers told of vendors who used to come from Paletwa, many miles north, to sell them cotton in their villages. For unknown reasons these vendors no longer make the trip. Occasionally the small market in Mrauk Oo has cotton for sale, but it is quite expensive for weavers to purchase. The period of December to March is the traditional time for the sale of the cotton crop, but when we explored the market of Mrauk Oo in December 1997, no cotton was to be seen. Only vegetables and piles of cheap manufactured clothing, in styles inspired by the West, were offered for sale. If cotton is needed for a special weaving project, the only other available option is to travel north to the Mro or Khumi areas, namely Paletwa.

Khami dress

The upper-body garment for Khami women is a breastcloth, known as *ah khin* (fig. 20). It consists of a rectangle approximately 40 x 58 cm; elaborately patterned with multicolored yarns, it is sometimes edged with small glass beads and sequins (fig. 21). The Khami *ah khin* is distinctive from the comparable Mro garment in its two complicated supplementary warp stripes, called *ma laung sakitpat*. The weavers can produce an *ah khin* in one month if they work on it every day. Traditionally the *ah khin* is worn without any undergarment, but today a young girl wears it over a Western-style blouse (fig. 22). The women wear the *ah khin* breastcloth in the same manner as that described for the Mro.

Over the *ah khin* women wear a wide shoulder scarf, the *htip paum* (figs. 23, 24). Draped over the shoulders, it is worn down the front of the body in a shawl-like manner. The Khami *htip paum* has a brightly colored central design area, about 18 cm wide, with two warp-striped borders, also 18 cm wide, of plain-weave fabric. *Htip paum*, also used for carrying babies, are not worn by older women.

The Khami women's lower-body wrappers, called *taka seang*, are very similar to the Mro wrappers described above. The *taka seang* is a flat

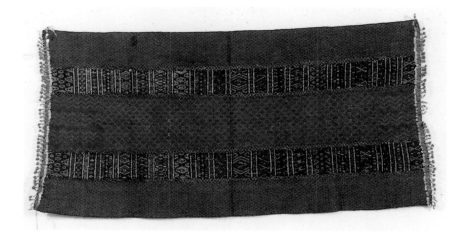

Fig. 20. Khami woman's upper-body covering or breastcloth (*ah khin*). These textiles join above one shoulder and wrap under the opposite arm. 67.5 x 35.5 cm.

Fig. 21. Detail of Khami *ah khin* shown in figure 20.

Fig. 22. Young Khami couple of Laung Shi Chaung village. Traditional male dress does not include an upper-body garment with the loincloth.

textile that wraps around the body, falling just below the knee and held in place by a belt. There are two different styles of belts with which to anchor the *taka seang*: one, the *kusa*, is composed of many strands of beads; the second type, the *sakruh*, is made of heavy metal beads which can be very elaborate and are sometimes made of silver. The *taka seang* usually has a black or dark background and is regularly patterned with brightly colored designs; sometimes there are glass beads along the bottom edge (fig. 25). One *taka seang* pattern that is distinctive consists of a zigzag pattern called *talung*, which fills the entire face of the wrapper. The *taka seang* that we have seen with the *talung* pattern were all woven in silk. Silk (*lacone*) is very expensive—when it can be found. Older women do not wear *taka seang*. Instead, they have a more somber, finely striped garment in dark neutral tones, the *inok* (fig. 17).

Traditional dress for men is an intricately woven loincloth, averaging about 17 cm in width. Called *thanipa* and/or *patari* (figs. 26, 27), these loincloths range from approximately 457 to 550 cm in length. The same complex weaving techniques used in producing the *ah khin* also appear in the two decorative trailing ends of the man's loincloth. The remaining central body consists of a very subtle black-on-black patterning.

Fig. 23. Khami woman's shoulder cloth, called *htip paum*. Unlike its counterpart in the Mro and Khumi dress, the Khami *htip paum* has no beads or bells along the selvedge. 194.3 x 45.7 cm.

Fig. 24. Detail of Khami *htip paum* shown in figure 23.

Fig. 26. Khami man's loincloth, known both as *thanipa* and *patari*. The two ends of these cloths are decorated for about 45 cm, with the same weaving technique as displayed in the Khami woman's *ah khin* (see figure 21). 411.5 x 14.6 cm.

Fig. 25. A group of Khami women from the Kyauk Taw area, a town where the Khami and Mro peoples overlap. The hats/headdresses are not a typical part of the traditional costume.

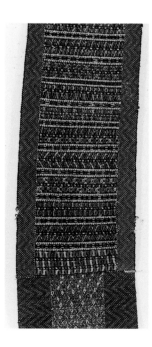

Fig. 27. Detail of Khami man's *thanipa* shown in figure 26.

Laytu and Zantu Dress

Of the remaining "mystery" garments, three were shown to the people of all three groups, Khumi, Khami, and Mro, as well as to other tribal groups in the area. The first of these garments is a short, cropped tunic-style upper-body garment, with red glass beads and cowrie shells decorating the bottom portion and beautifully patterned supplementary weft silk adorning the top (fig. 28). Many of this type have found their way into prominent collections in the United States with only "Chin" as a description. After questioning the people named above, the unanimous conclusion was that the tunic is a woman's upper-body garment from the Laytu people.

The Laytu are a group of the southern Chin/Zo who inhabit the central and lower parts of the Lemro River valley. Along with their exquisite upper-body garment, women wear a plain, black short skirt with a belt of metal disks. During a Laytu funeral ceremony, the relatives of the deceased pile traditional costumes around his or her body to show the wealth of family. These garments are later taken back by the rightful owners. In recent years the Laytu have been

Fig. 28. Laytu woman's beaded upper-body garment from the Lemro River area. 45 x 45 cm.

Fig. 29. Zantu woman's tunic from Myebon. Approximately 88 x 78 cm.

forcibly relocated for political reasons from their traditional mountainous river valleys on the Lemro to the western rice field areas of the Khami. Most of them found this move unbearable and have migrated back to their beloved homelands.[14]

The remaining two "mystery" pieces are long tunics or smocks. The first has a black or deep blue body patterned with brightly colored magenta supplementary weft and further embellished with buttons, glass beads, and sequins (figs. 29, 30). This type of garment is worn by women; it falls to around the knee and is belted at the waist with strands of glass or metal beads. The long tunic is worn by the Zantu (or Santu) who live on the lower parts of the Lemro River.[15] Their area stretches from Myebon, which is southeast of Sittwe, to Minbya, east-northeast of Sittwe. Local people call the Zantu the "Sea Chin" due to their proximity to the Bay of Bengal. The second type of tunic is worn by men (figs. 31, 32). The men's garments are more somber in color than the women's. The black background is striped in beautifully woven, geometrically designed bands of varying widths, in soft warm tones of madder and tan.

Today many of the northern Chin/Zo peoples have converted to Christianity, and in the river valleys of the south some villages have adopted Buddhism, but everywhere a few older people cling to old ways. F. K. Lehman (1963b) tells of the easy blending of the young, educated Christian men and women with the old traditionalists. The tolerance of the Buddhist philosophy has room for remnants of the old ways as well. Today observances are still made for major life experiences—birth, coming of age, marriage, constructing a new house, and death. Traditional costume is still required for most of these events. A modern holiday, called Union Day, has been added to the political calendar; it is celebrated on February 12 to commemorate the short-lived achievement of the unification of Burma's diverse racial groups by U Aung San, the father of modern Burma (contemporary Myanmar). At this time, people of all backgrounds wear their finest traditional costumes with pride.

Fig. 30. Detail of Zantu woman's tunic shown in figure 29.

Acknowledgments

The authors would like to thank the family of the Reverend S. T. Haugo and Nu Luan Za Cing for their knowledge of all Chin/Zo peoples and for their gracious hospitality; U Thein Win, for his excellent translations of Burmese and Arkanese into English and for sharing his vast knowledge of his country; U Tha Kyaw Aung, for translating Khami language into Burmese and English and for his guidance through the confusing waterways of the Mrauk Oo area; U Aung Tun Tha, the headman of Laung Shi Chaung village, and U Kyaw Zan, the headman of Maung Hna Ma village, for their hospitality and for introducing us to the weavers of their villages.

We are grateful to all the unnamed Khami, Khumi, and Mro weavers and people who educated us about their rich textile arts and cultures. We greatly appreciate the support and encouragement graciously provided in the United States by Dr. Mattiebelle Gittinger, without which this article would not have been possible. Special thanks are extended to Dr. Maude Southwell Wahlman for her many years of support and coaching on the proper way to conduct field interviews, and to Sylvia Fraser-Lu, Dr. Sarah Bekker, Dr. Kris Lehman, Dr. Vumson, and Pu Lian Uk for generously sharing their extensive knowledge of the peoples of Burma.

All photographs were taken by the authors.

Fig. 31. Zantu man's tunic.
Approximately 93 x 81 cm.

Fig. 32. Detail of Zantu man's tunic shown in figure 31.

About the Authors

Jay Bommer and Deborah Garner are husband and wife, owners of Tribal Spirit Traders, a company specializing in traditional arts of indigenous tribal peoples from around the world. For the past ten years they have been focusing their attention on building a comprehensive collection of traditional costumes from tribal groups living in Burma.

Notes

1. Any mistakes, translation errors, or misinterpretations of previously published material are strictly our own. We hope that this initial effort will encourage additional anthropological, linguistic, and art historical studies by scholars in these fields before all traces of the indigenous cultures are lost.

2. Chin is the term applied by English-speakers to linguistically related groups of Tibeto-Burman-speakers in the western hill regions of Burma. No single term had been used indigenously to designate these groups, but some called themselves Khyang, which in modern Burmese is pronounced *Khyin*, i.e., "Chin," and this became the English label for all. (Chin is the anglicized form of High Burmese pronunciation of "Khyan" [Brauns and Loeffler 1990, p. 35]). Locally, the term Zo, a component of many of ethnic group names, is used by some of the hill peoples to encompass all the groups. The authors have elected to use an amalgamation of the two, Chin/Zo.

3. The identification of Khumi, Khami, and Mro presents problems; some scholars think the Khumi and Khami are the same group. Although their textiles bear similarities, the differences are sufficient to retain the ethnic distinctions. It is generally conceded that the costume of the Mro was adopted from the Khami because other Mro living in Bangladesh and India do not share these traditions. (Brauns and Loeffler 1990, pp. 36, 37).

4. The Laytu and Zantu, known under a variety of other names in the literature, normally live farther north in the central Chin area. Their particular garment types contrast markedly from those of their neighbors in this southern area of Burma.

5. Khumi population centers were confirmed by interviews with Khumi informants as well as neighboring tribal peoples. Owing to suspicions and harsh treatment by the authorities toward locals who associate with outsiders, some personal and village names are being withheld.

6. Daw Nan Aung, a Khumi woman originally from Paletwa, gave us the names of the garments and accessories that complete the costume. The following garments were confirmed to be Khumi by several other Mro and Khami who live in close proximity to the Khumi.

7. Phonetic transliterations for the spelling of tribal names of individual garments discussed in this article were provided by our English-speaking translators, U Thein Win and U Tha Kyaw Aung; they were assisted by other individuals in each village.

8. This loincloth style is shared by Khumi, Matu, and Haka Chin/Zo peoples. Anthropologist F. K. Lehman (1963b, p. 87) noted that the Matu people of Matupi and the Khumi of Paletwa share cultural similarities.

9. Among those interviewed concerning this issue were U Sar Khaung, a Mro man; U Pri Kwin, a Khumi man; and Daw Nan Aung, a Khumi woman.

10. St. John (1879) mentions Mro men wearing narrow blue loincloths.

11. Pu Lian Uk, an elected Member of Parliament of the Burmese government in exile and a former school teacher who taught for ten years in Paletwa, contributed his extensive first-hand knowledge of the region, including this information.

12. St. John 1879, pp. 68–70.

13. See St. John 1879 for more detailed information on cotton production in this region during the colonial period.

14. Field interviews in Mrauk Oo and Teinnyo.

15. Field interviews in Mrauk Oo and Sittwe; correspondence with Pu Lian Uk.

References

Bessaignet, Pierre

1958   *Tribesmen of the Chittagong Hill Tracts*. Asia Society of Pakistan, Dacca.

Brauns, Claus-Dieter, and Lorenz G. Loeffler

1990   *Mru: Hill People on the Border of Bangladesh*. Birkhauser, Boston.

Carey, B. S., and H. N. Tuck

1976   *The Chin Hills: A History of the People, Their Customs and Manners, and Our Dealing with Them, and a Gazetteer of Their Country, Rangoon*. Originally published by FIRMA KLM on behalf of Tribal Institute, Aizawl, in Calcutta, 1869.

Enriquez, C. M. D.

1924   *Races of Burma*. Government of India Central Publication Department, Calcutta.

Fraser-Lu, Sylvia

1988   *Textiles of Southeast Asia*. Oxford University Press, Singapore.

Grant-Brown, G. E. R.

1913   *Burma Gazetteer: Upper Chindwin District*, vol. A. Rangoon.

Hall, D. G. E.

1964   *A History of Southeast Asia*. Macmillan Press, London and St. Martin's Press, New York.

Hardiman, J. P.

1912   *Burma Gazetteer: Lower Chindwin District*, vol. A. Superintendent of the Government Printing and Stationery, Rangoon. Reprinted by Central Press, Rangoon, 1967.

Haugo, Rev. S. T.

1971–72 Some Random Thoughts about Our People, Our Language, Our Culture, *Chin Literature and Culture Subcommittee Magazine*, 1971, pp. 8–12. Bengal Printing Company, Rangoon.

Lehman, F. K.

1963a   Anthropology in the Chin Hills, *Guardian*, vol. 104, pp. 39–40. Rangoon.

1963b   *The Structure of Chin Society*. University of Illinois Press, Urbana.

Lewin, T. H.

1869   *The Hill Tracks of Chittagong and the Dwellers Therein*. Bengal Printing Company, Calcutta.

Lowis, C. C.

1919   The Tribes of Burma, Burma no. 4, *Ethnographic Survey of India*, pp. 19–23. Rangoon.

Luce, George H.

1959   Notes on the People of Burma in the 12th and 13th Century A.D., *Journal of the Burmese Research Society*, vol. 42, pp. 52–74. Rangoon.

1961   *Translation of the Manshu; Book of Southern Barbarians, 862, by Fan-cho*. Data Paper no. 44, Southeast Asia Program. Cornell University, Ithaca.

Min Naing, U

1960   *Races of Burma*. Ministry of Culture, Rangoon.

St. John, M. R. F.

1879   *British Burma Gazetteer*, vol. 2.

Stevenson, H. N. C.

1944   *The Hill Peoples of Burma*. Burma Pamphlets, no. 6. Longmans Green, London.

Textiles of the Southern Thái of Viêt Nam

Michael C. Howard and Kim Be Howard

While a great deal of research has been conducted and much written about the textiles of the Tái-speaking peoples of Laos and Thailand, the textiles of the Thái in Viêt Nam are poorly studied and documented. This is especially true of the more southerly Thái living in the provinces of Hòa Bình, Thanh Hóa, and Nghê An, despite their possessing a very rich textile tradition with a vital place in the comparative study of Tái textiles.[1]

The textiles of these Thái are ignored in the main English language surveys of Southeast Asian textiles. Nor are they given much attention in the Vietnamese, French, and English literature focusing on the minority peoples of Viêt Nam, which deal primarily with the better known Northern Thái of Son La and Lai Châu Provinces. Thus, the popular image of Thái dress is that of the Black Tái women of these two provinces with their silver-buttoned, tight-fitting blouses, long black skirts, and colorfully embroidered black headcloths. Few people are even aware of the dress of the Thái to the south that more closely resembles the costume of the Thái in Houa Phan and Xiêng Khoang Provinces in neighboring Laos.

The present article provides a survey of the textiles of the southern Thái in Viêt Nam,[2] focusing on the types of textiles made by them and their use. We also present a brief overview of changes that have taken place, especially the impact of external factors such as commercialization in recent years. In addition, we examine the influence of Thái textiles on neighboring Môn-Khmer-speaking peoples.

The Southern Thái of Hòa Bình, Thanh Hóa, and Nghê An Provinces

There are over three million speakers of some ten Tái languages in Viêt Nam (Grimes 1996, pp. 799–807; Dang, Chu, and Luu 1993, pp. 111–141; and Nguyên 1997). These include about two million Tày, Nùng, and Sán Chay (or Man Cao Lan-Sán Chi) who speak Central Tái languages; about 50,000 Giáy (or Nhang) and Bô Y (or Bouyei) who speak Northern Tái languages; and a little over one million Thái, Lào, Lü, Lào Khrang, and Phu Thái (or PhuTái) who speak Southwestern Tái languages. The Central Tái-speaking peoples live mainly east of the Red River (Sông Hông) with the largest concentration in Cao Bang and Lang Son Provinces. The Northern Tái straddle the Red River and are found mainly in Lào Cai Province and immediately adjacent areas. The Southwestern Tái-speaking peoples live in the northwestern part of the country in a strip along the Laotian border from northern Lai Châu Province, through Son La Province, northwestern Hòa Bình Province, and south to the western portions of Thanh Hóa and Nghê An Provinces (fig. 1).

Fig. 1. The region in northern Viêt Nam occupied by the Thái.

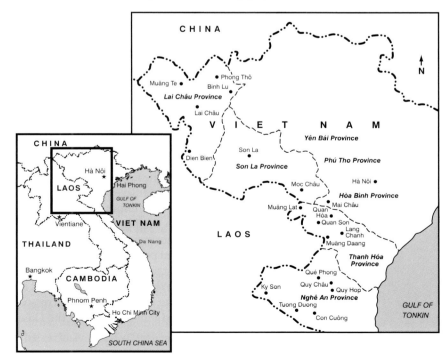

survey of Thái clothing focuses on the Northern Thái, but it does include information on the Thái of Mai Châu.

Viêt Nam has two national museums devoted to the study and display of the material culture of its ethnic groups (Howard 1999). The older of these, the Museum of Nationalities (Bao Tàng Van Hóa Các Dân Tôc Viêt Nam), in Thái Nguyên, has an extensive collection of Thái material, but no Southern Thái material is displayed or illustrated in its catalogue. The newly established Museum of Ethnology (Bao Tàng Dân Tôc Hoc Viêt Nam) in Hanoi (Hà Nôi), however, has sought to provide a more comprehensive picture of the Thái: its own staff, along with foreign scholars under its sponsorship, have undertaken several field trips to Nghê An and Thanh Hóa provinces. Included in this museum's displays of Thái material are Tái Muäng and Tái Thanh costumes, and examples of these are illustrated in its catalogue (Nguyên 1998, pp. 34–35).

Textiles of the Southern White Tái of Mai Châu, Muäng Lat, Quan Hóa, and Quan Son

In general, the Southern Thái until recent decades were more isolated from the outside than the Northern Thái. This was especially true during the period of French colonialism. Among the Southern White Tái of Hòa Bình and Thanh Hóa provinces, those living in Mai Châu District have been perhaps the most subject to external influences. During the French period their valley was connected with the outside by road in 1936. In recent years, while travel to other Southern Thái areas by foreigners continues to require the permission of provincial authorities, access to Mai Châu is unrestricted, and government officials have sought to develop the valley (about a four-hour drive from Hà Nôi) as a tourist destination.

The Mai Châu District village of Lác has emerged as an important center for producing and selling handwoven textiles to foreign and domestic tourists, shop owners in Hà Nôi and Saigon, as well as to textile dealers from Laos and Thailand (Howard 1998, pp. 17–18). This development is a result of a combination of the community's strategic location (being within day-trip range of Hà Nôi), government policy to promote tourism in the area, and local entrepreneurship. In addition to selling their own textiles, the villagers offer a variety of textiles from Thái and Muòng communities in northwestern Thanh Hóa Province.[7] It is interesting to note that while the selling of traditional handwoven textiles is of considerable economic importance to Ban Lác, acculturative influences over the past few decades have led villagers themselves largely to abandon wearing traditional dress that is identifiable as Thái.

Fig. 2. Tái Dam woman weaving. Quan Son District, Thanh Hóa Province.

Among the Southern White Tái living in northwestern Thanh Hóa Province, Muäng Kasa was a particularly important political and cultural center in the past, but destruction by aerial bombardment in the early 1970s and subsequent acculturative influences associated with the growth of the new administrative center of Quan Hóa have led to the disappearance of many attributes of traditional Thái culture, including the virtual cessation of producing handwoven textiles and wearing identifiable Thái dress.[8] Traditional Thái textiles and dress are in greater evidence in the more isolated communities in Quan Son and Muäng Lat districts (fig. 2).

The Quan Son District was established as a separate administrative entity in 1997. It has a total population of just over 31,000 people who live in 90 villages. Its population is 89 percent Thái. An estimated 80 percent of the Thái women in Quan Son District still wear distinctive Thái dress (fig. 3), although a growing number of the women wear Lào-style skirts that are obtained from Laotian traders. Generally, textile production in Quan Son District is greater in villages at higher elevation nearer to the Laos border, where there is less land available for agriculture, than in villages at lower altitudes with greater potential for agriculture.

Many of the older textiles of the Tái Dam in Thanh Hóa Province have already been sold to traders from Laos or Mai Châu, but many types of tradition-based textiles continue to be produced and worn. Although some villages near the main highway in Quan Son District have been receiving regular visits from textile traders from Laos for the past few years, most textile production is still for domestic consumption.

Prior to 1954, Thanh Hóa Tái Dam and Tái Mai Châu society had distinct class differences that divided people into nobles and commoners. Class distinctions were reflected in personal adornment. For example, only nobles were allowed to wear satin, and commoners could wear silver earrings but not gold. The length of men's trousers also varied according to class: the upper class wore them long, down to the feet, and commoners wore them above the feet.

Male fashion among these Thái can be roughly divided into three periods.[9] The first can be called the traditional period; it extends roughly from the 1940s back at least into the latter part of the nineteenth century, and possibly earlier (no information is presently available prior to this time). The second period, sometimes called "modern," refers to outside influences around

Fig. 3. Two Tái Dam women in Ban Ngum, Trung Thuong Commune, Quan Son District, Thanh Hóa Province. One woman is wearing a plain black *seen*, while the other is wearing a *seen muk ko* with *mee* patterning. Both wear headcloths, one black and the other indigo, which feature embroidered patterning (not seen in the photo).

the 1940s that were considered modern. During that period, commercial fabrics became more readily available and the style of some clothing changed. These were modifications of traditional fashions, however, and not a complete change of style of dress. The third period marked the abandonment of recognizable Thái dress and the adoption of generic modern-style clothing. In some communities, this break with tradition began in the 1950s but elsewhere did not take place until more recently; and in some more isolated communities older men still wear more traditional clothing.

The traditional male shirt (*seu-uh teen*) is made of cotton cloth that is dyed black or dark indigo. It has long tight sleeves, a round stand-up collar, and fastens down the side. The style of these shirts changed in the 1940s. The new fashion was for them to fasten in the center, like those of the Northern Thái, and for the pockets to be decorated with a thin red or blue line.

Traditional dress for men also included a long coat (*seu-uh sao*) when it was cold or for weddings and other special occasions. The coat

Fig. 4. Tái Dam loom set up to weave cloth for waistbands. Quan Son district, Thanh Hóa Province.

was made of cotton and either left white or dyed black or dark indigo. The traditional style opened in the center, but the new fashion in the 1940s had it opening down the side. Wearing such coats appears to have nearly ceased in the 1950s, except in very isolated villages.

Traditional men's trousers are baggy and are folded and tied at the waist. They are made of cotton cloth that is dyed black or dark indigo. Short trousers (*sawng kum*) were commonly worn while working in the fields. For other occasions, longer trousers (*sawng sao*) were worn. Male attire also sometimes included a headcloth (*po hoo-uh*) that was worn folded and knotted in the front. It is made of plain white cotton cloth. In the past, such a headcloth was always worn when visiting as a sign of respect. This fashion had almost disappeared by the 1950s.

Women's dress has been more conservative than men's fashion, but it too has undergone changes. Unlike men, however, many women continue to wear distinctive Thái dress up to the present. Traditional women's dress among the Southern White Tái of Thanh Hóa Province, in particular, includes a wider array of items than that of the other Thái groups. Several types of textile that were once made by other Thái, including those of Mai Châu, are still being made by this group of Thái. There are a number of traditional skirt styles and we have yet to decipher the association of their specific decorative motifs with particular locales (except in a few cases). All are made of three segments: a waistband, a central body, and a hem piece.

The waistbands (*hoo-uh*) of the Southern White Tái should perhaps be called a breast covering since formerly blouses were not worn and this segment of the skirt was attached roughly at the waist and covered the breasts (figs. 3, 4).[10] Sometimes these are made of pieces of plain cotton cloth, but more often patterned cloth is used.

Decorative waistbands have three distinct segments. The two top segments are made of cloth woven specifically for use as waistbands. These segments are decorated with supplementary-warp patterning and are woven on a special narrow loom. In the past the two upper segments were woven separately and then sewn together. In more recent times they are often woven as a single piece and sewn together with the third segment. The uppermost segment features geometric patterns. Simple ones may be woven in only two colors (blue and gray or black), while more complex ones may employ four or five colors. Among the more common motifs found on these upper segments are the *mak een* (square) and *ka nawng ma* (stairs or steps). Some also have an eight-pointed star pattern that is said to depict the flower of the eggplant. The middle segment tends to be more brightly colored than the upper one and usually features animal motifs. The most common motifs encountered in recent years depict various forms of dragon (*toh ngawk*).[11] Other animals depicted include a snake with two heads, turtle, bird, peacock, phoenix, fish, frog, spider, and butterfly. The dragon motif seems once to have been reserved for members of the noble class. Although this restriction disappeared decades ago, its association with nobility may have contributed to its subsequent popularity. Some informants have commented that it used to be possible to identify provenance of a skirt by the style of the dragon motif, but none was able to do so. The bottom segment is made either of a plain piece of cloth or from a strip of cloth with alternating bands of geometric supplementary-weft patterning in white on an indigo ground and figurative weft-ikat patterning in white with alternating indigo and red grounds. This strip is cut from a larger piece of cloth of a type that is also used in the body of some skirts. In the past Thái women in Mai Châu and Thanh Hóa Province sometimes wore skirts with only the upper two segments, or even only the uppermost one. In general, however, the ideal was to wear a skirt with all three segments.

There are six basic types of cloth used to make the body of the skirt (seven, if you count the plain black pieces of cotton cloth sometimes used). It should be noted that such skirt cloth is usually cut from a longer roll of cloth up to 20 meters in length. The simplest of these is a relatively dark-colored piece of cloth with black weft yarns and warp yarns in predominantly dark colors (black, brown, and purple), but also with a few lighter-colored ones, and sometimes very simple warp-ikat patterning.[12] When worn, the stripes are horizontal. Sometimes embroidered geometric patterns, usually in rows, in colorful thread, are added toward the bottom. A skirt made from this type of cloth is known as a *seen tah lai* or *seen tah lan* (fig. 5). A second type of cloth is the same as the above but with the addition of scattered weft-ikat (*mee*) patterns in white. The patterns are usually representational, of people, animals, or flowers. Skirts made from such cloth are sometimes also called *seen tah lan* or *seen mee* (fig. 6).

Fig. 5. Southern White Tái (Tái Dam) piece of cotton cloth for *seen tah lai*. 71 x 150 cm. Quan Son District, Thanh Hóa Province. Some stripes have simple warp ikat patterning. The lower part has embroidered patterns in commercial silk thread. The piece was made in early 1997, along with a number of other pieces of cloth, by a woman for her daughter's upcoming wedding.

Fig. 6. Southern White Tái (Tái Dam) material for *seen tah lan* or *seen mee* (folded in half in the photo). 142 x 61 cm. Ban Ngàm, Trung Thuong Commune, Quan Son District, Thanh Hóa Province. There are black cotton weft yarns and alternating black, purple, and yellow warp yarns to create stripes. The ikat patterning features two motifs: *bok bin nung* (papaya seed) and *bok kah kim* (called "pliers," but the weaver does not know the original meaning). The embroidery with silk thread includes *bok lai tah kai* (chicken eyes star leaf), *toh vet* (tick), and *toh ua* motifs. The cloth was made for Tet (New Year in the lunar calendar) in 1998.

The third type of cloth features plain or warp-ikat horizontal stripes similar to the first type, with purple being the predominant color, with the addition of supplementary-warp (*muk*) patterning using white yarn. There are five widths of *muk* bands, which are referred to by number (*sahm, see, hah, hohk,* and *jet*), and these give the skirts different names. The overall name for this type of skirt is *seen muk lai* (fig. 7). Rows of

embroidered geometric patterns in brightly colored thread are sometimes added at the bottom of these cloths as well.

The fourth and fifth types of cloth are similar. Both have patterned horizontal and vertical stripes. The most complex of the two features a combination of supplementary-warp patterned stripes that frame rows of small rectangles with alternating weft-ikat (*mee*) and supplementary-weft patterning. The weft-ikat (fig. 8) patterns commonly feature human figures, while there is considerable variation in the supplementary-weft patterning. On occasion, the latter also features human figures, but geometric patterns are more common. The simpler version of the two lacks the weft-ikat patterns. The generic name for a skirt using either of these types of cloth is *seen muk ko*. Those with weft-ikat patterns may be called *seen muk mee ko* or simply *seen mee* (fig. 9).

The sixth type of skirt is made from cloth with weft-ikat patterning in wide bands, usually with alternating red and indigo backgrounds, in between narrower bands with plain stripes and often stripes with geometric supplementary-weft patterning. The weft-ikat bands commonly include dragon motifs. The general name for skirts made from this type of cloth is also *seen mee* (figs. 9–11). Thin strips of this type of cloth, as noted above, are also often used as the lower part of skirt waistbands.

Seen muk ko and the latter type of *seen mee* almost always have a separate hem piece added. This is sometimes a feature of *seen muk lai* as well. The most common type of hem piece is a plain narrow piece of indigo-dyed cloth. Sometimes more elaborate hem pieces are worn, including ones with extensive discontinuous supplementary-weft patterning with *seeho* (sometimes spelled *siho*), *ngawk, nak,* and other traditional motifs.

The Southern White Tái of Mai Châu in particular, as well as those in Quan Son and other less isolated communities in Thanh Hóa Province, also wear skirts with a plain black or dark indigo body and no hem piece (fig. 12).

Women initially wore no blouse and either went bare-breasted or covered their breasts with the upper portion of their skirts. This style of wearing skirts is referred to as *hang ang*, meaning folded up to the breast. At some time in the past, some women adopted long-sleeved blouses with a rounded collar. Such blouses were especially common among women of the noble class. Many Southern Thái women, however, went from

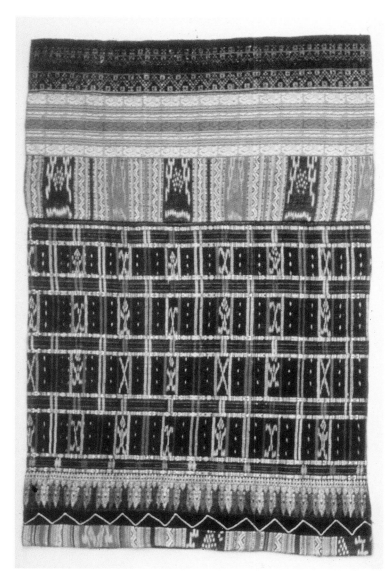

Fig. 9. Southern White Tái (Tái Dam) *seen muk ko*. 67 x 105 cm. Quan Son District, Thanh Hóa Province. There are two cotton waistband pieces added with supplementary-warp patterning and a third silk one with bands of weft-ikat patterning. The body is made of cotton with broad bands alternating with narrower bands. The broad bands show a combination of supplementary-weft and weft-ikat patterning featuring human figures. The narrower bands are plain weave with warp-ikat patterning and supplementary-weft (*muk*) patterning. A thin hem piece is added with bands of weft-ikat patterning. The skirt was made for Tet in 1997.

Fig. 8. Tái Dam woman tying thread to prepare for ikat dyeing. Ban Ha, Son Ha Commune, Quan Son District, Thanh Hóa Province.

Fig. 10. Southern White Tái (Tái Dam) *seen mee*. 68 x 72 cm. Thanh Hóa Province. The waistband has been removed. The body is made of silk and has alternating bands of weft-ikat and supplementary-weft patterning. The rust-colored ikat patterning features a very rare crane motif. The indigo ikat patterning features a *prasat phueng* (temple) motif. The hem piece is made of plain indigo cotton. The piece dates from before the Second World War.

Fig. 11. Southern White Tái (Tái Mai Châu) *seen mee*. 75 x 73 cm. Hòa Bình Province. The waistband has been removed. The body is made of silk with alternating bands of weft-ikat and supplementary-weft patterning. This weft-ikat pattern appears to be particular to the area around Mai Châu and adjacent Thanh Hóa Province. The hem piece is made of indigo-dyed cotton. The piece dates from the 1930s. Such skirts ceased to be worn in Mai Châu shortly after this time.

covering their breasts with the upper portion of their skirts directly to wearing modern-style generic blouses made of commercial cloth.

The everyday woman's headcloth traditionally was made of a piece of cotton cloth that was usually left white or sometimes dyed indigo blue. Occasionally these had a little embroidered patterning. There were also more elaborate festive headcloths with extensive supplementary-weft patterning employing a variety of motifs worn at least in some areas. Such headcloths are rarely made nowadays and are not commonly worn.

White Tái women of Thanh Hóa and Hòa Bình provinces also have a tradition of wearing a short-sleeved long cloak (*seu-uh teen sao*) on special occasions (fig. 13). In particular, these coats are worn by a woman at the funerals of her husband's parents and are worn by priests when praying at funerals. The upper portion of this cloak in the past was made of plain locally-made silk cloth, but over the past few decades it has

Fig. 12. Southern White Tái (Tái Mai Châu) tubular skirt. 70 x 101 cm. Mai Châu District, Hòa Bình Province. There are three waistbands: the upper one is indigo with white geometric patterning in cotton; the center one has stripes with geometric patterning using purple and yellow silk thread; the lower one is silk with variously colored vertical stripes. The body is made of plain indigo-dyed commercial silk. The body dates from the French period before 1954. The waistbands are newer than the body. Such a skirt would have been worn by an upper-class woman.

been more common to use commercial cotton cloth. The lower portion of the cloak is made from a separate, elaborately decorated piece of cloth, usually one with extensive supplementary-weft patterning. The cloth for this lower portion may be made by the woman herself, by her mother-in-law, or sometimes it is a particularly nice piece of cloth given to her by her husband (and obtained by him through trade).

Priests used to wear a cloth necklace (*thawng saanh*) that served as a magical charm or amulet at funerals (fig. 14). It is made of several pieces of cloth sewn together with a pouch in the center that is sometimes sewn closed; often embellishments such as pig tusks are attached. The pouch contains various potent items. These may include a tiger's tooth, a piece of the sky god's hammer (found when lightning hits a tree), and shells. Priests also would wear a special hat. These cloaks, necklaces, and hats are seldom worn today.

The Thái of these two provinces also produce a variety of textiles for domestic use out of long pieces of cloth (up to 20 meters long) made of either cotton or silk (fig. 15). Rolls or pieces of such cloth are often set aside to be cut up and

Fig. 13. Southern White Tái (Tái Mai Châu) woman's *seu-uh teen sao*. 60 x 143 cm. Ban Lác, Chiêng Châu Commune, Mai Châu District, Hòa Bình Province. The body is made of locally produced silk with black cotton trim. A separate piece of silk cloth with extensive supplementary-weft patterning is attached to the hem. This type of long coat is no longer worn in the area. The piece dates from before the Second World War.

Fig. 15. Southern White Tái (Tái Dam) piece of *khit*-style long cloth. 42 x 672 cm. Thanh Hóa Province. This was originally part of a longer piece. Lengths such as this can be used as coffin screens. Such cloths are also cut into shorter strips to make the centers of blankets and into thin strips to decorate mosquito nets. This example is made of silk with red warp yarns. Horizontal solid stripes are made using gold, green, yellow, and white silk weft yarns. Horizontal bands with gold-and white-colored silk weft yarns are used to create *toh ngawk* (dragon) designs. The cloth dates from the French era, or prior to the 1950s.

Fig. 14. Southern White Tái (Tái Mai Châu) *thawng saanh*. Overall length 90 cm, satchel width 17 cm. Ban Lác, Chiêng Châu Commune, Mai Châu District, Hòa Bình Province. The body and straps are made of several pieces of cotton cloth. The satchel in the center is sewn closed with something inside (considered to be magical charms). Two pig tusks are attached. Such charms are no longer worn in this area. This particular piece dates from before the Second World War.

Fig. 16. Southern White Tái (Tái Dam) cloth for *pha lai*. 39 x 325 cm. Ban Ngàm, Trung Thuong Commune, Quan Son District, Thanh Hóa Province. Made of white hand-spun cotton with indigo-dyed cotton weft yarns used to create patterns, the cloth features large diamond shapes which represent the *bok bin khoa horo* with a coffin in the center (the *bok* is the flower of the tree from which coffins are made). It also has smaller *toh bee* (butterfly) patterns. It was woven by Ngân Thi Nhat in the mid-1980s.

Fig. 17. Southern White Tái (Tái Dam) *pha lai* with red border. Ban Ha, Son Ha Commune, Quan Son District, Thanh Hóa Province.

used as needed. Cut into pieces 3 to 5 meters in length, they can be used as coffin screens. They are also cut into shorter pieces, and two of them are sewn together to make the centers of blankets that are lined and backed with plain cotton cloth. The cloth backing is usually left undyed. In the past, thin strips were cut from such long cloths and used to decorate the tops of mosquito nets.

There are two basic types of blanket (*pha*): *pha lai* and *pha khit* (the latter sometimes also called *pha daang* when it has a red background). *Pha lai* feature centers made from strips of white cotton cloth with supplementary-weft patterning using cotton yarn dyed either black or indigo blue (figs. 16, 17). *Pha khit* feature centers usually made from strips of red cloth with bands of supplementary-weft patterning (*khit*). In the past, the centers of *pha khit* were made of silk, but in recent years they have been made of cotton, sometimes with the patterning executed in brightly colored wool yarn (fig. 18). When used for special occasions or when certain motifs are especially noticeable, such blankets may also be named accordingly (e.g., *pha lai toh pee* for a *pha lai* blanket with a butterfly motif).

As was mentioned above, long pieces of cloth may be used to screen or cover coffins. Such cloths screen the coffin day and night and are buried with the coffin. It is generally considered appropriate to use red *khit* cloths for men and indigo or black cloths for women. Recently, the tendency has been to use pieces of plain commercial cloth for coffin screens.

The decorative strips of cloth attached across the tops of mosquito nets are known as *cha poy* or "heart-neck" (fig. 19). Such *cha poy* are rarely used any more, and decorations are usually made from commercial cloth.

Fig. 18. Southern White Tái (Tái Dam) contemporary three-panel wedding blanket woven in early 1998. Ban Ha, Son Ha Commune, Quan Son District, Thanh Hóa Province. The patterning of the blanket, or *pha baang*, is made with brightly colored pre-dyed wool yarn imported from Laos. In villages such as this, which are visited by merchants from Laos around the time of Tet to trade for textiles, such imported yarns are now widely used for decorative patterning.

Textiles of the Tái Muäng

Tái Muäng villages are found scattered throughout the northern and southern parts of Nghê An Province in Qué Phong, Quy Châu, Quy Hop, Con Cuông, and Tuong Duong Districts. As was noted above, the Thái population in Nghê An Province is around 210,000. Tái Muäng make up around 65–70 percent of this number, or about 145,000 people.

At this point, it is useful to mention two characteristics which distinguish the textiles of the Tái Muäng from those of the Tái Thanh (discussed in the next section). The first is the difference in the waistbands of women's skirts. The skirts of Tái Muäng women traditionally feature a plain white cotton waistband, while the skirts of Tái Thanh women have plain red waistbands. The second characteristic is that the motifs employed by Tái Muäng on their textiles tend to be representations of things, such as animals, flowers, mythical beasts, while those of the Tái Thanh are more abstract. It should be noted, however, that Tái Thanh sometimes copy Tái Muäng styles when making blankets and even skirts. This practice has become more noticeable in recent years with the emergence of a commercial market for Tái Muäng-style blankets and hem pieces.

The Thái of Nghê An Province, especially the Tái Muäng, were brought into the Thailand-centered regional textile market in the early 1990s. Textile traders from Laos first became active in Nghê An Province in 1991, and by the end of that year a variety of Tái Muäng textiles (skirts, headcloths, blankets, and coffin screens) had appeared for sale in Bangkok and Chiang Mai. The Laotian traders supplied scant information to the Thái dealers, who knew only that these textiles were supposedly "from somewhere in Laos, probably Sam Nua or Houa Phanh." Textile traders from Laos now make regular trips to Nghê An Province, and since about 1997 they have been joined by a few traders from Thailand.[13]

Since around 1995 Tái Muäng weavers, especially in Con Cuông and Quy Châu Districts, have also been receiving attention from Viêt Nam-based foreign and domestic nongovernmental organizations, such as Oxfam and Craft Link, which have encouraged the production of textiles for the tourist and expatriate handicraft market in Hà Nôi. Such textiles often differ from those produced for domestic use in overall quality, and the market for them remains fairly small and erratic. Nevertheless, the sale of such textiles has become a useful income supplement for at least some households.

Economic change in Nghê An Province over the past decade has led to the emergence of a more extensive local market for textiles than existed previously—again, primarily among the Tái Muäng. Thus, Tái Muäng women in Khê Thái Commune living along the main highway west of Con Cuông town now generally purchase material for their skirts and even embroidered hem pieces rather than making them. Many of these women stopped weaving in the 1970s, although almost all continued to embroider hem pieces. Then, a Viêt man opened a shop in 1990 that sold handwoven cloth and hem pieces bought from more isolated villages. Almost all of those who were still weaving soon stopped and the remaining few quit after a few more years, deciding that it was no longer worth the effort. Many women also no longer embroidered and simply purchased hem pieces from the shop.

Tái Muäng living along or near the main highway also sometimes purchase textiles from itinerant traders. These include not only Tái Muäng textiles but also textiles from Laos. For example, while many women in the Tái Muäng village of Cay Mé, Thanh Giám Commune, located along the main highway in Tuong Duong District, still weave and embroider, they also often buy textiles from itinerant traders from Ky Son District. In this case, not only do they obtain Tái Muäng and Lào textiles, but their weaving and style of dress have been influenced by Laotian fashion as a result of this trade. Thus, along with more traditional Tái Muäng clothing, it is now common for women in the village to adopt Lào-style shoulder cloths that they have either bought or made themselves and wear them around their waists at funerals and for other special occasions.

Tái Muäng women traditionally wore distinctive skirts both for everyday and festive wear. These are still worn by women in more isolated villages and by older women in villages along the main roads, but a growing number of younger women now wear such skirts only on special occasions.

The most common type of skirt (*seen lai*) is made of three separate pieces sewn together: a plain white waistband, a plain black cotton body, and a decorative hem piece (*teen seen*) with bright multicolored embroidered patterning (figs. 20, 21). The most common motifs found on more traditional embroidered hem pieces are variously

Fig. 19. Southern White Tái (Tái Dam) *cha poy* (portion only). 18 x 178 cm. From a village located between Quan Hoa and Mai Châu, Thanh Hóa Province. Black cotton warp yarns with stripes of variously colored cotton weft yarns with some supplementary-weft patterning. The cloth was made in the 1940s.

Fig. 20. Group of Tái Muäng women wearing plain black *seen lai* with embroidered hem pieces. Ban Cay Me, Thuong Duong District, Nghê An Province. One of the women is wearing a metal belt imported from Laos and two are wearing silk sashes. Only the oldest woman is wearing a plain cotton indigo headcloth.

Fig. 21. Tái Muäng woman wearing a plain black *seen* with embroidered hem piece and an embroidered black headcloth. Ban Yên Thanh, Luc Da Commune, Con Cuông District, Nghê An Province.

shaped stylized dragons. In recent years there are a much wider variety of highly individualistic embroidered patterns in a multitude of bright colors. The decorative embroidery of the hem pieces varies according to individual taste rather than by community or region. There is some regional variation in the width of the colored bands that border the embroidered area, with those in northern Nghê An Province tending to be wider than those in the south. The skirts are often lined with plain white cotton cloth.

Tái Muäng women in northern Nghê An Province also make two distinctive types of skirt—*seen man* and *seen bok*—the bodies of which are made of silk. Both the body and the separate hem piece of the *seen man* have supplementary-weft patterning which features alternating bands with plain stripes, and wider ones with geometric patterns as well as human and animal figures (usually the *toh sue*), known as the *man* technique (fig. 22). The body of the *seen bok* is woven with silk yarn and has wide vertical patterned bands alternating between red and indigo; in between these are thinner bands with stripes in a variety of colors (fig. 23).[14] The wide bands either all feature supplementary-weft (*khit*) patterning with large abstract floral and animal motifs or have the supplementary-weft patterning on the red bands and weft-ikat patterning on the indigo bands. The thinner bands have either plain stripes or plain stripes and rows of geometric patterning. *Seen bok* also have decorative hem pieces in *man* or other styles. Such skirts are time-consuming to make and are highly valued; they are worn only for special occasions (festivals, ceremonies, and market days). Only a few older women can still make these skirts, and most remaining examples are now treated as heirlooms; many have been sold to traders.

Fig. 22. Tái Muäng *seen man*. 70 x 90 cm. Quê Phong District, Nghê An Province. The waistband, made of plain black commercial cotton, replaced the original plain white waistband. The body and hem pieces are silk. The body and center of the hem features bands with *man*-style patterning, including elephants with human riders and *toh sieu* motifs.

Tái Muäng women also did not customarily wear blouses. The blouses they adopted were tight-fitting, with narrow long sleeves, a short waist, and rounded collar. Their blouse opens in the front down the middle and has metal buttons. It is usually made of plain black cotton cloth. Such blouses have fallen out of favor and are rarely worn today, even on special occasions. Most women now wear modern-style generic blouses made of commercial fabric.

Headcloths (*khan tai*) are worn by Tái Muäng women on special occasions. These headcloths are made of two pieces sewn together. At one end, a short piece is covered with supplementary-weft patterning in a variety of bright colors, and often has a braided fringe (fig. 24). This is attached to a much longer piece of black cotton cloth that is either plain or has a few small woven or embroidered decorations at the end. In the past, the background of the small decorative piece was either red or brown, from natural dyes. More recent pieces sometimes have other colors from synthetic dyes for a background.

To be worn, headcloths are folded twice into quarters. The style of wearing them tends to differ according to age: younger women wear them up, with the decorative end wrapped horizontally around the head, while older women wrap them so as to leave the decorative end hanging down at the back.

Two types of sash worn by women around their waist are a *sy eng lem* and a *sy huot*. The *sy eng lem* is made of unwoven strands of plain white cotton thread and may be worn as everyday wear (in the past these Tái Muäng were sometimes referred to as Tái Eng or Tái Sy Khao/white belt). The *sy huot* is colorful and worn on festive occasions (fig. 25). It is made of three pieces sewn together. A long center piece is made of colored plain cloth. The colors of choice for younger women tend to be red, while older women generally prefer yellow. The two smaller end-pieces are decorated with colorful stripes and geometric designs in supplementary-weft patterning. The sash is often folded over and sewn together where the ends of the center piece are joined.

Both headcloths and sashes are commonly given as gifts by a woman to her daughters and daughters-in-law. Many younger women no longer know how to make the older, more intricate types of these headcloths and sashes, which are now rarely worn and only during festive or ceremonial occasions.

Fig. 23. Tái Muäng *seen bok*, 70 x 90 cm. Ban Dông Minh, Châu Hanh Commune, Quy Châu District, Nghê An Province. The waistband is made of plain white cotton. The silk body features vertical bands of supplementary-weft patterning on backgrounds that alternate between plain red and combinations of red warp and black weft yarns. Among the motifs is the *mee pah*, or *mai pooh* (crab). The hem piece is in *man* style and is made of cotton. The body was woven in the 1940s. The original hem piece was sold in 1995 and the present one added.

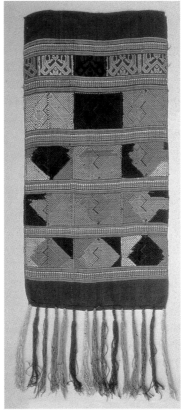

Fig. 24. Tái Muäng *khan tai* (end-piece only). 40 x 86 cm without fringe. Ban Nua Lang Xiêng, Yên Khê Commune, Con Cuông District, Nghê An Province. Made of silk with supplementary-weft patterning featuring chickens and dragons. This style of headcloth seems to be peculiar to this part of Con Cuông District, where they have not been made for at least several decades.

Fig. 25. A young Tái Muäng woman and her husband. Ban Cay Me, Thuong Duong District, Nghê An Province. The woman is wearing a silk sash (*sy huot*) and headcloth (*khan tai*) that were given to her by her mother. Both items are rarely worn in Ban Cay Me at present.

In the past, Tái Muäng men wore the usual black shirts and baggy black pants. Today, such clothing is worn only in quite isolated communities. During the period of French rule, from the late nineteenth century until the early 1950s, men also sometimes wore long coats for festive or ceremonial occasions and at school. These were plain black and fastened on the side. The long coats of men from wealthy families were often made of commercial cloth, while the coats of those from poorer families were made of handspun, locally dyed cotton. Since the 1950s, such coats have been used only to adorn the deceased (see below). Tái Muäng men in some areas also sport a colorful shoulder bag (*toong*) that is similar to those of the Northern Black Tái.

When the coffin of the deceased is displayed in the house, the sons sit on one side of the coffin and the daughters-in-law sit on the other. The women are expected to wear special clothing for the occasion. There are regional differences in the clothing worn for funerals between the Tái Muäng in northern and southern Nghê An Province. The traditional funerary dress of the village of Hóa Tien, Châu Tieng Commune, Quy Châu District, provides an example of the style common among Tái Muäng in northern Nghê

An Province. Deceased men and women are specially dressed for the funeral ceremonies. A dead man's funeral dress includes two coats. An inner, plain black cotton long coat has a stand-up collar, fastens on the side, and a plain white cotton lining. An outer long coat, made of thin plain white cotton cloth, opens down the front and has long sleeves with pieces of plain black and red cloth at the ends. A plain red cotton belt is worn around the waist. The outer coat probably represents an older tradition, while the inner coat seems to be a more recent adaptation.

A dead woman is dressed in a plain black cotton coat (*seu-uh nhao*) that opens down the front and has a plain white cotton lining which is worn over a plain black short-waisted blouse and two skirts. The outer skirt is known as a *seen lai mai*. It has a cotton body with checked patterning and an embroidered hem with a black background (fig. 26). This is a special skirt that is usually made by a woman's mother-in-law to be worn by the woman at her in-laws' funerals and for her own. A plain black *seen lai* is worn underneath the *seen lai mai*. Two headcloths are also worn. One of these is a plain *khan* and the other is a decorated *khan tai*.

Women also wear special clothing when attending the funeral of their in-laws. All daughters-in-law are expected to wear identical skirts. They wear either a *seen bok* or a *seen lai mai*. The *seen lai mai* is worn only at funerals. They also wear a plain red sleeveless cotton blouse with a plain white band at the bottom known as a *seu-uh daang*.[15] In Ban Hóa Tien, all daughters-in-law wear the same length of *seu-uh daang*, but in some other communities the eldest daughter-in-law wears a long one while the others wear shorter ones.

Tái Muäng women in Con Cuông and Tuong Duong districts have a tradition of weaving cloth with bands of supplementary-warp (*muk*) and weft-ikat (*mee*) patterning similar to those made by Southern White Tái in northern Thanh Hóa Province. In the case of the Tái Muäng, however, this cloth is used exclusively for making the center pieces of skirts to be worn at funerals, known as *seen pee* (fig. 27). The *seen pee* has the usual plain white waistband, a center portion with supplementary-warp (*muk*) and weft-ikat patterning of the *seen mee* type, and a hem piece that is either plain black or embroidered with a black background. In fact, the *muk* patterns in general are considered suitable only for clothing worn at funerals. These beliefs are not shared by Southern White Tái in Thanh Hóa Province, who

Fig. 26. Tái Muäng *seen lai mai*. 61 x 99 cm. Ban Hoa Tien, Châu Tieng Commune, Quy Châu District, Nghê An Province. This skirt was woven in the mid-1970s by a woman and given to one of her daughters-in-law to be worn at the woman's funeral. The waistband is made of plain white handspun cotton. The body is made of handspun cotton, as is the hem piece, which also has a wide black band in the center with silk-thread embroidery featuring dragon motifs.

attach no special significance to such skirts or to *muk* patterning, but they are found among the Northern Black Tái in the Diên Biên area. All daughters-in-law at the funeral are expected to wear identical *seen pee*, which are usually made by their mother-in-law.

In addition to *seen pee*, Tái Muäng women in these two districts should wear the traditional *seu-uh dahm*, the short-waisted, long-sleeved black blouse. Their hair is put up with pins, and they do not wear a headcloth. In Cay Mé village, Tuong Duong District, as a result of influence from Laos, women sometimes now also wear a Lào-style shoulder cloth around their waist (fig. 28).

In villages throughout Con Cuông and Tuong Duong Districts, almost no younger women know how to weave the supplementary-warp and weft-ikat cloth for the *seen pee*. In the village of Yên Thanh, Con Cuông District, for example, the last traditional *seen pee* was woven in the 1970s. Older pieces that have not been sold to traders are now kept as heirlooms, and few new ones are produced. Efforts have been made recently by a nongovernmental organization to revive ikat weaving in Yên Thanh, but such cloth is intended primarily for the commercial handicraft market and not for use in making *seen pee*.

Domestic textiles of the Tái Muäng include blankets and decorated mosquito nets. Strips of decorative cloth for mosquito nets (*cha poy* or *chuh poy*) traditionally were made by the bride's mother for her daughter to take to her new house. Such decorative strips are no longer commonly made or used.

The Tái Muäng make a wide variety of blankets. Their basic form is like that of other Southern Thái blankets. They have a border and backing of plain cotton cloth and a center comprised of one or two strips of decorated cloth. In addition to *pha khit* and *pha lai* (fig. 29) for blankets made of strips of plain woven cloth with supplementary-weft patterning (referred to as "with a stick rather than a needle" by one informant), the Tái Muäng also make *pha man* with supplemetary-weft patterning. As with other Southern White Tái, *pha khit* are sometimes referred to as *pha daang* when they have a red background. The *pha daang* of the Tái Muäng include blankets with realistic representations of animals and plants, and these may be called by the name of the main motif: for instance, *pha maybo* for a blanket decorated prominently with butterfly figures. Sometimes blankets are also named according to their function. Thus, blankets

Fig. 27. Tái Muäng *seen pee*. 58 x 106 cm. Ban Yên Thanh, Luc Da Commune, Con Cuông District, Nghê An Province. Such a skirt is made by a woman and given to one of her daughters-in-law to be worn at the woman's funeral. The waistband is made of plain white handspun cotton. The body is made of silk with weft-ikat and supplementary-weft patterning. The hem piece has a cotton background with embroidered patterning using silk thread featuring a dragon. This skirt was woven in the early 1970s using newly introduced synthetic dyes. It is one of the last ikat skirts made in the village by the older generation. Younger women have not learned the skill, although currently a nongovernmental organization is trying to revive ikat weaving for commercial purposes.

Fig. 28. Tái Muäng copy of a Lào-style shoulder cloth. Ban Cay Me, Thuong Duong District, Nghê An Province. Such textiles are a recent innovation found only in a few villages near the Laos border and are generally worn as sashes wrapped around the waist.

Fig. 29. Tái Muäng *pha lai*. 80 x 174 cm. Ban Ma Tom, Chi Khé Commune, Con Cuông District, Nghê An Province. The center portion is made of white silk and indigo-dyed cotton supplementary-weft patterning. The primary pattern is the *duon* (moon). This part is edged and backed by three pieces of patterned commercial cotton cloth. The center was woven in the 1940s by Luu Thi Dung, and the commercial cloth was added recently to replace pieces of plain white cotton cloth.

Fig. 34. Tái Thanh *seen ko*. 69 x 98 cm. Ban Dôc, Chi Khê Commune, Con Cuông District, Nghê An Province. The waistband is made of plain brown handspun cotton. The body has a cotton base with supplementary-warp patterning in silk. The upper and central portion of the body has bands with plain stripes like a *seen lan* in between wider bands; the latter are bounded at top and bottom with *muk* rows and in the center have alternating plain black areas and vertical stripes with supplementary-warp patterning in various colors. The lower portion has two horizontal rows featuring diamond-shaped supplementary-weft patterning in silk. It was woven in the 1930s by Vi Thi Quyén.

Fig. 35. Tái Thanh *khan tai*, made of three pieces sewn together. 37 x 198 cm without fringe. Ban Dôc, Chi Khê Commune, Con Cuông District, Nghê An Province. The center is plain black cotton with a band of embroidered patterns in silk thread at one end. Sewn onto this end is an extension that is made of plain black cotton cloth on one side and two pieces of plain white and brown cotton cloth on the other. Short strands of variously colored silk thread are attached to this as tassels. On the other end is a piece of reddish brown silk cloth covered in rows with supplementary-weft patterning to which have been added tassels made from colorful silk threads. It was woven in the 1930s by Vi Thi Quyén.

Tái Thanh women wear headcloths, known generally as *khan hoo-uh*, primarily for special occasions. The usual Tái Thanh headcloth is of a type called a *khan sieu*, which is made of a long piece of plain black cotton cloth with two or three tie-dyed small circles at each end and sometimes small embroidered decorative patterning. Tái Thanh sometimes wear more colorful *khan tai*, similar to those of the Tái Muäng (fig. 35). The latter are relatively rare today and are no longer made.

Tái Thanh men in the past wore the usual style of male shirts and trousers. Usually these were made of plain black cotton. Wealthier men's clothing might be made of silk and then was usually brown in color. With the availability of commercial cotton, men's shirts began to be made in different colors, although black was still considered appropriate for formal occasions as a sign of respect. Except in more isolated villages, such traditional male dress had pretty well disappeared by the 1960s. Men sometimes carry brightly colored shoulder bags.

The domestic textiles of the Tái Thanh include blankets and decorated mosquito nets. Decorative cloths for the top of mosquito nets (*cha poy*) are no longer made and are rarely seen. Patterned or plain commercial cloth is now used instead. Their blankets always have a backing and borders made of plain white cotton cloth. Blankets include: *pha khit* (fig. 36), *pha lai, pha sieo* (embroidered with a needle), and *pha man* (adopted from the Tái Müang). A woman brings as many *pha khit* with her as possible upon marriage and must present some of these as gifts to her new relatives on her husband's side. Longer pieces of *khit* cloth are sometimes used as coffin screens, but this is not a common practice any longer.

Fig. 36. Tái Thanh *pha khit*. 115 x 175 cm. Ban Dôc, Chi Khê Commune, Con Cuông District, Nghê An Province. This type of blanket is given by a woman to her mother-in-law. The center portion is made of two strips of *khit* woven silk cloth. This is edged and backed by three pieces of plain white handspun cotton. The cloth was woven between 1900 and 1910, and subsequently kept as an heirloom.

Thái Influence on the Dress of Neighboring Non-Tái

The Thái do not live in cultural isolation, and they share many aspects of the decoration of their textiles and styles of dress with neighboring non-Tái peoples. This is an interactive process, with the Thái borrowing some ideas and, in turn, others borrowing ideas or actual items from them. Especially among Northern Thái, there has been noticeable Chinese influence on their dress. The Thái in turn have had a strong influence on the dress of Môn-Khmer-speaking peoples living in their vicinity.

Some Môn-Khmer once lived in the area today occupied by the Thái; at the time when the two peoples came into contact, Môn-Khmer appear to have possessed only very rudimentary clothing and weaving technologies. The Thái displaced and conquered the local Môn-Khmer, who were often required to provide labor and tribute to Thái rulers. Many Môn-Khmer-speaking peoples were assimilated into Thái society, undergoing what Condominas (1990, p. 54) refers to as a process of "Tái-ization" that included the adoption of Thái dress. Even today, however, there are pockets of Môn-Khmer-speaking peoples living throughout the Thái area who have not been so completely assimilated. Nevertheless, the Thái have had a profound influence on the culture of these Môn-Khmer groups, including their material culture. Thus, the Kho-mú and O-du of western Nghê An Province have adopted the dress of neighboring Tái Muäng and Tái Thanh.

The Tái Muoi are especially interesting in regard to this relationship between Thái and Môn-Khmer. While the Tái Muoi are often categorized as a subgroup of Thái (Dang, Chu, and Luu 1993, p. 116), it appears that they were in fact originally Môn-Khmer speakers who adopted Thái culture and language to the point of identifying themselves as Thái.[17] Evidence of their Môn-Khmer heritage can be found in their house styles and basketry. In interviews with Tái Muoi women in Khê Thai Commune, Con Cuông District, who lived among Tái Muäng, we found that they had adopted Tái Muäng dress and produced embroidered hems with patterns like those of the Tái Muäng. However, they named their skirts according to the ethnicity of the maker rather than according to style, which cannot be distinguished: *seen Tái Müang* or *seen Tái Muoi*.[18] They have no tradition of making blankets.

Fig. 37. An elderly Li Hà woman, wearing cloth obtained from neighboring Thái. Ban Chou Son, Chou Kê Commune, Con Cuông District, Nghê An Province. Prior to moving to Ban Chou Son in 1973, she wore clothing made of plain brown cotton cloth which she obtained from the Thái and dyed herself with *cu nâu*. One such blouse is now used on a scarecrow in her garden.

A variety of small Vietic-speaking groups categorized collectively by the Vietnamese as Thô (there are about 50,000 of them) live close to the Thái and Muòng in central and western Thanh Hóa and Nghê An Provinces. Subgroups of Thô include Keo, Mon, Cuôi, Ho, Dan, Lai-Li Hà, and Tày Poong. The Thô grow hemp, which is used to make a variety of items, including nets, hammocks, and bags. Thô men in the past tended to dress in the style of neighboring Viêt or Thái, and in recent years they have generally been wearing modern generic clothing. Thô women living in Thanh Hóa Province dress more or less like neighboring Muòng, while Thô women living in Nghê An Province (in Tán Ky, Nghia Dán, and Con Cuông Districts) dress like either Viêt or Thái.

The Li Hà living in the village of Chou Son, Châu Khê Commune, Con Cuông District, provide an example of Thô patterns of dress (fig. 37). They were resettled from Khê Nóng Commune, near the Laos border, in 1973. The Li Hà have no tradition of weaving. When they lived in Khê Nóng, they collected a tuber called *cu nâu*, which is used to make brown dye traded or sold to Thái in exchange for thin, rough, plain, white cotton cloth. They dyed this cloth brown and made clothing from it. Women's dress at this time consisted of a plain wrap-around skirt and a short blouse. The blouse roughly resembled that of the Thái in form: it had narrow long sleeves, a round neck opening, and opened down the center, but with cloth, and not metal, buttons. This type of clothing was abandoned when they moved to Ban Chou Son, and now women dress like the neighboring Thái from whom they obtain their clothing.

Conclusions

The most obvious conclusion from the above discussion is that, despite major changes in recent years, the Southern Thái of Viêt Nam still produce a wide array of tradition-based textiles that continue to play a vital role in their culture. This situation has created an opportunity to conduct research that sheds important light on the textile heritage of the Thái people as a whole. This said, it is equally apparent that a great deal of the textile heritage of these people already has been lost or is in danger of disappearing in a very short time. The paucity of previous research and the speed with which changes are occurring among the Southern Thái at present, as well as the extent to which older textiles have been removed from the area without being documented, have generated a sense of urgency in pursuing research concerned with the textile traditions of the Southern Thái.

The present article presents an overview of our findings to date. Areas requiring attention in future research include a better understanding of specific local variations in textile production and use, and of the interaction among different subgroups, regions, and communities. Although some of the relevant data have been collected, putting together a comprehensive picture for the region as a whole has proven difficult. Another needed study is a more thorough comparative analysis of Southwestern Tái textiles in relation to the textile traditions of neighboring Tái-speaking groups, especially in Laos and on Hainan Island. Recent advances in comparative Tái studies in other areas, as demonstrated by many of the papers presented at the International Thái Studies Conference in Chiang Mai (1996) and the International Tái Studies Conference in Bangkok (1998), certainly provide an encouraging framework for such comparative studies.

In Laos, the obstacles to such an undertaking include the relatively poor state of anthropological research among Tái-speaking minority groups in Laos, as well as limited and sometimes contradictory data available on identification of such subgroups, and the paucity of fieldwork-based studies concerned with their textiles (see Gittinger, Chungyampin, and Saiyalard 1997).

Comparative studies of the textiles of the Li (or Hlai) of Hainan and the Southern Thái of Viêt Nam are of equal importance since it can be argued that the Li and Southern Thái weaving traditions represent survivals of what was probably once a far more widespread tradition among Tái-speaking peoples. Hans Stübel, in his pioneering work on the Li, offered some fairly general comparisons with textiles and weaving techniques in other parts of Southeast Asia (Stübel 1937, pp. 292–94). More recently, Gittinger and Lefferts (1992, pp. 32–34) have made points of comparison concerning Li weaving techniques and the evolution of the style of Tái tubular skirts. There is certainly potential for more comparative work along these lines.

Acknowledgments

Our research on the textiles of the Thái of Viêt Nam began in May 1995 with a brief visit to the Thái village of Ban Lác, Mai Châu District. We traveled with the late Bê Viêt Dang, then director of Viêt Nam's Institute of Ethnology. This and subsequent research has been sponsored by Viêt Nam's National Center for Social Sciences and Humanities, Institute of Ethnology, and Museum of Ethnology. Several Vietnamese anthropologists have been especially helpful. In particular, we would like to thank Nguyên Van Huy, Cam Trong, and Vi Van An of the Viêt Nam Museum of Ethnology and Pham Quang Hoan of the Institute of Ethnology. We also received welcome cooperation from provincial authorities in Thanh Hóa and Nghê An provinces and district officials in Quan Hóa, Quan Son, Quy Châu, Con Cuông, and Tuong Duong Districts in Thanh Hóa and Nghê An Provinces.

All photographs were taken by Michael C. Howard in 1997 and 1998.

About the Authors

Michael C. Howard is Professor of Anthropology in the Department of Sociology and Anthropology, Simon Fraser University, Burnaby, British Columbia, Canada. He is the author or editor of more than twenty books as well as numerous articles on the Asia-Pacific region. Among his relevant recent publications are *Textiles of the Hill Tribes of Burma* (1999), *Traditional T'ai Arts in Contemporary Perspective* (co-editor and contributing author) (1998), and *Textiles of Southeast Asia: An Annotated and Illustrated Bibliography* (1994).

Kim Be Howard is a dancer and choreographer who formerly worked with the Viêt Nam Theater of Song, Dance, and Music. She has a long-standing interest in the dances and costumes of Viêt Nam's ethnic minorities and is herself of mixed Tày and Thái descent.

Notes

1. Tái refers to people speaking those languages classified as belonging to the Tái subdivision of Daic languages (the other two being Kadai and Kam-Sui). Tái languages are further divided into Northern, Central, and Southwestern. Southwestern Tái languages are also divided into groups that include Chiang Saen, Northwestern, and Lao-Phutai. Thái refers to the official Vietnamese ethnic classification that includes speakers of Southwestern Chiang Saen Tái languages such as those listed in Grimes (1996, p. 806) as Tái Daeng, Tái Dam, and Tái Dón.

2. In a previously published survey of Thái textiles in Viêt Nam (Howard and Be 1999), we presented some preliminary data on southern Thái textiles. The present article is based on subsequent and more intensive fieldwork and is far more comprehensive than our earlier article.

3. The history of the migration of the Thái in Viêt Nam is based largely on discussions with Vietnamese anthropologists, especially Professor Cam Trong and Vi Van An, who themselves are ethnic Thái.

4. In fact, the term Tái Daang is not in general use as a name for a Tái subgroup in Viêt Nam. Rather, it is used specifically to refer to a subgroup of Tái living across the border in Houa Phan Province in Laos. According to 1987 census figures, the Tái Daang numbered about 53,200 and comprised some 70 percent of the Tái living in Houa Phan Province (concentrated in Muäng Xam To, Muäng Xoi, and Xieng Kho). According to Dào (1998), their traditions indicate two periods of migration to Houa Phan from the Muäng Kasa and Muäng Daang area (and perhaps from Muäng Khoong, Muäng Mun, and Muäng Ha as well): one occurred several centuries ago in connection with the "hedgehog rebellion" and another around the time of troubles with the Black Flags and Yellow Flags in the nineteenth century. In rituals Tái Daang often cite their coming from Muäng Kasa. Whether they were originally Black Tái or White Tái, or a mixture of the two, is unclear, but their textiles generally fit within the Southern White Tái tradition associated with the Tái of Muäng Kasa and, today, with Quan Son.

5. Grimes (1996, p. 804) states that there are 150,000 Phu Thái in northern Viêt Nam and that they are part of the Thái official ethnic community without giving further specifics. A map in Gittinger and Lefferts (1992, p. 25) shows Phu Thái living in Viêt Nam in the southwestern corner of Nghê An Province and adjacent northwestern Hà Tinh Province.

6. One is quite small and in the other a Tái Muäng woman is apparently misidentified as Tái Thanh.

7. The Muòng (it can also be spelled Müöng) are a Vietic-speaking minority whose culture has been heavily influenced by neighboring Thái; see Robequin 1929, vol. 1, pp. 100–118 and Cuisinier 1946.

8. Informants in Quan Hóa often commented on how much of Thái culture, including dress, had been lost locally and contrasted Quan Hóa with more remote Thái communities where many more traditional elements of Thái culture remained. This view is shared by Vietnamese anthropologists who have worked in the area; they find it necessary to travel to remote areas to conduct fieldwork on the more traditional aspects of Thái religious beliefs and other aspects of Thái culture.

9. Information on the history of male fashion among Tái Mai Châu is based on interviews with a variety of elderly Thái men in Mai Châu District. Likewise, the discussion on female Tái Mai Châu fashion is based on interviews with numerous elderly Thái women in Mai Châu District. In general, we found female informants to be more knowledgeable than their male counterparts and only a few older men could recall changes in male fashion with any precision.

10. There is a relatively extensive literature on the waistbands/breast coverings of the Muòng (see Cuisinier 1946, p. 226; Bui 1977; and Trân 1978). Bui provides a comprehensive study of the motifs. All the authors mention the influence of the Thái on this part of Muòng dress.

11. It is common in the literature on Thái textiles in Laos and Thailand to refer to dragon motifs as *nak*. The term *nak*, however, refers to an otter and not a dragon or *naga*, which is *ngawk*. In fact, both *nak* and *ngawk* motifs are used on Thái textiles and care must be exercised in making identifications.

12. Textile authors generally associate such warp-ikat weaving with some of the oldest weaving traditions in the region (see Bühler 1946; Fraser-Lu 1988, p. 42; Maxwell 1990, p. 75; and Howard ms.). It is also associated with use of the backstrap loom; among the Thái such warp-ikat patterning survived after adoption of frame looms.

13. The traders from Thailand sometimes have entered the area under the guise of scholars conducting research.

14. In Laos skirts of this type are identified with the Tái Moy and are called *seen chok khan* (see Bouynyavong, Pathoumvanh, and Chanthachit 1995, p. 74). The Tái Moy living closest to the Tái Muäng are those found in Muäng Xam To, Houa Phanh Province.

15. The Tái Daang in Houa Phan Province in Laos also have a tradition of wearing red funeral blouses, although these have been replaced with white blouses decorated with long strips of red cloth. The wearing of such red blouses may at one time have been a more widespred tradition among Tái in Nghê An, Thanh Hóa, and Houa Phan Provinces.

16. A *man baang* is illustrated in Gittinger and Lefferts 1992 (p. 134, fig. 3.47) and described as a "funeral cloth" possibly from Houa Phan Province in Laos (this place of origin is incorrect and is probably based on misinformation provided by textile dealers in Thailand or Laos to the buyer). The weaving technique is described in detail: "Three different color wefts…are inserted into each shed; that color needed for the design is brought to the surface where it is secured by a separate binding warp."

17. We would like to thank Vi Van An, of the Viêt Nam Museum of Ethnology, for first pointing this out to us.

18. These particular women stopped weaving their own cloth in 1990, when a shop selling cloth opened nearby, but they continue to embroider decorated hems. In the past they made their own cotton and silk thread and used natural dyes, but since 1990 they have bought pre-dyed thread from the shop.

References

Bê Viêt Dang, Nguyên Van Huy, and Chu Thái Son, editors

1992   *Các Dân Tôc Tày, Nùng o Viêt Nam. Viên Dân Tôc Hoc*, Viên Khoa Hoc Xa Hôi Viêt Nam, Hà Nôi.

Bounyavong, Douang, Bandit Pathoumvanh, and Chanthone Chanthachit

1995   *Infinite Designs: The Art of Silk*. Lào Women's Union and SIDA, Vientiane.

Bühler, Alfred

1946   Die Reservemusterungen: Versuch einer zusammenfassenden Betrachtung ihrer Technik, Enstehung und Herkunft, *Acta Tropica*, vol. 3, pp. 242–71, 322–66. Basel.

Bui Thiên

1977   Dêt Trang Tri Cap Vay Nguoi Muòng, *Nghe Dep Que Huong*, pp. 33–56. Ty Van Hoa Thong Tin Ha Son Binh, Hòa Bình.

Chu Thái Son and Dào Hùng

1991   *Vietnam: A Multicultural Mosaic*. Vietnam Foreign Languages Publishing House, Hà Nôi.

Condominas, Georges

1990   *From Lawa to Mon, from Saa' to Thái: Historical and Anthropological Aspects of Southeast Asian Social Spaces*. Department of Anthropology, Research School of Pacific Studies, Australian National University, Canberra.

Cuisinier, Jeanne

1946   *Les Mu'òng: géographie humaine et sociologie.* Institut d'Ethnologie, Paris.

Dang Nghiêm Van, Chu Thái Son, and Luu Hùng

1993   *Ethnic Minorities in Vietnam.* The Gioi Publishers, Hà Nôi.

Dào Van Tiên

1998   *Nguòi Thay Deng o Lào và Môi Quan Hê Van Hoá Lich Su Vói Nguòi Thái o Viêt Nam,* pp. 352–65. Edited by Câm Trong. Nhà Xuât Ban Van Hóa Dân Tôc, Hà Nôi.

Fraser-Lu, Sylvia

1988   *Handwoven Textiles of Southeast Asia.* Oxford University Press, Singapore.

Gittinger, Mattiebelle, Karen Anderson Chungyampin, and Chanporn Saiyalard

1997   Textiles and Textile Customs of the Tai Dam, Tai Daeng, and Their Neighbors in Northern Laos, *The Textile Museum Journal,* vols. 34–35 (1995–96), pp. 92–112. The Textile Museum, Washington.

Gittinger, Mattiebelle, and H. Leedom Lefferts Jr.

1992   *Textiles and the Tai Experience in Southeast Asia.* The Textile Museum, Washington.

Grimes, Barbara F., editor

1996   *Ethnologue: Languages of the World.* Twelfth edition. Summer Institute of Linguistics, Dallas.

Harmond, F. J.

1997   *Laos and the Hill Tribes of Indochina: Journeys to the Boloven Plateau, from Bassac to Hué through Laos, and the Origins of the Thái.* Translated from French by Walter E. J. Tipps. White Lotus, Bangkok. Originally published in *Le Tour du Monde,* vols. 38–39 (1878–79).

Hoang Luong

1983   *Hoa Van Thái.* Nha Xuât Ban Van Hóa Dân Tôc, Hà Nôi.

Howard, Michael C.

1994   *Textiles of Southeast Asia: An Annotated and Illustrated Bibliography.* White Lotus, Bangkok.

1998   Identity and Traditional and Tradition-based Textiles in Contemporary Thái Society, *Traditional T'ai Arts in Contemporary Perspective,* pp. 13–45. Edited by M. C. Howard, W. Wattanapun, and A. Gordon. White Lotus, Bangkok.

1999a   Vietnam's New Museum of Ethnography, *Arts of Asia,* vol. 29, no. 4, pp. 130–32. Hong Kong.

1999b   *Textiles of the Hill Tribes of Burma.* White Lotus, Bangkok.

ms.   Ikat Weaving and Ethnic Identity among Ethnic Minorities in Vietnam. Paper presented at the Joint NWRCSEAS-CCSEAS Conference, University of British Columbia, Vancouver, 1999.

Howard, Michael C., and Be Kim Nhung

1999   Dress of the T'ai Peoples of Vietnam, *Arts of Asia,* vol. 29, no. 1, pp. 93–105. Hong Kong.

Lê Ngoc Thang

1990   *Nghê Thuât Trang Phuc Thái.* Nha Xuât Ban Van Hóa Dân Tôc, Hà Nôi.

Maxwell, Robyn

1990   *Textiles of Southeast Asia.* Oxford University Press, Melbourne.

Ngô Dùc Thinh

1994   *Trang Phuc: Cô Truyên Các Dân Tôc Viêt Nam.* Van Hoa Dân Tôc, Hà Nôi.

Nguyên Van Huy

1997   *Mosaïque culturelle des ethnies du Vietnam.* Maison d'Edition de l'Education, Hà Nôi.

1998   *Vietnam Museum of Ethnology.* Vietnam Museum of Ethnology, Hà Nôi.

Robequin, Charles

1929   *Les Thanh Hoà: Êtude géographique d'une province annamite.* Les Editions G. van Oest, Paris and Brussels.

Robert, Romain

1941   *Notes sur les Tay Dèng de Lang Chánh (Thanh-Hoá-Annam).* Institut Indochinois pour l'Étude de l'Homme, Hà Nôi.

Stübel, Hans

1937   *Die Li-Stämme der Insel Hainan.* Klinkhardt & Biermann, Berlin.

Trân Tù

1978   *Hoa Van Muòng.* Nha Xuât Ban Van Hóa Dân Tôc, Hà Nôi.

Fig. 1. Chinchero man's cap knitted by Nilda Callañaupa in the 1980s. 64 x 27 cm. The Textile Museum 1990.24.2, Latin American Research Fund.

Men's Knitted Caps from Chinchero

Nilda Callañaupa and Ann Pollard Rowe

Fig. 2. Pre-Hispanic looped cap of undyed camelid fiber, possibly found at Ancón on the central coast of Peru. 17.5 x 18.5 cm. The Textile Museum 1961.30.67, gift of Burton I. Jones.

Men's knitted caps are in common use in many indigenous communities in the highlands of southern Peru and Bolivia (fig. 1).[1] They are worn instead of or underneath European style brimmed hats. The shape of the caps varies from one area or community to another, but usually they are pointed at the top, and often they have earflaps. Typically they have multicolored designs, similar to the weaving designs of the region. Usually very thin needles are used and the work is correspondingly fine. Some Textile Museum examples from the Cusco area have as many as 7 stitches and 8 rows per centimeter. In some communities the women knit, in others it is the men, and in others both men and women knit.

The local term for these caps in Quechua (the Inca language), ch'ullu (or ch'ullo) is not found in the earliest Inca dictionaries. The Incas are not recorded to have worn hats or caps, except for military helmets called 'umachuku, which were apparently made of leather.[2] 'Uma means "head" and chuku was an Aymara word referring to a kind of stiff (not form-fitting) hat worn in pre-Hispanic times in some Aymara-speaking areas in what is now southern Peru and northern Bolivia.[3] The modern Aymara word for the knitted caps is lluchu.

Looped caps, looking superficially similar to the later knitted ones, are nevertheless occasionally found in excavations of pre-Hispanic sites (fig. 2). Looping is an ancient technique in which the end of the yarn is put through the previous work, so it is much more laborious than knitting, in which a loop formed of yarn adjacent to the work is put through a previous loop.[4] Although some surviving looped pre-Hispanic caps are in simple looping (buttonhole stitch), the more elaborate example in figure 2 has the loops in vertical alignment, so that it looks like knitting ("cross-knit looping" in Emery's terminology). In looping, however, the loops are always crossed, while in knitting they may be either crossed or open. Most contemporary knitting, including that of the Cusco area, has a structure with open loops, which is not possible in normal looping. The cap in figure 2 is made in natural colors of camelid hair, with most of the yarns spun and plied in the opposite direction from both ancient and contemporary Cusco area practice.[5] The unused color floats loose on the inside of the cap, unlike most knitted caps made today. The extensions are tubular. Thus, this cap does not seem to be a direct antecedent of today's knitted ch'ullus, but it represents a general prototype.[6]

Knitting does not occur in the Americas prior to the European invasion. The date of its introduction into the Andes is unknown, but it must have been some time during the colonial period. The knitting technique is in fact a relatively recent invention even in Europe. The earliest datable examples of knitting that are generally recognized are two silk cushions from the royal tombs of Castile in northern Spain, dating to the second half of the thirteenth century.[7] One of the cushions has an Arabic inscription, and indeed other early examples of knitting consist of cotton socks found in Islamic Egypt, which are, however, impossible to date precisely.[8] It is therefore possible that the technique is of Islamic origin and was introduced to Spain as a consequence of its being under Islamic rule. The technique used by indigenous knitters in the Andes today has a number of features that are unlike modern knitting techniques familiar in North America and

Fig. 3. Old Chinchero man's cap. 46 x 20 cm. The Textile Museum 2000.34.1, gift of Edward and Christine Franquemont.

Knitting in Chinchero

Although knitted caps are still common in many Cusco area communities, they have not been worn since around 1940 in Chinchero. Prior to that time, in the earlier part of the twentieth century, intricately patterned caps were worn in the *ayllus* (sub-communities) of Cuper Alto, Ucutuan, Taucca, and Umasbamba (fig. 3).[10] In the other Chinchero *ayllus*, solid-colored caps were worn—red, dark pink, or white. Bags for money were knitted as well,[11] although money was also carried between the layers of the traditional women's hats. The bags are known to have been used by women, but it is unclear if they might have been used by men. Knitting was considered women's work in Chinchero.

Until some time in the 1910s or 1920s, knitted sleeves (*maqetos*) were worn by Chinchero men when working (fig. 4). Earlier sleeves had only black-and-white patterns, but later examples have designs similar to those on the lower parts of the caps, as in figure 4. They are clearly knitted from wrist to shoulder in the same manner as the caps. The sleeves are connected by a plain band to prevent them from slipping down the arms. The band in the sleeves illustrated is in garter stitch (presumably purled in both directions); it is continuous from the smaller of the two sleeves and the other end is sewn to the larger sleeve. It has a tuck sewn into it, presumably to compensate for stretching with use.

Although a similar style of knitted sleeves is still made in the Huancavelica area of Peru,[12] the authors have not seen them from other Cusco area communities. In his 1916 publication on body measurements of people from the departments of Cusco and Apurimac (the great majority from Cusco), however, H. B. Ferris illustrates eight men out of a total of 140 wearing knitted sleeves. Seven of these pairs of sleeves are monochrome, but one has black-and-white patterns.[13] The monochrome sleeves are longer than the patterned ones and have a flat garter stitch area at the top over the shoulders. Unfortunately, although some provenience information is given for the statistics, this information is not precisely linked to the illustrations, though it is possible that the patterned sleeves belonged to a man from around San Pedro de Cacha, south of Cusco. Thus, the wearing of knitted sleeves in the Cusco area seems not to be unique to Chinchero, but it was clearly not common and was dying out in the early twentieth century.

Europe, and probably represent older techniques that are now no longer used in Spain.

The general features of Andean knitting, known and mentioned in the available literature on knitting, include purling in the round on five needles, with the yarn carried around the neck and thrown with the left hand. The emphasis in this literature, however, has been how to replicate the general effects using simple modern techniques rather than detailed field recording of techniques actually used by indigenous people in the Andes. In fact, there is a significant amount of local variation in such techniques, due to regional stylistic differences.[9] This article will describe the techniques used in Chinchero, a town near Cusco in southern Peru, which we hope will provide an idea of the riches to be found in closer scrutiny of these traditions. The highlights include a method of handling three colors simultaneously and a distinctive starting border. We also present some new historical information.

Learning to knit

In 1980 I (Nilda Callañaupa) participated in an Earthwatch project organized by Edward and Christine Franquemont to record oral information from old people in Chinchero. The project was stimulated by a plan to build an international airport in the community, which fortunately has not so far come to pass. As part of the project, I had the opportunity to learn Chinchero style knitting from Doña Roberta Quispe, a sweet and very funny old lady in Cuper Pueblo (but born and raised in Cuper Alto), who had a nice relationship with my parents and grandparents (fig. 5). She was the only person I knew who still knew how to knit the Chinchero style man's cap at that time. In her youth she had knitted caps on commission from many people, including the authorities of Chinchero who wished to confer them on authorities visiting from elsewhere, and for saints' statues and statues of the baby Jesus in the church, etc. She stopped knitting when she was about 50 and her husband died. At around that time, the style of clothing was changing and fewer men were wearing the caps. Although she had not knitted for many years,

the Franquemonts asked her to knit caps for them, which became almost full-time work for her during her last years.

When I first visited her and asked if she could teach me how to knit, she laughed and said to me, "Do you really want to learn to knit? Do you think you have the patience to do it? People your age are no longer interested in traditional things like weaving and knitting.

Fig. 4. Old Chinchero sleeves. 33 x 14.5 and 35.5 x 15.5 cm, strap 61 x 5.5 cm. Collection of Nilda Callañaupa.

Fig. 5. Doña Roberta Quispe of *ayllu* Cuper Pueblo, Chinchero, knitting a cap. She is putting the yarn over the needle. Photo from the Chinchero Archives, courtesy of Edward and Christine Franquemont, 1980.

Those of us who never went to school are the only ones who care about our culture and traditions like knitting." But finally she told me that I could come back the next day. So the next day I visited her again, and this time I took my loom and some of my weavings to show her. Surprised, she invited me into her house and got out her knitting. The room was very dark and I could hardly see what she was doing, but she began to demonstrate, although without offering any explanations. She said to me, "Watch me and see if you still think you are interested. Knitting is for people with a lot of patience, and people of your age never have that talent. You children don't care anymore about the *ch'ullus* because you don't use them any more. Nobody appreciates the amount of work that is required to knit a cap." It was obvious that she liked to talk, but she was more interested in talking about her youth and her relationship with my family, and complaining about her health problems, etc., than in explaining what she was doing.

Finally, after a few hours of watching and pleasant conversation, she told me to bring my yarn and knitting needles. If I did not have knitting needles, she told me to gather cactus thorns, which is what she had used in learning to knit. The cactus is a species of *Opuntia*, but it does not flower, which makes it difficult to identify. Doña Roberta said she had learned from older friends when she was a shepherd, at about the age of sixteen. She watched them, decided she wanted to learn, and asked her friends to teach her. Her friends laughed at her and said that knitting was for real women and not for lazy girls. But if she really wanted to learn she could bring yarn and the five longest cactus thorns she could find on the next day. She practiced on small bags before she made men's caps.

This assumption of difficulty in learning is typical in Chinchero and in other parts of the Andean area. Instead of encouraging students as is usual in European cultures, the Chinchero teacher prepares her students to be tough. In order to make sure the student has sufficient determination to learn, the teacher gives the student to understand that it is necessary to pay attention, to practice, and to have patience. The teacher also assumes that the first piece will not be useful and will make the student use less well-spun yarn. The teacher or mother will not provide good yarn until the student learns or else the girl makes her own yarn. The lack of explanations is also typical. The student learns by watching, imitating, and practicing. I was very happy when

Doña Roberta agreed to teach me, and I imagine that others are as well.

When a woman does agree to teach, the student is expected to reciprocate by helping with whatever might be needed. For example, I used to go early in the morning to help cook the soup, and another time I helped cook lunch to take to the workers in her field. The custom is also for the student to take gifts to the teacher, whatever the student thinks she might need or have mentioned. I took my teacher coca leaves each time I visited her, as well as foodstuffs like sugar and coffee. Since my teacher was old, I also brought her medicine and provided personal help. It is also appropriate to give the teacher some special present on her birthday.

When I was growing up and learning to weave, my mother told me to take my first weaving to the big river, which for us is the Urubamba or Vilcanota River. The purpose of giving one's first weaving to the river is to bring good luck, to be a good weaver, and to weave one piece after another and not stop, just as the river is continually flowing.

Finally Doña Roberta began to teach me. She herself started the first steps of making the scalloped edging, telling me to continue and practice until I had learned it. Then I should come back, and she would teach me the next step. She emphasized very strongly how important it was that the knitting be tight. She said that this art was very enjoyable but also time-consuming. I learned not only knitting from her but also a lot about earlier life in Chinchero. During my lessons, she would say that it is time to cook and you have to help me, and she would give me a basket of potatoes to peel. It was also clear that she had patience for other things besides knitting. She was careful about everything she did.

She also taught her son how to knit. He is a single father (and now also a grandfather) and routinely does both men's and women's work. He is today the finest knitter in Chinchero, and he and I have taught about twenty other people, mostly women, but two other men, how to knit the caps. This new knitting is not exactly the same as the old style. The young people look for easier ways of doing the tricky things, so, for example, instead of knitting the scalloped edge, some make it with crochet. They have also changed some designs and added a few new ones. The newer caps are also not as tightly knitted. But today in Chinchero you can see more men wearing knitted caps than fifty years ago.

Knitting techniques

The yarn used is tightly spun and plied, in contrast to normal commercial knitting yarn, which usually has a relatively slack twist. Andean knitters add twist to commercial yarn, using a hand spindle, if they want to use it. The yarn is then wound into balls.

The knitting is done in the round on five needles, four to hold the work and one with which to transfer the stitches (fig. 6). The needles are usually made of wire, but sometimes bicycle spokes are used, though the latter are more often used for knitting sweaters. The needles are pointed on both ends in Chinchero, but in many other places in the Cusco area, one end of each needle is hooked.

The yarn is passed around the neck to maintain even tension. Although in some Andean communities, for example, on Taquile and Amantani Islands in Lake Titicaca, yarns of different colors are passed in opposite directions around the neck,[14] in Chinchero and some other communities, the yarns all pass in the same direction (left to right). In other communities where more than three colors are used, these yarns are not all passed around the neck. If the knitter is seated, the balls of yarn rest in her lap or on the ground next to her. If the knitter is standing, however, the balls may be tucked under the left arm (fig. 7). In figure 5, the yarn passes around Doña Roberta's neck, then under her shawl, and the balls are tucked under her arm as in figure 7, though they are not visible. Alternatively, some women tie the balls to their belts by passing a cord through the lower windings of the ball.

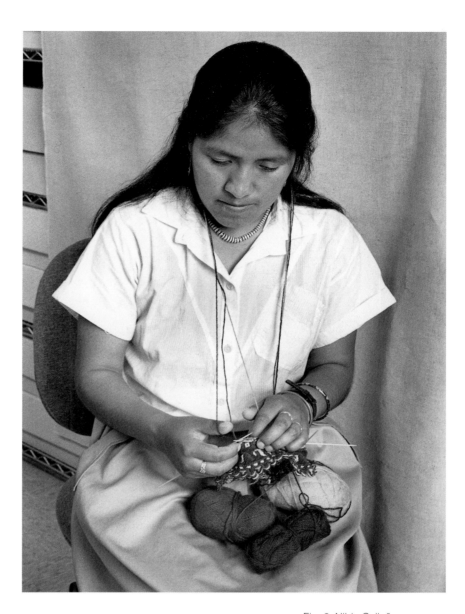

Fig. 6. Nilda Callañaupa knitting with three colors. She is switching the two unused colors, one on each thumb. The balls of yarn used are obviously machine-made, not traditional in Chinchero. Photo by Ann P. Rowe, 1990.

Fig. 7. Doña Roberta making the starting chain, holding two balls of yarn under her left arm. Photo from the Chinchero Archives, courtesy of Edward and Christine Franquemont, 1980.

Fig. 8. Throwing the center of three yarns after the other two have been switched. Photos in figs. 8–11 by Ann P. Rowe, 1990.

The work is done almost entirely in what is usually called purling in English (*tejer de detras* in Spanish) rather than what is strictly called knitting (*tejer a delante* in Spanish). Working on the inside face of the cap, the right needle is inserted in front of the left needle (if the knitter is right-handed), in the front of the stitch. The yarn is held in the left hand and put over the needle from front to back (figs. 5, 8), although in fact back to front gives the same result. When working with one color, the yarn is thrown by just lifting it with the left thumb. The stitches are not crossed.

In Chinchero three colors of yarn are alternated, and the colors are twisted with each other in every stitch so that there are no long floats on the back of the fabric. If the twist is always made in the same direction, the yarns get increasingly twisted; therefore it is necessary to change the direction of twist on a regular basis. The usual practice is to change directions whenever there is a color change in the pattern. If the yarns still get too twisted, the knitter just stops knitting and untwists them. The needle is inserted into the stitch before the threads are twisted. To twist the threads, the color to be thrown and purled is in the center, and the other two colors are switched with each other above the thread to be worked

(figs. 6, 9). Then the center thread is put over the needle to create the stitch (fig. 8). For example, the first or second finger of the left hand hooks around the right thread to pull it left, while the thumb of the right hand draws the left thread to the right (fig. 9). The left thread is held by the lower fingers while the thumb and first finger put the yarn over the needle (fig. 8). The right thread continues to be held by the thumb. In plain areas, additional yarns may still be twisted behind the work, in order that the texture remain the same as in the multicolor areas.

Decreasing is done by binding off a stitch of the background color at regular intervals, usually in the upper part of the designs. Increasing is done by picking up a stitch from the previous row and purling it. Increases are done mainly in a line between rows of pattern. To store unfinished work, the needles are all placed parallel (the free needle may be stuck through the work parallel to the others) and the yarns are wrapped around the ends of the needles and over the work in a figure eight (fig. 10). When adding a new color, the preferred method is to wrap the new yarn around one of the existing colors and knit both ends together for several stitches, until the short end is used up or can be cut off. Doña Roberta

Fig. 9. Hand position for switching the position of the two unused colors of yarn.

frowned on the method of tying the new thread to an existing one, later untying the knot, and darning in the end with a needle.

Making the starting border

The cap is begun by making the scalloped edging (*picas or puntas*) along the bottom. These notes tell how to make scallops with three colors, white, red, and green. Sometimes scallops with four or five colors are made (figs. 3, 4), and notes for these variations follow. The instructions are written for someone who is actually knitting, not observing. Instead of "right" and "left," I refer to the "first needle" and the "second needle." A right-handed person holds the first needle in the right hand and the second needle in the left. For a left-handed person, this would be reversed.

Creating a chain

The first step is to make a two-color chain. To tie the ends of the three yarns together, place them all side by side parallel and tie a single overhand knot with all of them. Alternatively, tie only the two colors to be used for the chain and add the third color later. Although one can put the yarns around the neck to make the chain

(fig. 11), Doña Roberta is not doing so in figure 7, since a looser tension does make this step easier.

1. Holding the first needle, with the knot below (you can hold it with the thumb and third finger), pass the red yarn behind the needle and over to the front, holding it in place with the first finger of the hand holding the needle.
2. Take the white yarn, pass it in front of the red yarn, then behind the needle and over to the front (fig. 11), holding it with the same finger and taking the tail behind the red yarn, where it can be held with the middle finger.
3. Insert the second needle into the back of both stitches (behind the first needle).

Fig. 10. Unfinished work prepared for storage.

Fig. 11. Knitting the chained starting border.

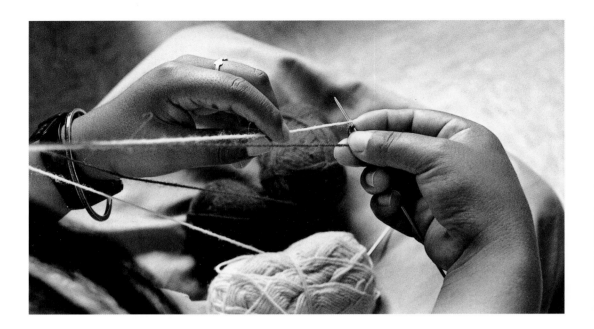

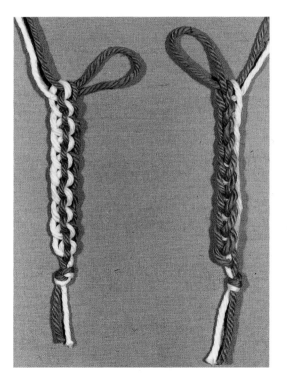

4. Take the red yarn, and pass it in front of the white yarn and around the first needle from back to front (actually front to back will yield the same result).

5. Pull this red loop through both the white and the red loops together. The white will show like a little bump.

6. Pull gently on the white yarn, but not too tightly or it will be too difficult to pick up stitches later. Also pull a little on the red yarn.

7. Take the white yarn from behind the red, pass it over the needle back to front, taking the tail behind the red yarn.

Repeat steps 3 through 7 nine times, but ending with step 6, for a total of ten stitches for the first scallop (fig. 12). A total of nine stitches are needed for each subsequent scallop. It is possible to make a long chain first, for many scallops, or to make one scallop at a time. The appearance of the chain includes a row of red stitches forming a simple chain, adjacent to a row of white overlapping stitches, adjacent to a row of red non-overlapping stitches, adjacent to a row of white non-overlapping stitches, which is in turn adjacent to the row of red chain stitches already mentioned. It is the white non-overlapping stitches that form the edge of the scallops.

Making the scallops

To begin knitting a scallop, pull the last loop so that it is big (1–2 inches long) and take the needle out of it. Orient the chain so that a row of non-overlapping white loops is framed by red loops.

1. Insert the first needle into the first white stitch (back to front). If this is difficult, fold the chain with the white loop on top.

2. Insert the first needle into the second white stitch, again back to front.

3. Place the second needle through this same (second) stitch behind the first one (front to back). Wrap the green yarn around the first needle back to front, and pull it through to

create a stitch (or pass the white stitch over the green one). Note that this is actually purling, not "knitting." Keep the green yarn in front of the work.

4. Insert the first needle (which is holding the green stitch) into the next white stitch of the chain (as in step 1 or 2).

5. Insert the second needle behind the first one through this same white stitch, wrap the green yarn around the first needle and pull the green stitch through, or pass the white stitch over the green one (as in step 2).

6. Repeat steps 4 and 5 three times until you have five green stitches in all.

7. Place the second needle through the front of the second stitch from the end and pass this stitch over the first one, off of the needle (bind off one stitch).

8. Repeat steps 4 and 5.

9. Place the second needle through the fronts of the second and third green stitches and pass them over the first stitch, off of the needle (bind off two together).

10. Repeat steps 4 and 5.

11. Repeat steps 9 and 4 and 5. There will be three green stitches on the needle.

12. Move the green thread to the back of the work. Place the second needle into the back of the last green stitch, pass the green yarn around the second needle, and pull the loop through with the second needle. Do the same with the remaining two green stitches. This is basically knitting backwards, that is, knitting (not purling) left-handed.

13. Move the green yarn to the front, and purl the same three stitches.

14. Pick up the next white stitch with the first needle, but don't work it.

15. Repeat from step 4 to 14 until you have enough scallops for a cap or bag of the desired size.

For five-color scallops (fig. 13), three colors of yarn are tied together for the chain. The chain is made as described above, but the third color is twisted with the red yarn before the yarn is thrown (see description of twisting above). After 10 stitches for the first scallop or 9 for subsequent ones have been made in this way, the color use is changed and the third color exchanges places with red. These two colors are exchanged after each scallop. The role of white remains the same.

Two additional colors can also alternate in filling in the scallops. The ends are tied together at the beginning. After the first stitch, the color not being used as filler is twisted with the one in use before the yarn is thrown. The color not being used for that scallop is dropped before the knitting backward starts. That color is picked up again to begin knitting the next scallop. Be sure to change the direction of twist with each color change. If doing these extra color changes, it is easier to make the chain for one scallop at a time.

The stripe-and-check border of the cap

The straight edge of the cap begins with a design called *ñaccha* (comb) or *k'utu* (a bump, such as a loop, stitch, or knot). First divide the scallops onto four needles. Hold the finished work in the secondary hand and transfer one stitch at a time to a needle held in the primary hand. It is not necessary to count the stitches—just distribute the work so it looks like about the same number of stitches on each needle. To make a tube, put the ball of red yarn through the large red loop at the end of the work; then pull the loop tight.

1. Using the red yarn, purl all the way around the cap. When all the stitches have been transferred to the new needle, move them to the middle of the needle before moving on. This will help prevent them from slipping off by mistake.

Fig. 13. Detail of the five-color starting border of the Chinchero sleeves in figure 4.

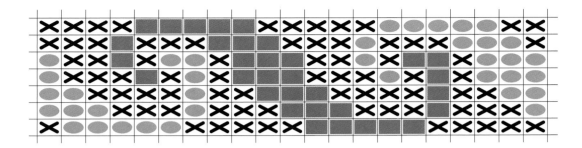

Fig. 14. Diagram of the fret pattern found in the first row above the border in Chinchero knitting. Diagram by Nancy Bush based on a sketch by Nilda Callañaupa.

2. With the same red yarn, knit another row. To knit with a single color, move the red yarn to the back of the work and place it over the left forefinger. Insert the first needle behind the second one, in the back of the stitch. If the previous row has been purled, it is hard to insert the needle behind, so one can insert it in front first and then move it to the back (underneath). To pass the yarn over the needle (front to back), it is only necessary to tilt the hand slightly. To pull it through, you can hold the thread between the first finger and thumb of the left hand, holding the needle with the lower fingers. Alternatively, you can hold the yarn with the right forefinger.

The next two rows alternate two blue and two white stitches, with the white stitches above each other and the blue ones above each other.

3. Add the blue yarn. To purl the first row of blue and white, these yarns must be moved to the inside of the work: put the balls through the square made by the needles. Drop the red and put the blue and white yarns around the neck. When changing colors, no special maneuver is needed. But when purling the second stitch of the same color, after the needle is inserted, cross the two colors before throwing the yarn, so that the unused color is held down, but not twisted. The hand motion used to cross the colors and throw the yarn is analogous to that used for three colors, but is not perfectly consistent.

4. Knit the next row. After knitting the first two blue stitches, move the yarn to the inside of the work, and move the white yarn to the outside in order to knit those two white stitches. Then move the blue back inside and the white outside, etc. This will create two-stitch long floats of each color on the back.

5. Before purling the next row of red (as in step 1), twist the red with the blue and white. Continue twisting the red with the blue and

white for several stitches before cutting off the blue and white.

6. Knit another row of red (as in step 2). This completes the border.

Purling the designs

The design band is begun by purling a row of green for the background. In the next row the alternation of three colors begins. White and green are already available, so a third color, yellow, is added.

The patterns are learned by counting the stitches in a previously knitted article. Figure 14 shows the fret design typically knitted in the row above the border. Soon, the knitter knows the patterns well enough to be able to work each row solely with reference to the previous one.

Making the top tassel

After completing the 3-color pattern, don't bind off, but divide the loops into three sections. Note that it is now necessary to decide where the earflaps will be. Purl three separate tubes, each a different color. For such small tubes it may be difficult to use five needles, so three or four can be used instead. When binding off, bind off one stitch from each side of the tube together, so that the tube is closed. Cut the lengths for the fringe, thread each one on a needle (or in groups of two or three), and put the needle through the cap so each length is centered. Then use a sewing needle and sew two rows of chain stitches over where the fringe was put through in order to secure it.

Making the earflaps

For the earflaps (*ninry*), pick up the requisite stitches from the first row of red at the top of the scalloped border. Purl back and forth (garter stitch) until the work will no longer be covered up by the border scallops. Then alternate rows of purling and knitting in the rest of the triangle. Make the border scallops separately (through the first two red rows) and then sew them on. Tack down the tips of the scallops on the hat by sewing them to the earflaps with a matching yarn.

Historical Speculations

The use of tubular purling on five (hooked) needles in multiple colors with the yarn held in the left hand and passing around the neck has also been recorded in this century in rural Portugal.[15] It seems likely that since the Andean countries were part of the Spanish, and not the Portuguese, empire, this technique was also formerly used in Spain, but it has apparently by now been replaced by modern techniques. Some of these same technical features have also been recorded in parts of Greece, Turkey, and rural Egypt;[16] it therefore seems likely that they were introduced to the Iberian peninsula by the Arabs.

The knitted sleeves provide a further clue about the Spanish source of this technique. The concept of separate sleeves is derived from Spanish costume. Women's dresses of the late fifteenth and early sixteenth centuries had detachable sleeves, and some of these were knitted.[17] Detachable knitted sleeves with multicolored patterns survived as part of the traditional women's costume in Orbigo in León, until early in the twentieth century.[18] León is not very far from northern Portugal, so this seemingly tenuous connection may have some significance as a possible source for the Andean techniques.

Addendum: Knitting in Guatemala

Ann Pollard Rowe

It is usually assumed in the literature on knitting that the technique used in Guatemala is similar to that used in the Andes. As it turns out, this is not the case. When working on The Textile Museum exhibition *Looping and Knitting, A History*, presented in 1997, I realized that our knitted wool bags from Sololá, Nahualá, and Zacualpa were made with the loops crossed (in the Z direction), in notable contrast to the familiar open loops of Andean knitting (figs. 15, 16).[19] I also found that the Guatemalan bags were knitted from the bottom up, whereas Andean bags are knitted from the top down. The bags in figures 15 and 16 have an interesting start at the bottom. The yarn zigzags from one side of the bag to another, with a twist (Z) into which the first loop is knitted, and a two-span float (Z) in the center. Some of the other bags have a simpler looped start. Most of the Guatemalan bags are worked in two colors, usually black and white, though the one in figure 16 is red and white, and our collection also includes one plain white

Fig. 15. Knitted wool bag purchased in Sololá, Guatemala, 1937–40. 39 x 40 cm, excluding strap. The Textile Museum 1964.65.140.

Fig. 16. Detail of the starting edge (bottom) of a knitted wool bag purchased in Sololá in 1940, but possibly made in Chichicastenango. The Textile Museum 1965.51.29, anonymous gift.

Fig. 17. Sololá man knitting.
Photograph by Marilyn
Anderson, 1976.

example. The Sololá bags and the one in figure 16 have the unused color carried under the main color on the back, similar to Andean practice, while the Zacualpa and Nahualá bags have the extra color floated on the back.

Checking the literature on Guatemalan textiles, however, I realized that no one has described the technique used, and the only person who has recorded it seems to be the photographer Marilyn Anderson.[20] At my request, Anderson supplied me with a photograph from the same contact sheet that shows the technique even better than in her previously published photograph (fig. 17). From this photograph, it is apparent that the bags are made in the round using five needles, similar to the Andean technique, but that the knitting is done from the right or "knit" side, in obvious contrast to the Andean method. The end of the needle visible between the man's legs appears to be hooked. The man is holding the yarn between his right thumb and first finger and it clearly does not pass around his neck. Although the balls of yarn are not actually visible, it appears that they are inside the bag. The details of inserting the needle and throwing the yarn are unfortunately unclear.

The differences in the knitting techniques of the Andes and Guatemala suggest that knitting was introduced into these areas from different places in Spain, and that there was regional variation in knitting techniques within Spain. While crossed knitting has not previously been noted in Spain, there are in fact relatively few early examples of Spanish knitting that have been preserved and published, so such a gap in our knowledge cannot be taken to be definitive. Crossed knitting is found in some Balkan and Turkish pieces (crossed either Z or S), so it certainly was known in the Arab world.

Additional information on this subject would be highly desirable. Part of the purpose of this addendum is to draw attention to the questions raised, in the hope that someone might investigate further. A more recent monograph on Sololá textiles says that the bags are knitted on a circular needle made of two bicycle spokes or regular knitting needles joined by a cord.[21] Thus it appears that the technique has been modernized in the ten years since Anderson took her photographs.

Acknowledgments

All information on Chinchero knitting is from Nilda Callañaupa, who is a native of Chinchero and wrote the initial draft of the article. In 1990 Nilda Callañaupa visited The Textile Museum and taught the techniques to Ann Rowe, who recorded it at that time. The technical text was thus edited by Ann Rowe on the basis of this experience, then checked again by Nilda Callañaupa. The introductory and concluding sections providing non-Chinchero background information and references are by Ann Rowe.

We are grateful to Edward Franquemont for his interest in the article and for providing the photographs in figures 5 and 7 as well as the old cap in figure 3. The photographs in figures 1, 3, 12, and 16 are by Franko Khoury. Those in figures 2 and 15 are by Jeffrey Crespi. Those in figures 4 and 13 are by Ann Rowe.

About the Authors

Nilda Callañaupa A. was born in Chinchero where she learned the textile skills traditional in her community. She holds a master's degree in the tourism program from the San Antonio Abad National University in Cusco and worked for nineteen years at Peruvian Andean Treks in Cusco in various capacities, ending as assistant to the manager. In addition, she has made many trips to the United States and Canada to give lectures and workshops on Andean textiles and contemporary Andean culture, including at The Textile Museum. In 1996 she founded the Center for Traditional Textiles of Cusco, of which she is the director and president. The Center, which works to preserve the traditional textile culture of the Cusco area, is affiliated with Cultural Survival in the United States and has also been recognized by the National Institute of Culture in Peru.

Ann Pollard Rowe is Curator for Western Hemisphere Collections at The Textile Museum. Affiliated with The Textile Museum since 1972, she has contributed numerous articles on both modern and ancient Peruvian textiles to previous issues of *The Textile Museum Journal*.

Notes

1. LeCount 1990 shows a broad range of examples.

2. Rowe 1997b, p. 29.

3. LeCount (1990, p. 26) is mistaken that Cieza de León uses the word "chullo." She references a translation, not a transcription of his text, which in fact uses the word "chuco," a hispanicized spelling of "chuku" (Cieza 1553, cap. 100, fol. 125; 1984, p. 274).

4. For a more detailed discussion of looping versus knitting, see Rowe 1997a, based on Emery 1980, pp. 31–32, 39–42, in turn based on Bühler-Oppenheim and Bühler 1948, pp. 93–99, 107–13.

5. The beige yarns are spun S and two-plied Z, while the dark brown yarns are spun S, two-plied Z, and two-replied S or vice versa. Both Inca yarns and contemporary Cusco area yarns are typically spun Z and two-plied S. In the looping, the loops are crossed Z. Harcourt (1962, pl. 71) illustrates a similar pre-Hispanic cap, said to have been found at the central coast site of Ancón, and which has ties that are missing in the Textile Museum piece. The cap might have been an import to Ancón, but it is hard to say from where.

6. LeCount (1990, p. 26, fig. 3.3) illustrates another interesting looped cap, said to be Uru, from northern Bolivia—geographically closer than the Textile Museum piece illustrated.

7. Rutt (1987, pp. 39–44) is a recent discussion, also providing references to earlier publications. These pieces are illustrated in color in Morral and Carbonell eds. 1997, p. 46, pls. 5–6, and p. 458, item 167, discussed pp. 43, 45 in the text by Montse Stanley. The same book also illustrates a pair of silk gloves from the grave of an archbishop of Toledo, who died in 1247 (p. 64, pl. 13, discussed p. 62).

It is noteworthy that this book, which draws primarily on collections in Spain, includes virtually nothing that appears to be antecedent to Latin American knitting. The few examples of pre-nineteenth-century two-color knitting shown are said to have floats on the back. Probably the explanation has to do with the book's emphasis on upper-class and city knitting, as opposed to the country and peasant traditions that are more likely to show some connection with country and peasant traditions in the Americas.

8. Rutt (1987, pp. 33–39) again provides references to earlier publications.

9. In addition to LeCount 1990, see, for example, Gibson-Roberts 1995.

10. See also LeCount 1990, p. 68, pl. 5, left; Meisch ed. 1997, pp. 127–28, cat. no. 207 (same piece as LeCount).

11. LeCount 1990, p. 68, pl. 5, top row, item 2, and p. 89, graph 3; Meisch ed. 1997, pp. 126–28 (cat. no. 206 is the same as in LeCount).

12. For Huancavelica sleeves, see LeCount 1990, pp. 12–13, figs. 2.4–2.6, p. 67, pl. 4; Noble 1995.

13. The patterned sleeves are shown in pl. VIII, figs. 51–52; the monochrome ones are pl. XVII, fig. 107 and pl. XLVI, fig. 106 (same man); pl. XXI, figs. 138–39; pl. XXI, figs. 140–41; pl. XXV, figs. 160–61; pl. XXV, fig. 162; pl. XXVI, fig. 167–68; pl. XXIX, figs. 187–88.

14. See, for example, Frame 1983, pp. 26–27.

15. Rutt 1987, pp. 22, 24, 203.

16. Besides Rutt, see Stanley 1986, p. 26; Edraos 1990.

17. R. M. Anderson 1979, pp. 190–95.

18. Ortiz Echagüe 1957, p. 185.

19. The Textile Museum's bag from Zacualpa is 1984.37.4, Latin American Research Fund; from Nahualá is 1983.18.2, gift of Bertoldo Nathusius (not new when given); a plain white bag, purchased in Sololá 1937–40, but possibly from Nahualá, is 1964.65.135. Osborne (1975, p. 271) says that wool bags are also knitted in Santa Catarina Palopó and Joyabaj.

20. M. Anderson 1978, fig. 215. Rutt (1987, p. 203) gives the impression that Lila O'Neale recorded this technique, but in fact she describes only the finished wool bags, and superficially at that.

21. Mayén de Castellanos 1986, p. 74; 1988, p. 78.

References

Anderson, Marilyn
1978   *Guatemalan Textiles Today*. Watson-Guptill Publications, New York.

Anderson, Ruth Matilda
1979   *Hispanic Costume 1480–1520*. The Hispanic Society of America, New York.

Bühler-Oppenheim, Kristin, and Alfred Bühler
1948   *Die Textiliensammlung Fritz Iklé-Huber im Museum für Völkerkunde und Schweizerischen Museum für Volkskunde, Basel (Grundlagen zur Systematik der gesamten textilen Techniken)*. Denkschriften der Schweizerischen Naturforschenden Gesellschaft, Band LXXVIII, Abh. 2. Basel.

Cieza de León, Pedro
1984   *Crónica del Perú, Primera Parte*. Pontificia Universidad Católica del Peru, Fondo Editorial; Academia Nacional de la Historia, Lima. Originally published 1553.

Edraos, Patricia Tongue
1990   Knitting Greek Style, *Threads*, no. 30 (Aug.), p. 51. The Taunton Press, Newtown, Connecticut.

Emery, Irene
1980   *The Primary Structures of Fabrics: an Illustrated Classification*. The Textile Museum, Washington. Originally published 1966.

Ferris, H. B.
1916   *The Indians of Cuzco and the Apurimac*. Memoirs of the American Anthropological Association, vol. III, no. 2.

Frame, Mary
1983   Faugustino's Family: Knitters, Weavers and Spinners on the Island of Taquile, Peru, *In Celebration of the Curious Mind: A Festschrift to honor Anne Blinks on her 80th Birthday*, edited by Nora Rogers and Martha Stanley, pp. 21–34. Interweave Press, Loveland, Colorado.

Gibson-Roberts, Priscilla A.

1995   Multicolored Knitting Techniques of the Central Andes, *Piecework*, vol. III, no. 1 (Jan.-Feb.), pp. 48–49. Interweave Press, Loveland, Colorado.

Harcourt, Raoul d'

1962   *Textiles of Ancient Peru and Their Techniques.* Edited by Grace G. Denny and Carolyn M. Osborne, translated by Sadie Brown. University of Washington Press, Seattle and London.

LeCount, Cynthia Gravelle

1990   *Andean Folk Knitting: Traditions and Techniques from Peru and Bolivia.* Dos Tejedoras Fiber Arts Publications, Saint Paul, Minnesota.

Mayén de Castellanos, Guisela

1986   *Tzute y jerarquía en Sololá.* Con la colaboración de Idalma Mejía de Rodas, capítulo final de Linda Asturias de Barrios. Museo Ixchel del Traje Indígena de Guatemala.

1988   *Tzute and Hierarchy in Sololá.* With the collaboration of Idalma Mejía de Rodas, final chapter by Linda Asturias de Barrios, translated by Ava Navin. Museo Ixchel del Traje Indígena de Guatemala.

Meisch, Lynn A. (editor)

1997   *Traditional Textiles of the Andes: Life and Cloth in the Highlands: The Jeffrey Appleby Collection of Andean Textiles.* Thames and Hudson, New York, and the Fine Arts Museums of San Francisco.

Morral i Romeu, Eulàlia, and Sílvia Carbonell (editors)

1997   *Mil anys de desseny en punt* (text in Catalan and Spanish). Centre de Documentació i Museu Tèxtil, Terrassa, Spain.

Noble, Carol Rasmussen

1995   Peruvian Maquitos: Colorful Sleeves Knit Traditions Together, *Piecework,* vol. III, no. 1 (Jan.-Feb.), pp. 42–47. Interweave Press, Loveland, Colorado.

Ortiz Echagüe, José

1957   *España: Tipos y trajes.* Tenth edition. Publicaciones Ortiz Echagüe, Madrid.

Osborne, Lilly de Jongh

1975   *Indian Crafts of Guatemala and El Salvador.* Second edition. University of Oklahoma Press, Norman.

Rowe, Ann Pollard

1997a   *Looping and Knitting.* Exhibition brochure. The Textile Museum, Washington.

1997b   Inca Weaving and Costume, *The Textile Museum Journal 1995–96*, vols. 34–35, pp. 4–53. Washington.

Rutt, Richard

1987   *A History of Hand Knitting.* Interweave Press, Loveland, Colorado.

Stanley, Montse

1986   *The Handknitter's Handbook.* David and Charles Publishers, Newton Abbot.

Fig. 1. Sections of two Ethiopian hangings from Magdala (left panel = BM1 (1868.10–1.22); right panel = BM2 (1973 Af38.1)). Silk, tablet-woven. BM1: 504 x 60 cm., BM2: 491 x 50 cm. British Museum, London. As published in *The Burlington Magazine*, June 1996. Photography by Michael Gervers.

Tablet-woven Curtains from Ethiopia: New Light on a Puzzling Group of Textiles

Martha Henze

The largest examples of tablet-woven textiles known came to light as the result of a dramatic military confrontation led by the British under Sir Robert Napier that took place April 13, 1868, at Magdala on the high plateau of north-central Ethiopia.[1] In the aftermath of the battle, which ended with the suicide of the flamboyant Emperor Tewodros II, the treasures he had looted from numerous churches and monasteries in his kingdom were salvaged from his ruined fortress. Richard R. Holmes, a member of The British Museum's Department of Manuscripts, had come with the expedition and had been provided with 1,000 English pounds to purchase valuable objects of special interest to the museum. Of objects auctioned to the British officers present for the benefit of noncommissioned officers and soldiers, Mr. Holmes acquired 350 Ethiopian Church manuscripts and other valuable objects. Among these was a single panel of an unusually large curtain woven of thick, colored silk yarn in a technique later recognized as tablet weaving.[2]

This unusual panel remains in the Ethnography Department of The British Museum (1868.10–1.22, hereafter referred to as BM1). In later years objects from Magdala such as crosses, censers, chalices, curtains, and other ecclesiastical objects have appeared in museums and English churches, but many may remain in private hands. Few heavy silken tablet-woven curtains were taken at Magdala. Many officers probably thought the heavy curtains were unsuitable for personal use and probably not worth the enormous effort to carry them home to England. The royal class were the only people in Ethiopia who could use objects of silk and the only ones wealthy enough to buy raw silk. There appears to have been only one workshop in which these curtains were manufactured. By the end of the eighteenth century, the technique declined and seems to have disappeared. Two other curtains

(besides BM1) have surfaced to date. One panel was acquired by The British Museum in 1973 (1973 Af38.1, hereafter referred to as BM2) from a descendant of an officer at Magdala. A third silken curtain, made up of three panels, was donated to the Royal Ontario Museum (ROM) in Toronto by the son of a British officer, present at Magdala, who had emigrated to Canada in the late nineteenth century (ROM 922.26.1).

No scholarly attention was paid to these curtains until the early 1990s when Dr. Michael Gervers set in motion a thorough study of all three of these extraordinary curtains in collaboration with Dr. Ewa Balicka-Witakowska.[3] Except for an undocumented sighting in Ethiopia in the 1960s,[4] these museum objects were for many years the only known examples of this textile rarity. While it seemed clear that all three had been taken from Ethiopia at the same time, there were no clues to the identity of their weavers. Although the curtains appeared to be of an ecclesiastical nature, there was no firsthand evidence to explain how or where they were made or used. Colonel G. A. Sweny, who acquired the curtain now in the ROM, was told that his curtain came from a church in Gondar, the royal capital of Ethiopia in the seventeenth and eighteenth centuries. Neither silk weaving nor tablet weaving is known to have been part of the traditional culture in Ethiopia at any period up to the present.[5]

New evidence came to light in February 1995 when Paul B. Henze, a retired American Foreign Service officer and historian of Ethiopia, was shown a hanging of three panels of silken curtains much like the London and Toronto museum objects while he was photographing manuscripts and icons at a monastery church in northern Ethiopia.[6] He and I discovered three additional examples of similar tablet-woven curtains, of cotton rather than silk, during two research trips to Ethiopia in 1998 and 1999. The purpose of this paper is to summarize the information published by Balicka-Witakowska and Gervers (1996) and to report the results of our field research to date.

Silk Tablet-woven Curtains from Magdala

The figured panel in The British Museum

The single panel (BM1; fig. 1, left) selected for the British Museum by Richard R. Holmes at Magdala measures 504 cm in length and varies in width between 54 and 62 cm (almost 17 x 2 feet). The panel required the use of 349 tablets with 4 warp yarns per tablet.[7] Its length is divided visually into three parts, each with designs rendered in red against a white or yellow ground. Thin blue stripes set off the central section from the others. The panel appears to have been the central panel of three; remnants of connecting threads can be seen on the selvedges. The central and widest section of the panel used a bleached white thread as background which causes the red figures and patterning to stand out more clearly than those on the narrower side sections where yellow is used.

Fig. 2. Detail of BM1 (fig. 1) showing two royal figures. As published in *The Burlington Magazine*, June 1996. Photography by Michael Gervers.

Decoration on the BM1 panel is a composition of figural scenes bordered at top and bottom by geometric patterning of various kinds. The most prominent figures[8] of the white-grounded section are arranged in three registers and, judging from their attributes of crowns, patterned apparel, and attendants, the three persons represented appear to be of royal stature (figs. 1, 2). Three lower registers depict rows of warriors. In the first row of five figures, each is armed with a curved sword at his waist and holds a tall staff cross; in the second row, four warriors carry round shields, wear an animal-skin over the shoulder, and hold two sheathed spears; five warriors in the third row are outfitted with curved swords, cartridge belts and matchlock guns.

The nonfigural panel in The British Museum

The single panel (BM2; fig. 1, right) donated to The British Museum by a descendant of a Magdala officer in 1973 is nonfigural and measures 491 cm in length and varies between 48 and 56 cm in width. The panel required the use of 290 tablets with 4 warp yarns per tablet. Ten tablet-woven loops have been sewn at fairly regular intervals along one long edge indicating that the curtain was hung with the stripes viewed horizontally at some point in its history. As the ROM curtain and others discovered recently were clearly made to be viewed vertically, suspended by loops sewn along the narrow top end, it seems probable that BM2 was originally made to hang that way also. Some of the loops now sewn to the long edge of BM2 may have been borrowed from another panel of the same type and used together with those woven for BM2's narrow end. The panel, shown in vertical position in figure 1, consists of five narrow bands of geometric ornamentation using red and yellow yarn with a narrow stripe of pale indigo blue color separating them. The bands are made up of larger sections of the same geometric patterns used as infill ornamentation in BM1.[9]

The three-paneled curtain in the Royal Ontario Museum

In physical appearance the ROM curtain (ROM 922.26.1; fig. 3) very closely resembles the British Museum objects. It measures 535 cm x 212 cm, each of the three vertical panels being approximately 70 cm wide (a little wider than the two panels in The British Museum). Each panel required the use of over 350 tablets using more than 1,400 twisted silk threads. The panels are woven of very thick blue, yellow, red, and bleached white spun-silk yarn in the same tablet weaving techniques as used in the British Museum examples. The ornamentation of each panel is arranged in a series of registers that alternate geometric patterns and figural elements. Some of the latter are human figures, while others are ecclesiastical objects sometimes similar in type to those in BM1. The central panel here is the most important; in its detail of a crowned queen and enthroned king it appears to have been influenced by, or to be related in some way to, the BM1 panel. Balicka-Witakowska and Gervers (1996, p. 380) suggest that the ROM hanging may have been woven in a Gondar workshop somewhat later than BM1 but may represent the same royal personages. The rendering of some figures in the ROM panel is less precise and the spatial arrangement less carefully measured than in BM1, indicating a possible decline in workmanship. The assemblage of three processional crosses and censers in the lower left side panel may be seen as a symbolic representation of the Crucifixion, together with the darkened sun and the moon shown as green and red rectangles. The opposing side panel very clearly depicts the Crucifixion, with human figures instead of crosses. These two figural assemblages, together with the ceremony depicted in the upper right panel, reinforce the religious character of the scenes on this curtain. The authors interpret the scenes as depicting the celebration of a mass attended by royal patrons, rather than a court scene as in BM1.

Because of the images on BM1 and the ROM triptych, and the very expensive materials of which they are made, it seems reasonable to conclude that the "Gondar" curtains from Magdala were woven under royal patronage in the second quarter of the eighteenth century. BM2 is probably a side panel from a similar curtain.

The Abba Gerima Silk Curtains

On February 21, 1995, Paul Henze visited the ancient monastery of Abba Gerima located a few miles south of the town of Adwa in the province of Tigray (fig. 4). To his amazement, among the heap of dusty carpets pulled out of a corner of the treasury for his examination were long panels of colorful silk. These resembled those he had first seen when Michael Gervers presented a paper about the ROM curtain at the Second International Conference on the History of Ethiopian Art in Nieborow, Poland, in 1990. What he had found were two more examples of the tablet-woven "Gondar"-type curtains now in The British Museum and in the Royal Ontario Museum.

The two Abba Gerima curtains measure 375 cm in length; each is made up of three panels 66 cm wide (figs. 5, 6). One curtain (AG1, fig. 5) has no figural panels but is made up entirely of geometric patterning—wavy lines, zigzags, concentric diamonds, checkerboard blocks, solid blocks of color and stripes—worked in the same clear blue, red, green, and yellow heavy silk as the museum objects (AG1 most closely resembles

Fig. 3. Section of the Royal Ontario Museum silk curtain. As published in *The Burlington Magazine*, June 1996. ROM 922.26.1, Royal Ontario Museum, Toronto.

the BM2 panel). The second hanging (AG2, figs. 6–8) has a central panel with two rows of five cross-in-diamond patterns and two rows of five ecclesiastics wearing neck crosses, holding in one hand a cross and in the other a prayer stick (fig. 7). Figures are shown across the width in a color pattern of red on what appears to be undyed silk, blue on red, red on yellow, again blue on red, and finally greenish or faded blue on what appears to be bleached white. The remainder of the central panel bears the same general geometric patterning that covers the two side panels which are without figures. In brief, they are visually of the same group as the so-called Gondar pieces.[10]

The Abba Gerima monks were delighted to relate what they knew about the curtains, which they said had been given to the monastery in the reign of Ras Mikael Sehul who lived from c. 1686 to 1780. An aggressive Tigrayan ruler, he used his strength to ally himself with the more prestigious Gondarene royalty. Ras Mikael played matrimonial politics as well, marrying when already in his seventies a daughter of Mentewab (empress 1721–30 and regent 1730–69).[11] After a brief period of meddlesome attempts at king-making, he was defeated by rival figures and, losing all influence, was forced to return to his home province to spend his declining years. He died there at a ripe old age (Prouty and Rosenfeld 1994, pp. 231–232). It is tempting to speculate that this wily old ruler who associated himself with the Gondar court during the period in question might have seen the silken curtains hanging in one of the royal churches, come to covet the luxurious objects, and managed to bring a set back to his home area to give to his favorite religious establishment, the monastery of Abba Gerima. At the very least, Ras Mikael Sehul provides a tangible connection between Gondar and Abba Gerima and could lend weight to the hypothesis that the Magdala curtains were from the royal court at Gondar.

The interview at Abba Gerima in 1995 demonstrates the nature of research in areas such as this where history is largely kept in the memory and passed on orally. The monks of

Fig. 4. Treasury building of the Abba Gerima monastery in the northern Ethiopian province of Tigray, where the two silk hangings (AG1 and AG2) were laid out for observation and photographing in 1995.

Fig. 5. Full-length view of the nonfigural three-paneled silk curtain (AG1) found in the Abba Gerima monastery.

Abba Gerima told Paul Henze that the curtains had hung for many years in the sanctuary. Loops of blue and yellow tablet-woven fabric are sewn at intervals on the folded-over top edge. A simple pole of hard wood would have been attached between two pillars of the church to hold the curtains, as the modern curtains are hung today. The monks said that they were not using them any longer because the weight of the silk made them too hard to draw easily. When asked where the curtains were made and by whom, the monks replied that they were woven near Adwa by a people called "Seglin" (phonetic spelling) who were not Ethiopian and came from somewhere else. Asked if these people were Muslim and what language they spoke, they said they did not know. They thought the people had lived in a village south of Adwa called Mai Zbi (Hyena Water), but there was none there now.[12] Efforts to find traces of a group of foreign artisans bearing the name "Seglin" working in this region in the middle of the eighteenth century have not yet borne fruit.

Fig. 6. Full-length view of silk curtain with two registers of figures (AG2, reverse) found in the Abba Gerima monastery.

Fig. 7. Detail of section of AG2 depicting two rows of Ethiopian religious figures, each holding a cross in the right hand and a prayer staff in the left.

Fig. 8. Detail of AG2: cross-in-diamond patterning in central panel.

Analyses of Dyes

The three-paneled curtain in the ROM underwent a thorough structural analysis by Mary Frame, an independent textile scholar who resides in Vancouver, British Columbia, Canada, prior to its conservation and dye analysis by the Canadian Conservation Institute (CCI) in Ottawa (Frame, 1993). The dyes of the ROM hanging were analyzed by that laboratory in 1993 and 1994 (Moffatt and Miller, 1993; 1994). Peter Collingwood was commissioned to undertake a study of the structure of the two hangings in the British Museum (BM1 and BM2) and completed the work in early 1999.[13] The CCI was recently commissioned to analyze dyes contained in yarn from the Abba Gerima silk curtain AG1. The tests identified dyes on fibers of the Abba Gerima sample that have the same chemical compositions as those obtained from the ROM "Gondar" hanging. The dyes identified were madder, indigo, brazilwood, and a plant of the *Rhamnus* genus. The report concludes: "It cannot be determined from the analytical results whether the dyed silk from the various artifacts came from the same workshop or time period" (Moffatt and Miller 1999).

These dyestuffs were surely available in an important commercial center such as Gondar in the eighteenth century. It is likely that the silk yarn was either dyed abroad before export or was dyed in Ethiopia with imported or local dyes. Although scientific analyzes to date have not answered all the questions surrounding these eleven panels of tablet-woven silk, which have so many visual elements in common, they have confirmed that the panels were made from the same material and in the same technique. Furthermore, a field interview indicates that the panels were almost certainly hung between pillars to conceal the *maqdas*, the most sacred part, of the churches for which they were made. The interview at Abba Gerima offered a small clue to the identity of the weavers and a possible location of production.

More Ethiopian Tablet-woven Church Curtains

The cotton curtains in the church of St. Gabriel Wukien

In February 1998, Paul Henze and I traveled in the state of Tigray to a region called the Tembien (fig. 9), which lies northeast of the Semien Mountains between Gondar and Adwa. Our goal was to visit some of the rock-cut churches which had just been made accessible by new roads. Not visible from the valley below, the large monastic church of St. Gabriel Wukien lies about 30 meters up a cliffside of red volcanic stone and has magnificent views across the broad valley to the rugged bulk of Worqamba (Mountain of Gold), whose slopes conceal several other rock-cut churches.

The St. Gabriel Wukien church was hewn according to a basilical plan with columns, arches, and domes between four bays—a fine example of the dozens of churches carved into living rock in the heartland of Ethiopia.[14]

As we walked through the ambulatory carved around three sides of the church and stepped over the threshold to enter, we were stunned by an unexpected reward for our climb. Peering through the late afternoon gloom into the unlit nave, we were able to make out a wall of curtains stretched between columns across the far end concealing the holy-of-holies, or *maqdas*. Even from a distance of about 12 meters, we could make out through the dust-filled air the figures of priests with crosses and soldiers with weapons with which we were familiar from the ROM and BM silk hangings (figs. 10–13).

It was clear to us at the outset that the curtains hanging in St. Gabriel Wukien, though woven in the same technique and similar in decoration and size to the silken "Gondar" and Abba Gerima pieces, were woven of cotton yarn by artisans of far less skill. The most exciting aspect of the discovery is that these were the first examples of this unusual type of textile found *in situ*.

Three complete curtains were hung side by side from a wooden pole or, in two cases, from a thick cord strung between the stone pillars across the nave. They were suspended by loops of leather or fabric roughly sewn across the panels at points of stress. One tablet-woven loop remained; this appears to have been the original mode of hanging. All other loops had been

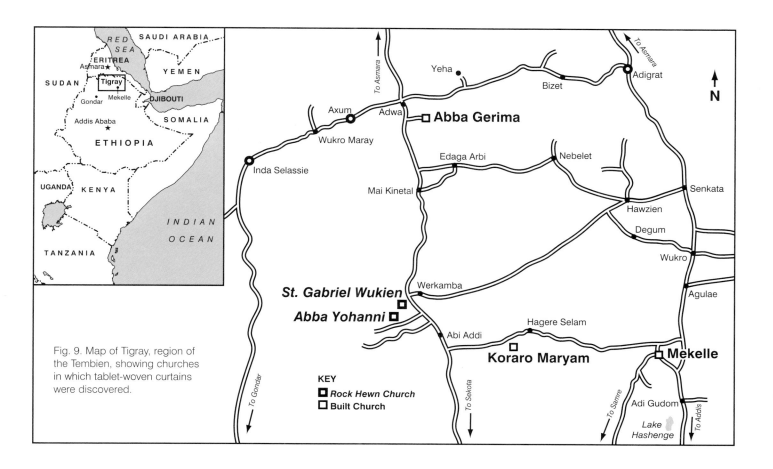

Fig. 9. Map of Tigray, region of the Tembien, showing churches in which tablet-woven curtains were discovered.

KEY
◻ *Rock Hewn Church*
◻ *Built Church*

Fig. 10. First view of cotton tablet-woven curtain of four panels (GW1) hanging *in situ* in the rock-hewn church of St. Gabriel Wukien in the Tembien region of Tigray. Note that illumination is provided only by candles or flashlight in this fifteenth-century church.

Fig. 11. Section of GW1 curtain showing the religious figures, soldiers, and crosses that relate these cotton tablet-woven curtains to the silken "Gondar" curtains in the Royal Ontario Museum and The British Museum. One clearly sees the representation of the Crucifixion in the third panel: there are the three crosses and colored squares that represent the darkened sun and the moon.

Fig. 12. Detail of GW1: double-faced complementary-warp structure.

Fig. 13. Detail of GW1: geometric patterning of the fourth panel in the dress of the two priests.

replaced at least once during the years of use, evidence of the burdensome weight of such curtains, which caused the monks of Abba Gerima to put aside their silken ones. The bottom edges of all panels showed signs of having been worn or trimmed from time to time, no doubt because the fabric's weight caused them to sag onto the straw-covered stone floor. The pervasive dust of a century or two surely added to their weight. At some point in recent years a flowered polyester curtain had been stretched on a nylon cord in front of the old tablet-woven hangings.[15]

Two of the St. Gabriel Wukien curtains (GW1 and GW2) are made up of four narrow panels each, approximately 370 cm long and 46 cm wide. The third curtain (GW3) is of similar length and comprises three panels with geometric patterning only. The left-hand panel of GW1 (figs. 10–13) has three registers of figures at eye level with a block of concentric diamond design above and a block of chevron patterning below. Uppermost (fig. 12) is a poorly drawn architectural element framing two white-robed figures, one a priest bearing on his head what appears to be a *tabot*, the holy tablet sanctifying the church; the second is a smaller figure bearing a staff-cross as large as himself. Both figures stand in a frame which may represent the entrance of the *maqdas*. The register below shows three warriors wearing cartridge belts and holding matchlock guns like those in BM1. A third register has three figures with spiky headdresses; each holds in the left hand what is probably meant to represent a fly whisk (figs. 10, 11).

The second figural panel of GW1 has an assemblage made up of a large diamond-shaped processional cross flanked by two smaller crosses, all of interwoven design (figs. 10, 11).[16] The appearance of a square form at either side of the uppermost point of the large cross recalls the interpretation by Balicka-Witakowska of a similar assemblage on the lower left panel of the ROM curtain as symbolic of the Crucifixion with the sun and the moon (Balicka-Witakowska and Gervers 1996, pp. 380, 383). This entire panel, which bears a lower range depicting four hand-crosses, is especially well-drawn as if showing that the artisan was weaving the shape of objects entirely familiar to him.

The last figural panel of GW1 includes a register depicting two elegantly robed priests wearing ecclesiastical crowns, holding pierced diamond-shaped hand-crosses in one hand and elaborate censers in the other (figs. 10, 13). A small dark hatless figure fills the width;

perhaps there was no space for a third priest as in the first register of the ROM's central panel. In a low register, two large diamond-shaped hand-crosses alternate with three smaller ones (fig. 10).

The second four-panel curtain at St. Gabriel Wukien (GW2) includes two panels completely filled with registers of various geometric patterning, like those used as infill on figural panels of the curtains at the Abba Gerima monastery church and the Gondarene ones now in the ROM and BM. These at St. Gabriel Wukien are rendered in shades of dyed brown and cream-colored natural cotton.

Only one register of figures decorates the left-hand central panel of GW2 (fig. 14). In it, two crowned priests hold censers in their left hands and tall processional crosses of a rounded form topped by a small cross in their right. The third figure wears no crown, but his staff seems to hold a crown aloft. A well-drawn hand cross floats above his head (fig. 15, left).

The right-hand central panel of GW2 (figs. 14–17) contains several puzzling elements. At the upper edge of the panel are two figures that could rarely have been seen from the floor below (fig. 15). They are grotesque, apparently six-armed elongated figures dressed only in a garment which extends below the knees. Each stands with one arm uplifted. Between the figures is what might be a piece of furniture with carved legs. Although rendered in an awkward manner, this assemblage is reminiscent of the depiction of the enthroned king and attendant "angels" in the top figural register of BM1.

Figures in the central register are quite distorted (figs. 14, right, and 16). Two small figures hold disproportionately large staff-crosses; one wears a scimitar at his belt and the other holds a fly whisk in his left hand. The central figure is represented by a huge head with spiky hair, two eyes, and a mouth, attached to a cross-topped staff taller than the other two figures. The lowest register (fig. 17) contains four spear-bearers: two tall figures bearing rectangular shields and spears with leather-shrouded spearheads, and two shorter figures holding smaller spearheads. Above them are two ewers which may depict jugs of holy water.

The third curtain at St. Gabriel Wukien (GW3) is made up of three nonfigural panels which may have lost a fourth at some time in the past (fig. 18). This curtain had been torn, patched, and shortened, and was used at the edge farthest from the sanctuary.[17]

During a visit to Tembien in March 1999, we revisited the church of St. Gabriel Wukien. On this visit, the head priest added a few bits of lore to our interpretation of the figures. He pointed out that the priestly figure carrying the tabot-like object on his head was Abba Daniel, founder of the monastery, who was buried in the church.[18]

Fig. 14. Section of adjacent registers of two panels of GW2. These figures reveal the inexperience of the weavers who appear to be trying to copy with mixed success the figures of the silken "Gondar" curtains.

Fig. 15. On the right, the upper section of one of the figural panels of GW2 showing two abstract "angels" similar to those guarding the royal figure of BM1 and an interesting use of geometric patterns.

Fig. 16. Detail of GW2: distortions in the creation of human figures.

Fig. 17. Detail of GW2: spearbearer panel.

The cotton curtains of the monastery church of Abba Yohanni

During our second visit to St. Gabriel Wukien, we asked the head priest if he knew of any other church in the region that possessed curtains similar to those that hang in his church. He answered immediately that nearby Abba Yohanni had some, but they were not as complete as those in St. Gabriel Wukien. Within a few hours we had driven around the mountain and ascended the cliff-face into which the church of Abba Yohanni is carved. There we found two curtains, in poor condition but still hanging in place before the *maqdas* (figs. 19–21). Panels of plain-weave fabric had been hung on the suspension pole together with the tablet-woven brown and white panels. Some of these hung in front of the tablet weaving, and in some instances the plain-weave panel was sewn to the tablet-woven panel. As a result of this arrangement and the unusual height of the ceiling, the curtain panels were intertwined, obstructing visual examination. For a precise description, the hangings will have to be taken down and sorted to establish which panels originally were made to be joined together.

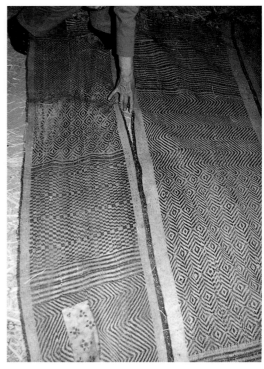

Fig. 18. Sections of three-paneled nonfigural curtain (GW3) being examined in the ambulatory of the church of St. Gabriel Wukien.

It was immediately apparent that these curtains, while they shared some elements with those of St. Gabriel Wukien and the "Gondar" examples, were in several ways quite different. The brown and white tablet-woven panels were of a finer, more tightly spun cotton yarn than those of St. Gabriel Wukien.[19]

One Abba Yohanni curtain (AY1) presently consists of a tablet-woven panel, about 22 cm wide, with a wider panel, about 40 cm wide, of identical vertically striped plain-weave fabric attached to each edge. The tablet-woven panel (fig. 19) is divided visually into at least six sections separated by several horizontal stripes. At the very top, a tiny portion of a stepped motif is barely visible. This is followed by a section of what seems to be zigzag patterning which is followed by an interesting design of stacked stepped motifs. The major feature of the panel is an undyed section with a well-executed arrangement of hand-crosses in brown. The assemblage features a central cross with a perforated diamond head atop a long straight staff which ends in a square base. Its staff is flanked on each side by a grouping of one medium-sized cross of the same type with four small crosses positioned above one another in pairs. Below the cross-filled register is another further block of zigzag patterning. It is possible to glimpse a corner of a lower register that may be part of an interlace cross like those in the more complete curtain, AY2.

Fig. 19. View of a three-paneled curtain (AY1) in the church of Abba Yohanni, not far from St. Gabriel Wukien. A tablet-woven panel combined with two plain-weave panels may have replaced other tablet-woven pieces.

Fig. 20. The upper portion of a four-paneled curtain (AY2) in the church of Abba Yohanni. One panel of plain weave appears to have replaced, or been substituted for, a fourth tablet-woven panel. Not only are the interlace and geometric patterns very well executed here, but the cotton yarn is much finer and more tightly spun than that used in the curtains of St. Gabriel Wukien.

Fig. 21. Detail of AY2, lower portion of curtain shown in figure 20. Note the fine quality of the paintings on the adjacent wall, indicative of the past glory of this rock-hewn church carved from a sheer cliff face.

Fig. 22. Remnant of the tablet-woven curtains of the stone-built church of Koraro Maryam, central Tigray. The degraded quality of the weaving is seen in the very thick soft yarn of the frayed edges.

The second curtain (AY2) is made up of two full-length panels, one of tablet weaving and one of the vertical-striped plain-weave fabric flanked by two remnants of geometric-patterned tablet weaving (figs. 20, 21). The remnant to the left, approximately 1.5 meters long, features a large checkerboard design set between a long diamond-patterned section above and a wave pattern below. Panel two has the same vertically-banded plain-weave design as AY1. The third panel, tablet-woven, has a top register of geometric pattern set off by narrow horizontal bands from the main figural register. Here a natural-colored stepped diamond form with alternating dark and natural diamond shapes inside it stands out against a dark square. The next register, again set off by bands, features a large square filled by a finely executed, interlaced cross pattern against a natural ground (fig. 20). Below it is a large section of repeating stepped diamond patterns, with a cross in the center of each. Another well-executed interlace pattern fills the next register and is followed by a large section with the same stepped diamond pattern.

The fourth panel, a remnant of about one meter in length, has a short lattice-patterned section at the top, followed by a long panel of an all-over grid pattern of repeating cross shapes. Both the first and fourth panels appear to have been cut off rather than being worn out or torn.[20] Our informant could not provide any information about the origin of the curtains or their significance to his church.

The curtain panels in Koraro Maryam

As we followed a newly built highway from west to east across the Tembien of central Tigray, we planned to visit three churches new to us which, we were told, had unusual manuscripts that we might be able to photograph. The route is very scenic, passing through valleys and then ascending to *ambas*, or flat-topped mountains, surrounded by ranges of higher peaks. On top of one of these *ambas* we sighted the stone-built church of Koraro Maryam, an old church that had been completely rebuilt by its prosperous community in 1965–66 after a disastrous fire had destroyed the original building.[21]

The manuscripts, which the priests showed with great pride, were indeed interesting, dating from the second half of the seventeenth century. At our request, they brought out several discarded silk garments made "in the Turkish manner," popular with Ethiopian nobility in the eighteenth century.

As we toured the new church building, I noticed a pile of nondescript cloths draped over a lectern. One of them proved to be the remnant of two curtain panels, tablet-woven of brown and white cotton yarn similar in thickness to that used in the curtains of St. Gabriel Wukien (fig. 22). Each panel was 37 cm wide, and one now measured 123 cm in length. Of the other, only about 35 cm remained. The longer piece is made up of two sections divided by horizontal stripes; one of overall concentric diamond patterning above a section of natural brown and white checkerboard design. On the plain ground of the smaller piece one can discern parts of three stick-like figures, which bring to mind the "angel" figures of BM1 and the uppermost section of GW2.

The oldest priest was pleased to answer questions about the curtains which he said he had seen complete and hanging across the *maqdas* as late as 1942–43, but they were so damaged by the later fire that they were discarded except for this piece. When we asked if he knew who made them, he unhesitatingly replied, "Seglin from Adwa." He thought they were Ethiopian Christians but he wasn't sure. As if to confirm our suspicion that this unusual textile was used in more places than we first thought, Memhir Gebre Meskal offered this: "They [the curtains] were brought to three churches at the same time—to Koraro Maryam and to one to the East and one to the West." He gladly gave us the names of both churches, which we unfortunately did not have time to pursue on this journey.[22]

Concluding Remarks

At this point in the investigation, one can say with certainty that for some undetermined reason and for an extended period of time, probably in the middle of the eighteenth century, an unidentified group of artisans in northern Ethiopia produced large, exceedingly complex woven curtains by the nontraditional tablet-weaving technique for several churches in the region between Gondar and Adwa. I have seen no examples of tablet weaving other than these curtains in any museum, market, church treasury, or in daily use. Various twining skills are used in basketry and net-making in Ethiopia, but there are no bands or other pieces of cloth made in the tablet-weaving technique.[23] Nor has any evidence turned up in archaeological excavations. Both the woven structure and designs needed to represent the iconographic message are complex. The structure required a large number of tablets (304 for each panel), which must have been carefully orchestrated. It is probable that royal personages commissioned the very expensive silken textiles. Perhaps they were intended to commemorate some significant occasion or were made as gifts to favored religious establishments. The curtains found in the Abba Gerima monastery church are clearly of the same quality as those in The British Museum and the Royal Ontario Museum. Since they have only two registers of figural design, they may have been part of an assemblage that featured a third curtain of more complex design, in the manner of the BM1 and ROM examples. The cotton hangings at St. Gabriel Wukien and elsewhere appear to be crude attempts to reproduce the complex figural patterning of the "Gondar" silk hangings (the ROM and BM panels). It is almost as if the designer or weavers had been shown the precisely woven silk panels by a patron of more modest means who wished to make an impressive gift to his local church. The weavers seem to have selected certain figures that they thought were within their competence and put them together in a random arrangement with no effort to depict an actual ceremonial occasion. For the present, we can only record their existence and await the discovery of other examples that may shed light on who wove these unusual textiles, and how and why they came to be woven.

Acknowledgments

The purpose of this article was to bring together all currently existing information about these unusual tablet-woven textiles from Ethiopia. The authors of the original article about the "Gondar curtains" published in *The Burlington Magazine*, Ewa Balicka-Witakowska, art historian and orientalist at Uppsala University, Sweden, and Michael Gervers, historian at the University of Toronto and research associate at the Royal Ontario Museum, gave their generous support and invaluable advice. Dr. Gervers also made available for citation the unpublished structural analyses by Mary Frame and Peter Collingwood, and dye analyses prepared by the Canadian Conservation Institute in Ottawa.

Peter Collingwood enthusiastically contributed his expert knowledge of tablet weaving wherever it may appear and patiently sorted out the nonweaving author's efforts at description. Paul Henze not only provided transport and photographic skill but shared his deep knowledge of Ethiopian culture and history. I would also like to thank the members of our research party—Stanislaw Chojnacki, Tafari Wossen, Tabotu Wolde-Mikael, Kebede Amare, and our assistant, Soloman Denboba—for their good company and patience, and all the anonymous Ethiopian monks and priests who graciously helped us record their prized possessions.

All photographs were taken by the author's husband, Paul Henze, between 1995 and 2000, unless otherwise credited.

About the Author

Martha Henze developed an interest in textiles while living abroad in Ethiopia from 1969 to 1972, and in Turkey from 1958 to 1959, and again from 1974 to 1977. During the past ten years, she has traveled extensively throughout Ethiopia with her husband, Paul Henze, often accompanied by Professor Stanislaw Chojnacki, a recognized authority on Ethiopian Art and a founder of the Institute of Ethiopian Studies (IES) at Addis Ababa University. In four exploratory trips, she has undertaken a project to record and conserve historical textiles during which time she studied the tablet-woven curtains discussed here. She has also located several groups of Anatolian kilims and carpets dating from the late seventeenth to the early nineteenth century, found in churches in northern Ethiopia.

Notes

1. In 1864, the Ethiopian Emperor Tewodros II, feeling himself snubbed by Queen Victoria, had imprisoned the British consul in his fortress of Magdala. Over three succeeding years he seized several other Europeans and their families. Many books have been written about the British Expeditionary Force led by Sir Robert Napier to gain their release. A full account can be found in Bates (1979). Balicka-Witakowska and Gervers (1996) include a summary of the Magdala event as it relates to their study of the tablet-woven curtains brought from there.

2. Tablet weaving is a technique of combining warp and weft, characterized by the use of flat tablets, or cards, for the production of the shed. These tablets, usually square and made of some stiff material, carry the warp through holes punched in their four corners. Because all the tablets have to be gripped together by the weaver's hands, the technique has only rarely been used for textiles wider than a few centimeters, e.g., for narrow bands. As it requires only the tablets, a beater to force the weft into position, and some means of tensioning the warp, the technique has had a wide distribution from the sixth century onward, but mainly in northern Europe, the Middle East, and the Far East (Collingwood 1982).

3. The first article about the ROM curtain appeared in Gervers 1995, pp. 34–39. A fuller analysis of the British Museum and ROM curtains was published in Balicka-Witakowska and Gervers 1996, pp. 375–85.

4. A French scholar, M. Guy Annequin, reportedly photographed silken curtains at the monastery of Abba Gerima in the 1960s, but there is no trace of a written description or photograph taken at that time (personal communication, Michael Gervers 1999 and Jacques Mercier 2000).

5. Except for these hangings, tablet weaving is undocumented and unknown in Ethiopia. While there are many references to the popularity of silk garments among royal and religious figures in Ethiopia, there is no reference to the actual weaving of silk fabrics. From a very early period, foreign-made luxury goods were exchanged for exports of ivory, incense, gold, and slaves (Pankhurst 1968, pp. 256–67, 382–83; Pankhurst 1990). The authors of *North African Textiles* give a misleading impression of the incidence of silk weaving in Ethiopia based on the existence of the three examples of silken panels now in The British Museum and the Royal Ontario Museum (Spring and Hudson 1995, pp. 31, 38).

6. Paul Henze has studied Ethiopian history and culture for over thirty years and is the author of numerous articles on the subject. His most recent book, a comprehensive history of Ethiopia, is entitled *Layers of Time* (2000). Since 1991, he has traveled to remote regions to photograph manuscripts, wall paintings, and other treasures of Ethiopian Orthodox churches. These photographs will be added to the archive of the Ethnographic Museum and Art Gallery of the Institute of Ethiopian Studies (IES) at Addis Ababa University.

7. The measurements and warp count of the British Museum pieces cited are taken from the unpublished reports by Peter Collingwood (ms.). These vary slightly from the measurements available to Balicka-Witakowska and Gervers (1996).

8. Balicka-Witakowska and Gervers (1996, pp. 384–85) present a hypothesis that identifies the human figures as the Ethiopian King Bakaffa of Gondar, who reigned from 1721 to 1730, and his much longer-lived wife Empress Mentewab, who wore the crown as regent for their son, the third figure, until he ascended the throne with the name of Iyasu II. The authors present a clear case for this hypothesis by describing historical events and identifying objects such as crowns, style of dress, weaponry, and religious symbols with types customarily seen in Ethiopia at this period in Gondarene history.

9. These patterns require using two techniques of tablet weaving. The oblique stripes, zigzags, small diamonds, and cross-stripes are produced by turning all the tablets together in one direction with reversals at the pattern turn. To produce human figures, large checkerboards, and other small motifs, some of the tablets must be turned twice forward, then twice backward while the rest turn twice back, twice forward (Collingwood 1982, pp. 227–32). This produces a double-faced design with colors seen in reverse on the back. The resulting structure shows complementary sets of warp in 3-span floats in alternate alignment (Emery 1994, pp. 150–51).

10. See the section on Analyses of Dyes, p. 90.

11. See note 8 above.

12. This information is from notes taken by Paul Henze at the time of his interview with the monks of Abba Gerima, on February 21, 1995.

13. The full report of the structural analysis of the British Museum curtains completed by Peter Collingwood in late 1999 awaits publication by Gervers and Balicka-Witakowska.

14. Except for the eleven churches of Lalibela, said to have been carved at the beginning of the thirteenth century, and a few in Tigray, there is little evidence on which to base the age of these rock-hewn churches. Until the 1960s, few had even been recorded by foreigners. In the decades since, two hundred or more have been located, photographed, and described in the province of Tigray alone. Others have been found as far south as Addis Ababa in Shoa, though most of these are no longer being used. Lacking written records, scholars must rely on knowledge of the evolution of Christianity in other parts of the world and Ethiopia's own historical and artistic development to assign the foundation of these churches to a particular century.

15. In more recently built Ethiopian churches where the *maqdas* is a square central structure reaching the central peak of the roof, holy pictures are painted on its walls. Between services these are concealed by lightweight curtains of modern commercial fabric.

16. The church of St. Gabriel Wukien has a superb example of such a diamond-shaped cross in its treasury. Professor Stanislaw Chojnacki, director for many years of the museum and library of the Institute of Ethiopian Studies at Addis Ababa University, made many helpful suggestions regarding identification of the puzzling elements of the curtains of St. Gabriel Wukien. He is the author of *Major Themes in Ethiopian Paintings* (1983) and contributor to major publications on traditional and modern Ethiopian painting and ecclesiastical art objects.

17. As we departed, the priests gave me a small piece of the curtain that had been separated from one of these panels earlier. Peter Collingwood kindly examined the sample and confirmed that it was indeed double-faced tablet weaving, made of natural and brown-dyed cotton (see note 9 above).

18. Daniel of Wukien was originally from Shoa and moved north to Tigray to establish his own monastery in Tembien. Abba Daniel was "respected by King Zara Yakob," a fact which would establish the founding date of St. Gabriel Wukien in the first half of the fifteenth century (Kinefe-Rigb Zelleke 1975, p. 68).

19. Peter Collingwood studied the detail photographs and a small fragment of the Abba Yohanni pieces and confirmed that these curtains are also woven in both plain and double-faced tablet weaving techniques (see note 9 above) and are of unusually finely spun cotton.

20. Their appearance lends some credence to the tale told by the priest that during the Italian occupation (1930s) an officer had cut off the lower parts of the panels, saying he would replace them.

21. The Ethiopian Calendar date would be 1958, which is seven to eight years behind the Gregorian Calendar.

22. Our guide from the Tigray Tourism and Information Office in Mekelle offered to make these journeys at his first opportunity.

23. See note 5 above.

References

Balicka-Witakowska, Ewa, and Michael Gervers
1996   Monumental Ethiopian Tablet-woven Silk Curtains: A Case for Royal Patronage, *The Burlington Magazine*, June, pp. 375–85. Burlingon Magazine Publications Ltd., London.

Bates, Darrell
1979   *The Abyssinian Difficulty*. Oxford University Press, Oxford and New York.

Chojnacki, Stanislaw
1983   *Major Themes in Ethiopian Paintings*. Franz Steiner Verlag, Wiesbaden.

Collingwood, Peter
1982   *The Technique of Tablet Weaving*. Watson-Guptill Publications, New York.

ms.   Structural Analysis of British Museum reg. no. 1868.10–1.22. The British Museum, London, 1999.

ms.   Structural Analysis of British Museum reg. no. 1973.Af38.1. The British Museum, London, 1999.

Emery, Irene

1994   *The Primary Structures of Fabrics: An Illustrated Classification.* Watson-Guptill Publications/Whitner Library of Design, New York and The Textile Museum, Washington.

Frame, Mary

1993   *The Gondar Hanging: Structure and Construction.* The Canadian Conservation Institute, Ottawa.

Gervers, Michael

1995   The Death of King Bakaffa: A Story Told in Silk, *Rotunda*, vol. 27, no. 4, pp. 34–39. The Magazine of the Royal Ontario Museum, Toronto.

Henze, Paul

2000   *Layers of Time: A History of Ethiopia.* C. Hurst & Co., London and St. Martin's Press, New York.

Kinefe-Rigb Zelleke

1975   Bibliography of the Ethiopic Hagiographical Traditions, *Journal of Ethiopian Studies*, vol. 13, no. 2. Institute of Ethiopian Studies, Addis Ababa University, Addis Ababa.

Moffatt, Elizabeth, and D. Miller

1993   *Analysis of the Dyes of the Gondar Hanging.* CCI Analytical Report, ARS no. 3178.1. August 18, Canadian Conservation Institute, Ottawa.

1994   *Analysis of the Dyes of the Gondar Hanging*, part II. CCI Analytical Report, ARS no. 3178.3. May 25, Canadian Conservation Institute, Ottawa.

1999   *Analysis of the Dyes on Silk Fibres from Three Ethiopian Artifacts.* CCI Analytical Report, ARS no. 3534. August, Canadian Conservation Institute, Ottawa.

Pankhurst, Richard

1968   *Economic History of Ethiopia, 1800–1935.* Haile Sellassie I University Press, Addis Ababa.

1990   *A Social History of Ethiopia: The Northern and Central Highlands from Early Medieval Times to the Rise of Emperor Tewodros II.* Institute of Ethiopian Studies, Addis Ababa University, Addis Ababa.

Prouty, Chris, and Eugene Rosenfeld

1994   *Historical Dictionary of Ethiopia and Eritrea.* African Historical Dictionaries, no. 56. The Scarecrow Press, Inc., Metuchen and London.

Spring, Christopher, and Julie Hudson

1995   *North African Textiles.* Smithsonian Institution Press, Washington.

A Group of Possibly Thirteenth-Century Velvets with Gold Disks in Offset Rows

Milton Sonday

A provocative question from two colleagues— "What do we know about thirteenth-century Persian velvet?"—initiated the research that led to this paper. I began to respond seriously upon learning which velvet had prompted the question and what other researchers' opinions had been. A report that I assumed would be straight-forward on what could be a very rare fabric quickly grew into an all-consuming project.[1] It soon became obvious that the first example I studied belonged to a large and tightly related group. Numerous variations within the group, however, forced me to deal with concepts fun-damental to pattern weaving, the weaving of velvet in general, and various details concerning the weaving of individual textiles within the group. Consequently, this presentation focuses on conceptual and detailed aspects of the structure and techniques of the velvets in question. For date and attribution, I have relied upon pub-lished works relevant to the period in which these velvets may have been woven.

The velvets that make up this group are patterned with gold disks in offset rows; the disks are nestled within voided areas of cut pile. The disks illustrated in figures 1 and 2 are about 1.2 cm wide and the surrounding cut pile is red. This group of velvets has traditionally been dated to the fifteenth and sometimes to the four-teenth century. Most have been called Italian, others Spanish, and one attributed to regions east of the Mediterranean.[2] A thirteenth-century date and a non-European attribution has been proposed by Anne Wardwell and Lisa Monnas, but little has been said about how the pattern was woven (Wardwell 1988–89; Monnas 1993). Wardwell (1988–89, p. 111), writing about Eastern Islamic silks of the thirteenth and fourteenth

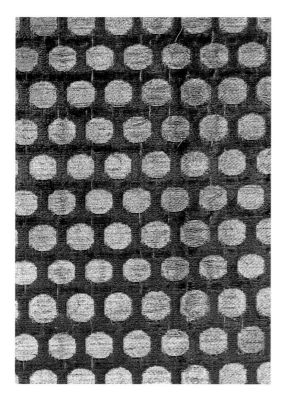

Fig. 1. Front (left) and back (right) of velvet patterned with gold disks in offset rows surrounded by cut pile. The section illustrated measures 21 cm warp x 15 cm weft. The width of each disk is about 1.2 cm. Cooper-Hewitt, National Design Museum, Smithsonian Institution, New York 1902–1–385, Gift of J. P. Morgan. Art Resource, New York. Photo by Jill Bloomer.

Fig. 2. Detail of the front
(left) and back (right) of
the velvet shown in figure 1.
Section shown measures
6.5 cm. warp x 4.5 cm weft.

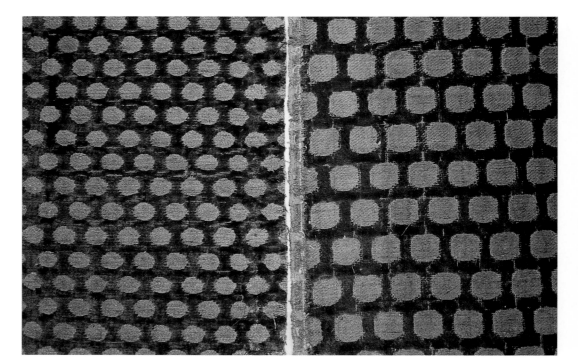

Fig. 3. Two pieces in the
collection of the Koninklijke
Musea voor Kunst en
Geschiedenis, Brussels,
from the Errera Collection:
(left) TX 465, disks 1.1 cm
wide, (right) TX 464, disks
1.4 cm wide; note side finish.
Photo by Chris Verhecken-
Lammens, courtesy of the
Koninklijke Musea voor Kunst
en Geschiedenis, Brussels.

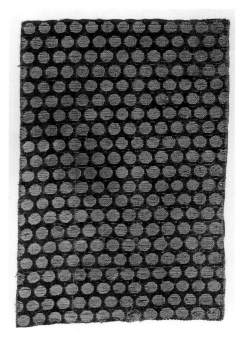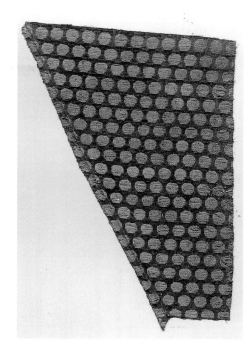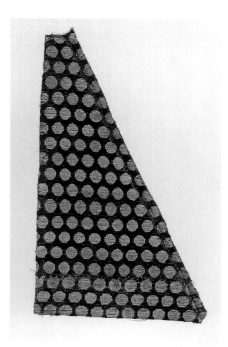

Fig. 4. Three pieces in the Cleveland Museum of Art, from left to right: 1918.225, 1918.30a, 1918.30b. A small strip is sewn to the bottom edge of 1918.30b. Disks of all pieces are slightly wider than 1 cm. The Cleveland Museum of Art, 2001, Dudley P. Allen Fund.

centuries, says: "There is no question that textiles with this pattern were produced in the late thirteenth and fourteenth centuries because they are described in the 1295 inventory of Boniface VIII, the 1311 inventory of Clement V, and the inventory in 1341 of the church of San Francesco in Assisi." Wardwell refers to a painting by Simone Martini that is the subject of an article by Lisa Monnas (1993). Now in the Museo Nazionale di Capodimonte in Naples, it was executed in 1317, perhaps for Santa Chiara in Naples. Monnas (p. 166) begins by saying that "it shows St. Louis of Toulouse enthroned, receiving a heavenly crown from two angels hovering above his head, whilst simultaneously conferring the crown of Naples upon his kneeling brother, Robert of Anjou." St. Louis is shown wearing a cope patterned with offset rows of gold disks in the main scene, as well as in one of the five smaller scenes below, in which he is shown on his death bed (see color plate, p. 105). Monnas remarks that St. Louis's cope "looks to have been closely observed from real cloth" and suggests as a model one of the velvets in the group in the collection of the Victoria and Albert Museum, her figure 8, saying: "the artist has carefully imitated the stepped effect of the weave, transforming circles into octagons" (p. 170). The pattern has also been noted on the dress of Salomé in a fourteenth-century mosaic in St. Mark's basilica, Venice (Davanzo Poli 1995, no. 83, p. 101). In a painting by Andrea Orcagna in the Galleria degli

Uffizi, Florence—a commission awarded around 1367—the pattern fills four small roundels, two set into the top of each of the wings of the triptych (Sangiorgi 1920, p. 117).

A surprisingly large number of actual examples of such velvets survive and more may yet be found.[3] Notable among them are the chasuble in the Art Institute of Chicago (Mayer-Thurman 1975, no. 44, p. 130), a chasuble in the Musée de Tissus, Lyon (Cox 1900, pl. XXX), and a 234-cm long textile, with full selvedge-to-selvedge width, in the Museo Nazionale del Bargello, Florence. The actual number of fragments or lengths is larger than the number of accessioned items because a given object may be composed of several pieces sewn together. For example, one in the Hispanic Society, New York (H954), is a patchwork of fifteen pieces, some of them tiny. Another in this institution (H955) is a patching together of four pieces, with two additional small pieces sewn to the back. Are the pieces, large and small, in these thirty collections from the same bolt of cloth? If not, might they be from the same loom?

That these velvets are not products of the same loom is clear when two velvets with disks different in size and configuration are placed side by side. Such is the case with the two pieces in Brussels (fig. 3).[4] The contours of the disks of these two pieces are different, much more so than with pieces in other collections. The three pieces in the Cleveland Museum of Art

Collection	Disk width (cm)	Pile count/cm ⟷ x ↕
Cleveland 1918.30b	1.1–1.2	17 x 8
Brussels TX 465	1.0–1.1	16 x 9
Cleveland 1918.225	1.1–1.2	16 x 9
Cleveland 1918.30a	1.1 –1.2	16 x 9
MMA 46.156.72	1.2	16 x 9
Private collection, London	1.2	16 x 9
Cleveland 1918.30c	1.2	16 x 9
Boston MFA 93.376	1.2	16 x 9
Private collection, London	1.2	16 x 8
Hispanic Society H955 (no.3)	1.3	15 x 11
Textile Gallery, London (no.1)	1.2	16 x 9
Cooper Hewitt 1902-1-385	1.2	15 x 10
V&A 545a-1884	1.3	15 x 10
V&A 545b-1884	1.3	15 x 10
Hispanic Society H955 (no.2)	1.3	14 x 11
Bargello F127 (no.1)	1.3–1.4	15 x 10
Brussels TX 464	1.4	15 x 11
Hispanic Society H954 (no.2)	1.4	15 x 11
Hispanic Society H955 (no.1)	1.4	15 x 10
Cooper Hewitt 1896-1-59	1.4	14 x 9
Stibbert, Florence	1.5	Not counted

Table I
Width of disks and pile counts.

(fig. 4), also photographed together, at first glance appear to be identical. Actually, there are four pieces: an additional small piece is sewn to the bottom of 1918.30b, which, for my purposes, I labeled "c". Visually determined differences among disks are difficult to establish when disks are not side by side. To facilitate comparisons, photographs must be taken at the same scale. The narrow range of disk widths and pile counts is shown in Table I. Ultimately, we must rely on technical features to identify those velvets woven on different looms and to propose some features of the loom or looms that might have been used.

This study, based on examples I have actually seen, includes those in collections in New York in the Cooper-Hewitt Museum, the Hispanic Society, and The Metropolitan Museum of Art;

the Cleveland Museum of Art; the Museum of Fine Arts, Boston; the Victoria and Albert Museum; The Textile Gallery, London, and a private collection in London; Koninklijke Musea voor Kunst en Geschiedenis, Brussels; plus Museo Nazionale del Bargello and the Stibbert Museum, Florence.[5] Two in Italy are published (Buss and others 1983, pp. 130–31) with an analysis by Marina Milenelli.[6]

The discussion here follows the progress of my work on these velvets as I became increasingly involved, piece by piece. I did not follow a predetermined set of criteria for analysis. Only as I neared deadlines did I have a set of criteria— criteria that readers are free to use in order to continue research on this fascinating group of velvets.

Color plate. Detail of the predella of Altar of St. Louis of Toulouse, executed in 1317 by Simone Martini. St. Louis, shown on his deathbed, is wearing a cope patterned with offset rows of gold disks. Museo Nazionale di Capodimonte, Naples.

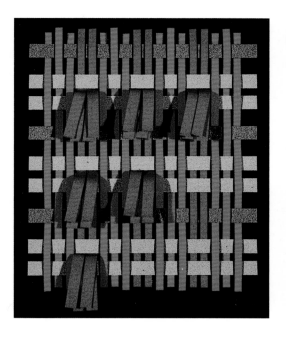

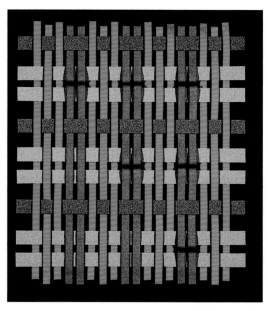

Fig. 5. Diagram of the front (left) and back (right) of the plain-weave foundation of the lampas/velvet. Every fourth warp of the set of warps of the plain weave is used for pile. Note the pairing of wefts in one shed of the plain weave that forms a vise for the pile warps pulled up between them. This weave, with pile, can be considered the foundation of a lampas.

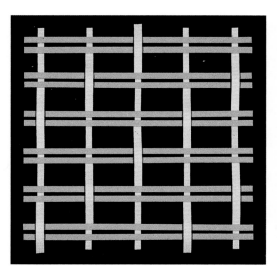

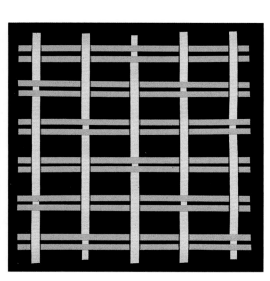

Fig. 6. The supplementary weave of the lampas/velvet: (left) weft-float face—a 1&2 Z-twill; (right) warp-float face—a 2&1 S-twill.

Fig. 7. The interlacing sequence of the set of warps of the twill with the set of wefts of the plain weave—the means by which the two weaves of the lampas are connected. Note that this interlacing sequence ignores the pairing of wefts in the plain weave. (left) weft-float face of the twill; (right) warp-float face of the twill.

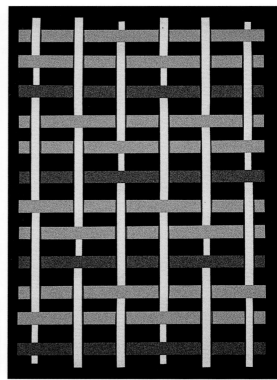

Fig. 8. The interlaced connection of the 1&2 Z-twill—the supplementary weave of the lampas with its paired gold wefts—with only the set of wefts of the plain weave; weft-float face of the twill (left), warp-float face of the twill (right).

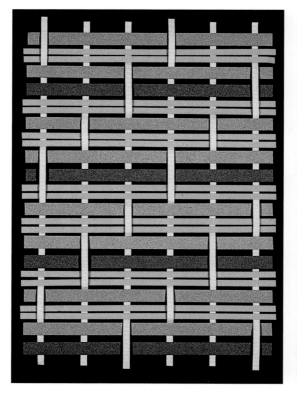
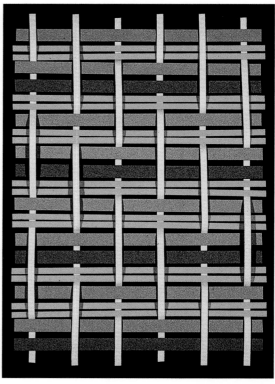

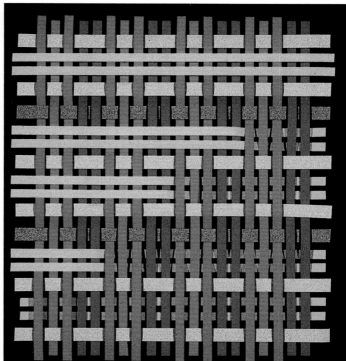

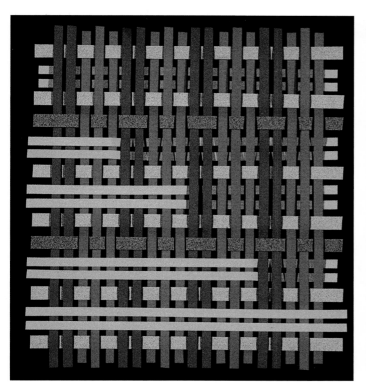

Fig. 9. The lampas technique without the set of warps of the supplementary twill weave. This shows how units consisting of a pair of pile warps and three non-pile warps control the position of gold wefts to the front (left) or to the back (right).

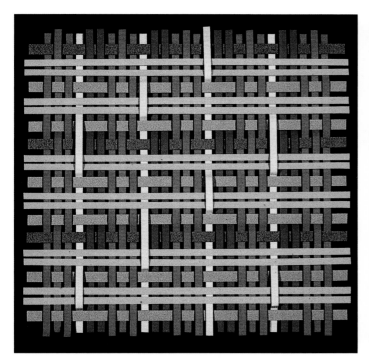

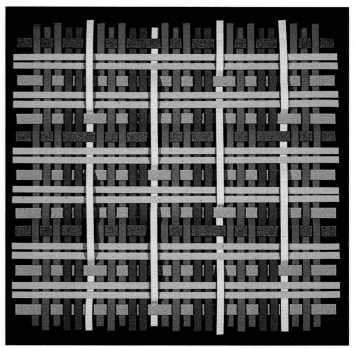

Fig. 10a
Structural detail of lampas/velvet showing area of a gold disk as seen on the front with the weft-float face of the twill. The warp order from left to right shows three non-pile warps, one warp of the supplementary twill, a pair of pile warps, etc. See also, figure 12.

Fig. 10b
Structural detail of lampas/velvet showing area between gold disks as seen on the back with the warp-float face of the twill. The warp order from left to right shows three non-pile warps, a pair of pile warps, one warp of the twill, etc. See also, figure 13.

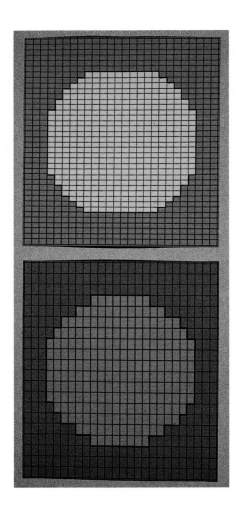

Fig. 11. Contour of the two components of one of the disks shown in figures 1 and 2: (top) the gold disk that fills the void; (bottom) the area voided of pile.

Fig. 12. Full structural detail of the front of the lampas/velvet: (left) at the left edge, gold wefts dip to the back of the cloth next to the three non-pile warps thereby leaving a gap; (right) at the right edge, gold wefts dip to the back next to a pair of pile warps, where overlapping pile obscures this edge of the gold disk.

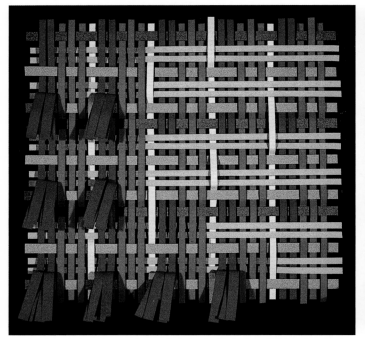 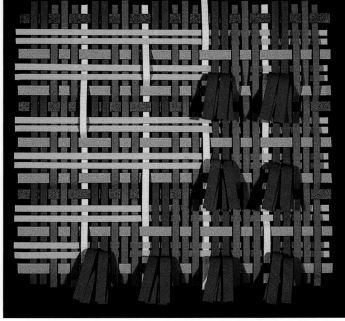

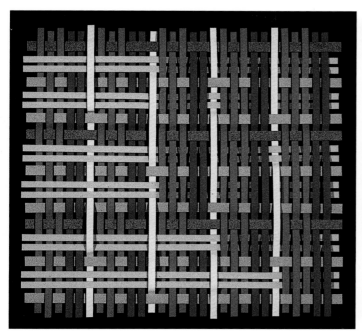

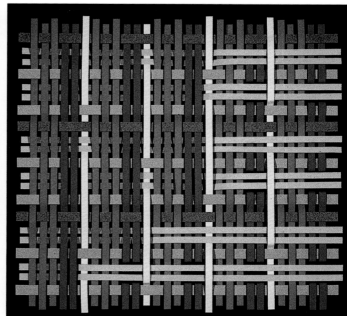

Fig. 13. Full structural detail of the back of the lampas/velvet: (left) the reverse of figure 12, right; (right) the reverse of figure 12, left.

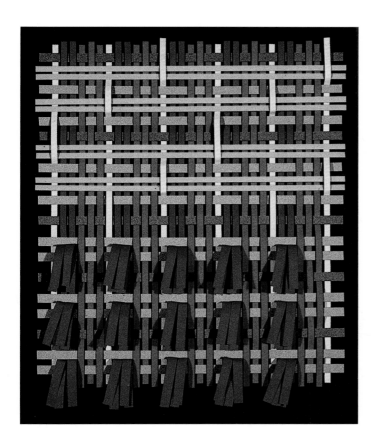

Fig. 16. Full structural detail of the front showing the bottom edge of a disk in which a voided row of pile warps precedes the first gold weft of the disk, thereby creating a narrow gap between pile and gold.

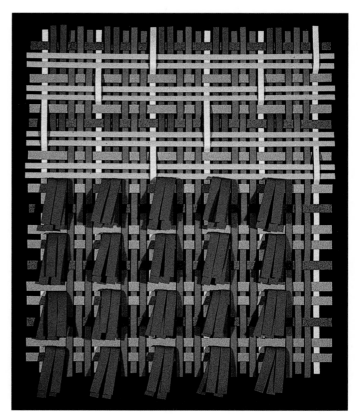

Fig. 18. Full structural detail of the front showing the bottom edge of a disk in which a non-voided row of pile precedes the first gold weft of the disk, thereby eliminating the gap shown in figures 16 and 17.

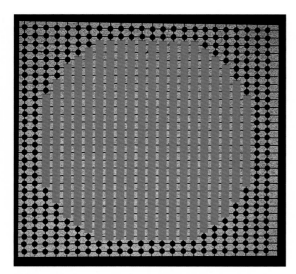

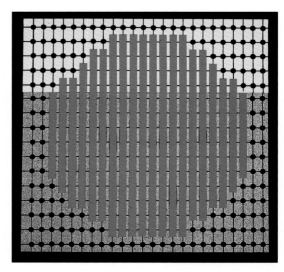

Fig. 22. Diagram of a variation in the contour of the void of the "basic" disk shown in figure 21.

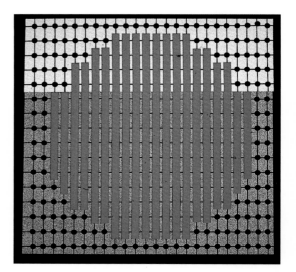

Fig. 23. Diagram of another variation in the contour of the void of the "basic" disk shown in figure 21.

Fig. 21. Diagram of the contour of the two component parts of a "basic" disk in figures 1 and 2, as analyzed from the back: (top) the gold disk; black dots indicate which pair of pile warps and groups of non-pile warps were raised to position pairs of gold wefts to the back. The gold wefts that would be on the back are not shown; (bottom) the void; black dots indicate which pile loops were pulled up on the front.

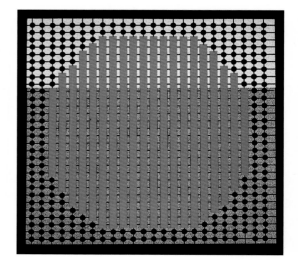

Fig. 24. Diagram of a variation in the contour of the gold disk of the "basic" disk shown in figure 21.

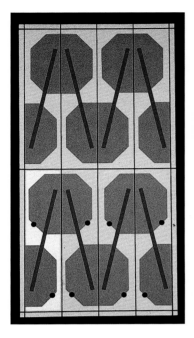

a

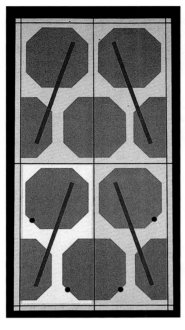

b

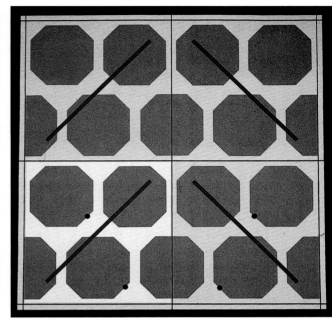

c

Fig. 25. Diagrams showing how disks in offset rows could have been repeated: (a) repeat unit with half of a disk from each row mirror-imaged on vertical axes; (b) repeat unit with a full disk from each row mirror-imaged on vertical axes; (c) repeat unit with two full disks from each row mirror-imaged on vertical axes; (d) repeat unit with one full disk from each row set with others side-by-side and others end-to-end, or in a straight repeat; (e) repeat unit with two full disks from each row in a straight repeat.

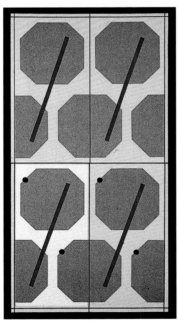

d

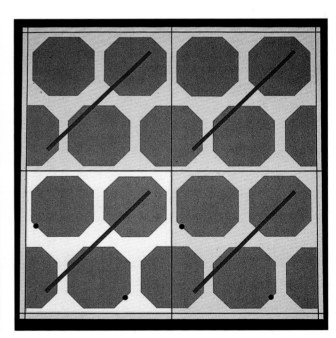

e

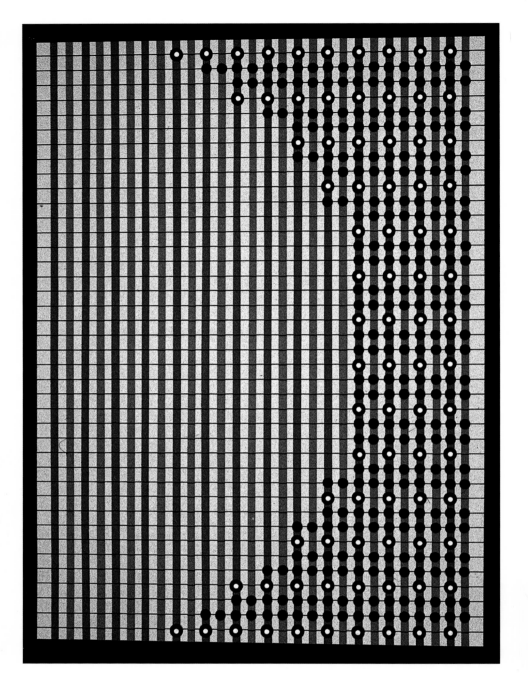

Fig. 27. Half unit of the "basic" disk, the component parts of which are shown in figure 21. Pile warps alternate with groups of three non-pile warps. Weft order: one pile rod followed by two sheds for gold wefts. Dots with white centers represent lifts of pile warps. Smaller dots represent the lifts of pile and non-pile warps needed to position pairs of gold wefts to front or back.

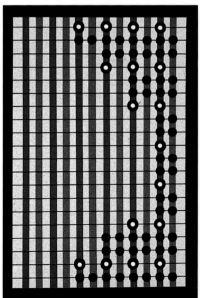

Fig. 28. Half unit of a hypothetical disk that will be used for diagrams in figures 29 and 33.

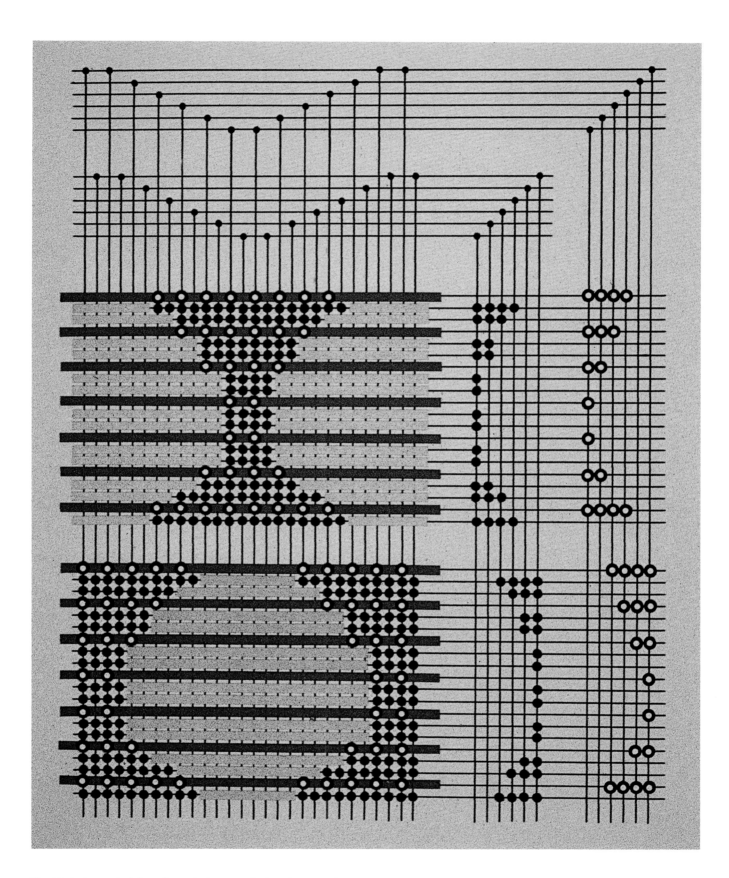

Fig. 29. A plan or draft for a theoretical set-up of a loom's pattern harness.

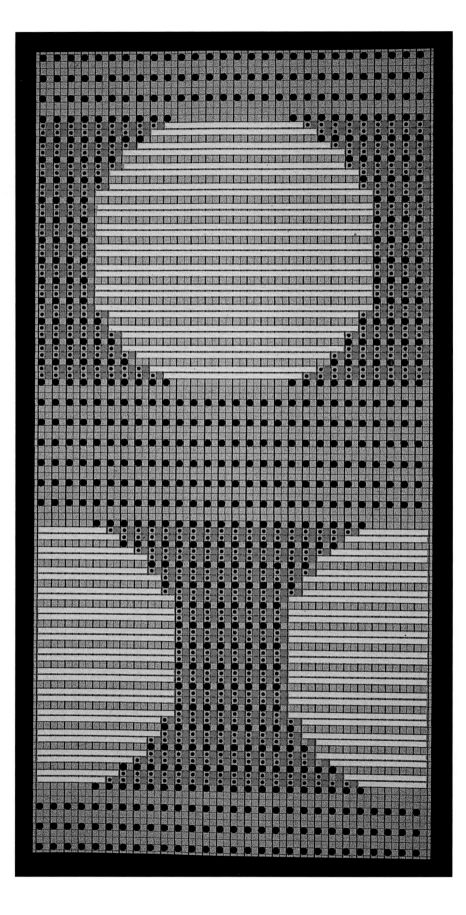

Fig. 30. Diagram of two offset "basic" disks. The repeat unit shown in figure 27 was mirror-imaged on axes that fall between warp pattern steps, or on double-pointed axes as demonstrated in figure 29.

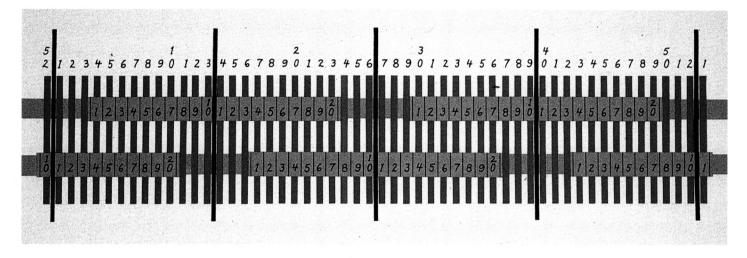

a

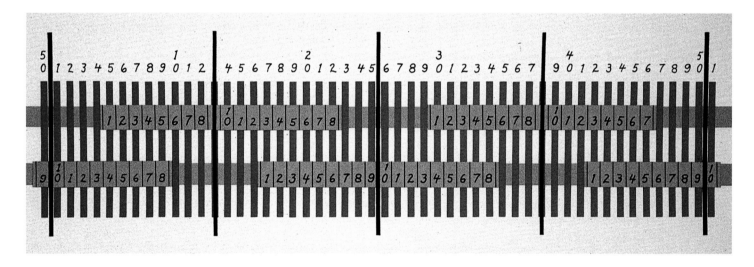

b

Fig. 31. Diagrams showing how disks were centered in the two straight repeats (see Table II).

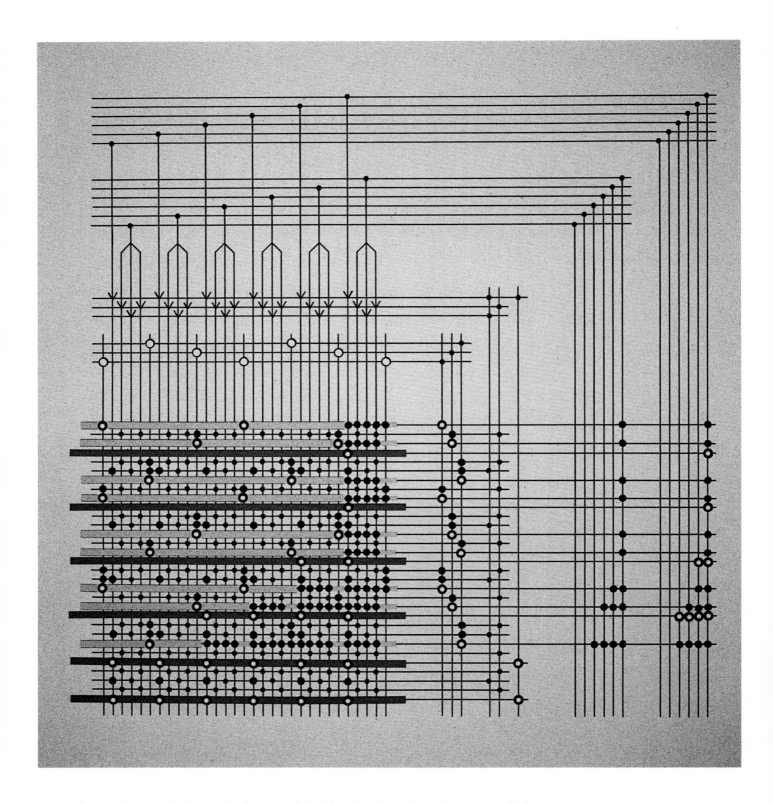

Fig. 33. Theoretical plan or draft for weaving the lampas/velvet (see figure 29 for the pattern harness with its two sets of six cross cords or shafts at the top). Below the pattern harness, the structure harness has three shafts for the plain weave and three shafts for the twill, each with an appropriate number of treadles. Three shafts for the plain-weave foundation are threaded with a set of warps that includes those that are pile warps and those that are non-pile warps in reverse order that makes it possible for only the pile warps to be lifted by means of one treadle. The other two treadles are used for the plain weave that requires all pile and non-pile warps to be lifted (see n. 14). The three shafts for the twill are threaded with the set of warps of the twill in continuous order.

a

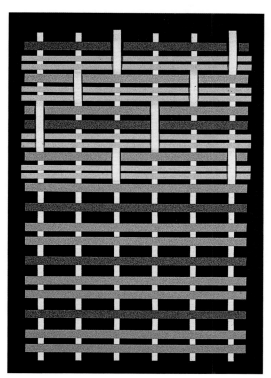

b

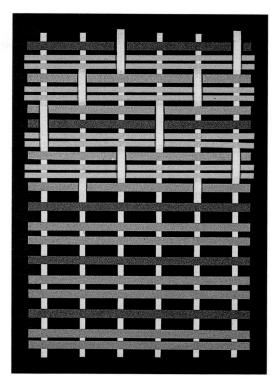

c

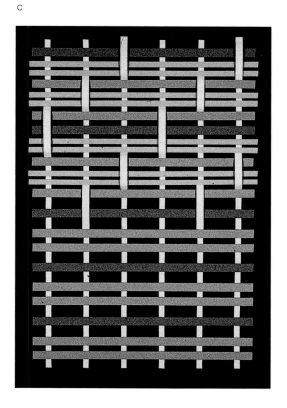

Fig. 34. Diagrams showing three options available to the weaver to start and stop the interlacing of the warps of the twill with its pairs of gold wefts and with wefts of the plain-weave foundation for an interlaced connection. Differences may be noted where the twill warps start to interlace with the first pair of gold wefts. When twill warps are not interlacing with foundation wefts, they float free on the back of the lampas/velvet in the bands between rows of disks, as in figures 20 and 36a-c: (a) interlacing starts with the first pair of gold wefts; (b) interlacing starts with one foundation weft before the first pair of gold wefts; (c) interlacing starts with two foundation wefts before the first pair of gold wefts.

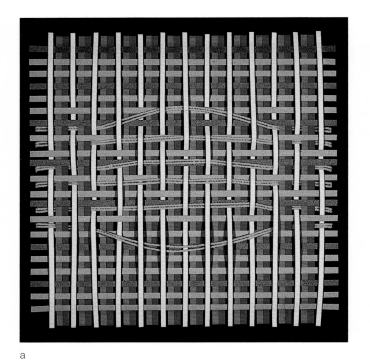

a

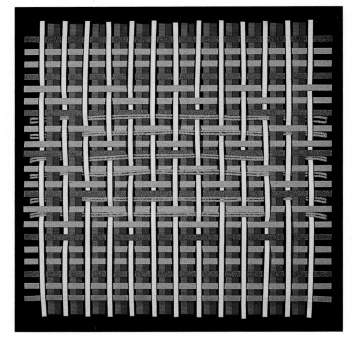

b

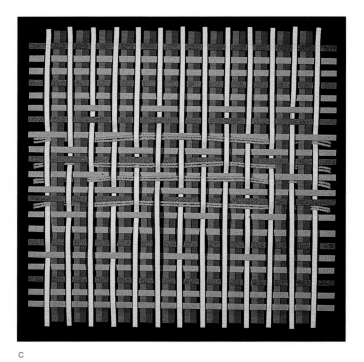

c

Fig. 35. Diagrams showing the starting and stopping of the interlacing of the warps of the twill with its pairs of gold wefts and wefts of the plain-weave foundation for an interlaced connection as seen on the back of the lampas/velvet. The gold wefts represent those that form the hourglass shape between disks: (a) the first pair of gold wefts that forms the bottom edge of the hourglass shape curves down; the last pair of wefts that is the top curves up; (b) the first pair of gold wefts is horizontal; the last pair of gold wefts is horizontal; (c) the first pair of gold wefts is horizontal; the last pair of gold wefts is horizontal.

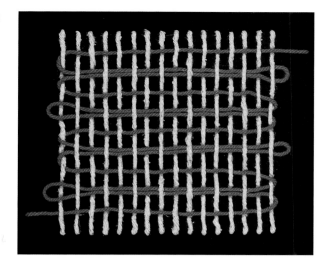

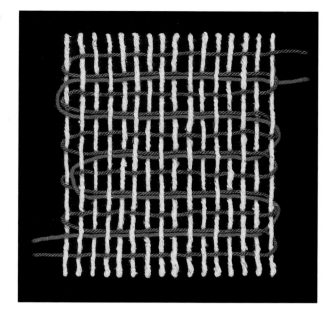

c

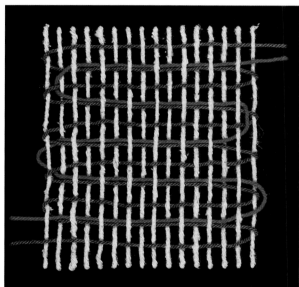

d

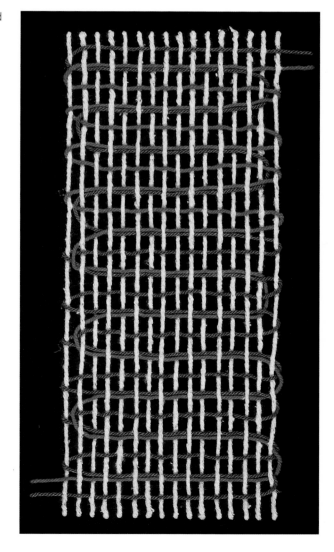

Fig. 37. (a) A plain weave with paired wefts in every other shed woven with one shuttle; (b) a plain weave with paired wefts in every other shed woven with two shuttles, variation 1; (c) a plain weave with paired wefts in every other shed woven with two shuttles, variation 2; (d) a plain weave with paired wefts in every other shed woven with two shuttles with variations 1 and 2.

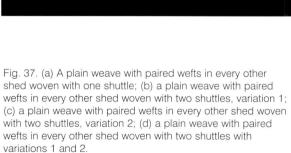

The pattern, when looked at closely (fig. 2), is composed of disks, more octagonal than circular. Small hourglass-like shapes remain as negative space between disks, and narrow horizontal bands separate rows of disks. The fronts and backs of these three areas will be looked at in detail in order to understand the unique features of the fabric. Disks are offset approximately on a 60-degree diagonal.

Shared features include the following: cut pile slants down and slightly to the left, gold wefts are bound on the front in a 1&2 twill, and gold wefts are paired in each shed of the twill. The gold wefts of these pieces are composed of narrow strips of "gilded" animal material (parchment, membrane, or leather) wound in the Z-direction around a yellow (possibly also pale rose, tan, or orange) silk core that has a Z-twist (Indictor 1988, Table 2, p. 9). The narrow strips of animal material almost completely cover the silk core. It is generally assumed that gilded animal material was not used for woven silks after the fifteenth century; this provides a terminal date for the weaving of the velvets in this group.

Three features can easily be seen on the backs of the textiles (figs. 2, 36a-c). First, gold wefts are used only as needed in bands for the rows of disks. Second, gold covers the hourglass-shaped spaces between disks in each row. Third, a set of beige (yellow?) silk warps float on the back between rows of disks.

Other shared features require closer observation. The warps for pile are a cool red silk and are used in pairs. The non-pile warps are a warmer red silk. All warps have a firm Z-twist and are similar in diameter, although irregular. The sequence of these warps (the warp order) is one pair of cool red pile warps (one pile warp pair) to three warm red single warps (non-pile). The dye for the cool red has been determined to be that of the insect cochineal, and for the warm red, the madder plant.[7]

It should be noted that the color of the pile warps of the example in the Museum für Angewandte Kunst in Vienna is blue-green. Difference in color by itself does not indicate a different loom. A set of warps of another color can be tied onto a set already on a loom. Similarly, a weft can easily be changed simply by using a thread of another color.

The study that follows is divided into two sections. The first discusses features that can be determined by looking at the fabric, including structure, warp order, weft order, details of the two basic patterning techniques, the contour of disks and their layout, and clues that might help to determine a repeat system. The second section covers more theoretical features, including a consideration of loom types that satisfy the requirements set by specific interlacing orders, a discussion of repeat systems, and a proposal for how a loom might have been warped and set up to weave these structures and pattern.

Studies of structure and technique alone will not allow us to determine the origin of a single cloth or a closely related group of cloths. Therefore, I conclude with a discussion in which I summarize aspects of Anne Wardwell's work in order to bring this group of velvets patterned with offset rows of gold disks into clearer perspective.

Surfaces and Their Structure and Basic Techniques

I begin by taking the velvet apart—warp by warp, and weft by weft—and continue by putting everything back together in the form of weaving plans, so as to consider the cloth as a whole.

As stated above and as seen in figure 2, the front of these fabrics has two surfaces, cut pile, and gold wefts bound in 1&2 twill order. The back has three surfaces determined by characteristics of the twill. First, the backs of gold disks have no gold wefts. Second, gold wefts bound in 2&1 twill form the hourglass-shaped spaces between disks. Third, the narrow bands between rows of disks are not covered by gold wefts and are "veiled" by free-floating warps of the twill, most of which are worn off in each of the examples studied.

The first aspect to be discussed is the nature of the pile. The warps that form pile are derived from plain weave (fig. 5). The over-one/under-one sequence of plain weave is achieved by all warps: the pairs of warps that make pile working together as one structural unit and the three single non-pile warps, each a structural unit. On the front of the fabric, selected pairs of warps for pile are pulled up as a loop between a pair of wefts in one shed of the plain weave, which I will term shed "a". These pairs of wefts act as a vise that helps secure the pile in the plain weave. As a result of pulling a pile warp pair up as a loop between the pair of vise-wefts, the non-pile warps immediately to left and right of the pile warp also act as a vise by passing over the pair of wefts that form the vise of shed "a". In accordance with plain weave, appropriate pile and non-pile warps go over the single weft of shed "b", schematically shown as a darker weft in figure 5.

The plain-weave interlacing sequence and tiny holes—the points at which pile warps were pulled up on the front as loops—are clearly visible on the back, thus making it easy to count warps and wefts. The spacing of warps and wefts in all the diagrams in this study is based on the count of pile of Cooper-Hewitt 1902–1–385, which is 14 to 15 (across the warp) by 10 (along the warp), or about 145 per square cm.

The weft order, or the sequence of making sheds for weaving only the velvet, is shown in figure 5. Reading up, or in the direction of weaving, the sequence is: the first of the pair of foundation wefts in shed "a", the rod or gauge over which pile warps were looped, the second of the pair of foundation wefts in shed "a", and then the weft in shed "b", etc.

Interpreting the basic structure of the velvet as a plain weave, in which every fourth warp of one set of warps is pulled up as a loop, runs counter to the interpretation that pile warps are a supplementary set of warps, or a set of warps added to a foundation with its own set. This in itself I find intriguing.[8]

Techniques for making and cutting pile loops to produce an allover surface texture or pattern are fairly straightforward. Three pairs of pile warps are shown in figure 5. All were lifted for shed "b" of the plain weave. When needed for pile, they were also lifted individually between the vise-wefts of shed "a". Areas with no pile, in other words, areas that were "voided," were filled with gold wefts. Obviously then, the take-up, or rate at which individual pile warps were used, differed from one to the other and, collectively, was much greater than the take-up of non-pile warps. Therefore, we can imagine a loom with a warp beam holding the non-pile warps under appropriate tension and another device for holding pile warps under considerably less tension.

A second patterning technique was used for the gold wefts forming the disks that fill the areas voided of pile—a technique that requires a step-by-step explanation. Following more recent usage, it is called *lampas*. I define lampas, a centuries-old technique, as a combination of two weaves, a foundation weave and a supplementary weave that is attached to it. From my point of view, to qualify as a lampas, each of the two weaves must be able to stand on its own if theoretically separated. The foundation is probably always dominated by its set of warps, and the supple-

mentary weave is probably always dominated by its set of wefts. In the case of this lampas, the foundation is the plain weave/velvet and the supplementary weave is the 1&2 twill with pairs of gold wefts.

The warps that float on the back of the velvet (figs. 2, 36a–c) are those of the set that bind the gold wefts of the supplementary weave in twill order. The interlacing of these warps with pairs of gold wefts can be considered its own fabric which is a 3-unit twill: on the front face a 1&2 Z-twill and on the back face a 2&1 S-twill (fig. 6). They are also the warps that attach the twill to the velvet (fig. 7).

The direction of the supplementary twill may vary from piece to piece. The direction is S in Brussels TX 465 and the six pieces studied in The Textile Gallery, London. Of the five pieces that make up Bargello F127, the direction of one small and one medium-sized piece is Z. But the twill direction is S for one tiny bit, another small piece, and the length. According to a brief description provided by the Musée des Tissus, the direction of the twill in the chasuble in Lyon is S, but it is not known how many pieces make up the chasuble. Three features determine a twill's direction: the diagonal sequence of the threading, the tie-up, and the order in which treadles are used. Without a loom it is impossible to determine which of these governed the supplementary twill's direction. A single workshop or workshops within a specific area may or may not have unvaryingly used the same twill direction.

Having established the integrity of the two weaves, each with its own sets of warps and wefts—the plain-weave foundation with pile warps and the supplementary 1&2 twill with gold wefts—it is the precise way in which the attachment is achieved that further qualifies the type of lampas. The attachment is achieved by means of the warps of the supplementary weave interlacing with the wefts of the foundation weave, or not, as the case may be. This lampas has an interlaced connection of the two weaves.[9]

The twill fabric is attached to the plain-weave/velvet foundation in an interlacing order as illustrated in figure 7, which has only wefts of the foundation and only warps of the twill. Figure 7 demonstrates that the interlaced connection of the lampas/velvet foundation and the twill has nothing to do with the pairings of foundation wefts that act as vises for pile.

Figure 8 is essentially the same as figure 7, but the gold wefts of the 3-unit twill are added to illustrate the order of the set of wefts of the plain weave and the set of wefts of the twill. Starting at the bottom, in the direction of weaving, the weft order is: two foundation wefts, the first paired gold wefts of the twill, one foundation, the next paired gold wefts of the twill, etc. It is best not to dwell here on the precise interlacing sequence of the twill warps with its gold wefts and the wefts of the foundation, discussed below.

The pairs of gold wefts of the twill are positioned either to the front or to the back by all the warps of the foundation, which, in this case, include the pairs of pile warps and the groups of three non-pile warps. This is demonstrated in figure 9 by a diagram in which the set of warps of the twill is omitted.

Figure 10 introduces the first diagrams of the full structure of the lampas/velvet to show warp order and how pairs of gold wefts appear on front and back. The diagram on the left (fig. 10a) presents an area of a gold disk as seen on the front with the weft-float face of the twill. The warp order from left to right shows three non-pile warps, one warp of the supplementary twill, a pair of pile warps, etc. A warp of the twill is to the left of a pair of pile warps. Chris Verhecken-Lammens notes that the warp order in Brussels TX 465 positions a warp of the twill to the right of a pair of pile warps. While this is a minor point, it does indicate another warp set-up and a different length of cloth. I did not find the Brussels variation of the warp order in other pieces I was able to double-check. The diagram on the right (fig. 10b) presents an area between gold disks as seen on the back with the warp-float face of the twill. Here, the warp order from left to right is three non-pile warps, a pair of pile warps, one warp of the twill, etc.

A Basic Disk

Patterns of all woven fabrics must conform to the squared relationship of warps and wefts and are, therefore, composed upon and conform to a squared grid. This explains why woven patterns, when looked at closely, have stepped edges. A pattern grid is made up of individual units; its width is determined by the nature of the warp pattern step, and its height is determined by the nature of the weft pattern step. Figure 11 shows the two components of a disk of figures 1 and 2: at the bottom is the void in the velvet; at the top are the gold wefts of the disk that fill the void. The width of each warp pattern step is governed by factors having to do with warps that pattern or control a weft or wefts that pattern. Significant

factors include their diameter and number of warps or wefts per unit of measure. In the case of this velvet, it is the pairs of pile warps that pattern by having been lifted to form loops. For example, figure 5 shows three pairs of pile warps individually controlled for pattern, and in figures 12 and 13 there are five. In other words, there is a pair of pile warps in each warp pattern step of the velvet. In the case of this lampas, each warp pattern step has a pair of pile warps and three warps that are lifted to position the pairs of gold wefts of the twill to front or back of the foundation. There are five such warp pattern steps in the four diagrams that make up figures 12 and 13. We have already established that pile warps pattern independently. Therefore, the groups of three non-pile warps are also independently controlled. Both pile and groups of three non-pile warps must be used together for lampas, but they are not always coordinated so the edges of disks meet the edges of the voids that they fill. Such is the case with Brussels TX 464 where there is a gap surrounding gold disks and pile. I noticed this feature in other pieces as well.

The set of warps of the twill is not needed for the pattern and, therefore, is not included in the discussions of patterning techniques.

A pattern grid is completed by weft pattern steps, the height of which is determined by thickness, count per unit of measure, etc., of the wefts that pattern. In this lampas there are two: the rows of rods acting as wefts over which the loops of pile warps were formed, and the pairs of gold wefts of the twill.

The count of warp pattern steps of the two components of the disk shown in figure 11 is the same (15 per cm). The count of the weft pattern steps of the two components is different. That of the velvet is 10 loops or rods per cm, but that of the gold is 20 sheds of the supplementary twill. The count of the gold weft pattern steps is higher because there are two sheds of the twill between each row of pile. Each shed of the twill has a pair of gold wefts. Thus, the stepping off of the pile to form circular voids is much coarser than the stepping off of the gold wefts for the disks that fill the void.

We can now look at close-up views of the edges of disks. The model in figure 12 shows a pile warp pair on the left of the three non-pile warps in each warp pattern step of the lampas; the gold wefts forming the left edge of a disk dip to the back next to the group of three non-pile warps. This is visible on the front of the fabric (fig. 14). At the right edge, gold wefts dip to the back next to pile warps. This is not easy to see on the front of the fabric because pile warps are slightly slanted to the left, thereby obscuring this edge of the disks. Where gold wefts dip to front and back is much clearer on the back, but left-right positioning of pile and non-pile warps is reversed (fig. 13).

The combining of the weft pattern steps of the velvet and lampas techniques can be expressed in terms of the weft sequence or weft order, part of which may be seen on the back of the fabric (fig. 15). Although two twill sheds or two pairs of gold wefts between rows of pile are visible, it is not clear just where the rods or gauges that form and determine the size of the loop or length of cut pile are inserted in the weft order. The weft order is also not easily seen, but I have determined that it follows the first vise-weft in shed "a" of the plain weave and precedes a pair of gold wefts of the twill (figs. 12, 13). The weft order, perhaps better expressed as the order in which sheds are made, is a repeat of the following weaving sequence from bottom to top; where it begins and ends is arbitrary:

- shed "a" of the plain weave plus a continuation of the previous shed of the twill for insertion of a foundation weft;
- velvet pattern selection and lift for insertion of rod or gauge;
- lampas pattern selection and lift plus next shed of the twill for insertion of a pair of gold wefts;
- repeat of shed "a" of the plain weave plus same shed of the twill;
- lampas pattern selection and lift plus the next shed of the twill for a pair of gold wefts;
- shed "b" of the plain weave for which pile and non-pile warps are lifted plus the same shed of the twill for insertion of a foundation weft;
- repeat of the sequence.

The features that distinguish the left and right sides of a disk are common to all the disks I examined, but the bottom edge varies in two ways. In the first variation (fig. 16) the disk begins with a row of pile that is voided. The result is a narrow gap between the previous full or non-voided row of pile and the first pair of gold wefts of the disk. This can easily be seen on the front (fig. 17). In the second variation (fig. 18) the disk begins with the first pair of gold wefts that are brought to the front to form a disk. These wefts

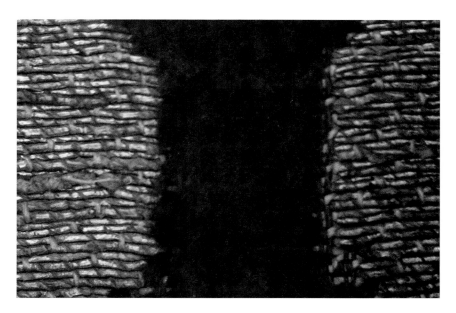

Fig. 14. Detail of the front of a disk in figures 1 and 2, showing the left and right straight edges of the central third of the disk.

Fig. 15. Detail of the back of the straight edge of the central third of a disk showing weft order, including pairing of gold wefts in each shed of the twill.

are tightly packed against the previous non-voided row of pile because both the pile and the gold wefts are held between the vise-wefts of shed "a" of the plain weave. Both variations could be woven on the same loom.

All disks I have studied end with a voided row of pile at the top which creates a gap similar to the gap at the bottom. This feature is consistent, no doubt because a close juxtaposition of the last gold weft of the disk would have been covered by the overhanging pile of the subsequent non-voided row (fig. 19). The gap at the top is covered by overhanging pile.

Some velvets have a curious feature: short vertical dashes that are not regularly spaced across the width of the fabric. These can be seen in Cooper-Hewitt 1902–1–385 (fig. 1) and Brussels TX 464 (fig. 3, right). I noted them also in the pieces in the Stibbert and in the larger piece in the Bargello, but not across the entire width. Some are vertically aligned and others are not. Exactly what causes the dashes is not always clear. Those that are vertically aligned appear to have been caused by a pairing of non-pile warps of more than three non-pile warps in the warp order. Those that are not vertically aligned might have been caused by a slight difference in tension among the three non-pile warps that are between pairs of pile warps. A slightly higher tension on the warp in the middle (the warp that is raised for shed "b") might have caused the two warps to the left and right (the warps raised for shed "a") to separate, thereby creating a gap between pile warps.

Fig. 19. Detail of the top edge of a disk showing how pile, slanted down, slightly obscures the last pair of gold wefts of the disk.

Fig. 17. Detail of the bottom edge of a disk showing the gap between a voided row of pile and the first pair of gold wefts of the disk as demonstrated in figure 16.

Disk Variations

Regardless of the details of their edges, all disks are octagonal (fig. 20) and can be divided into three sections: a bottom third with a horizontal base and slanted sides, a middle third with vertical left and right sides, and an upper third with slanted sides and a horizontal top. The lower third of the void shown at the bottom of figure 11 is 4 weft pattern steps high, the center third is 6 weft pattern steps high, and the top third is 4 weft pattern steps high. The octagon made by pairs of gold wefts is 7 weft pattern steps high in the lower third, 12 weft pattern steps high in the central third, and 7 weft pattern steps high in the upper third. Both components are 20 warp pattern steps wide. For the remainder of this discussion, when I refer to a width in terms of

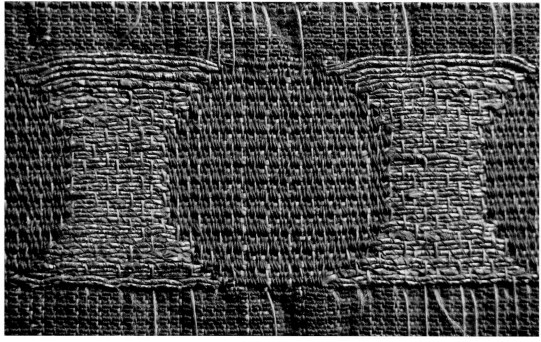

Fig. 20. Detail of the front (top) and back (bottom) of a disk in figures 1 and 2.

warp pattern steps, I will indicate the alternation of pile and non-pile warps as, for example, in this disk: 20 & 20. The disk, specifically its components, can be divided into equal halves vertically and horizontally. Were the vertical lines that divide the disks of Cooper-Hewitt 1902–1–385 also the axes of mirror-imaging used for weaving them? Were pattern sheds used in reversed order on horizontal axes? These questions forced me to examine more disks in this and additional pieces.[10]

Figure 20 gives close-up views of the front and back of a disk. These are schematically interpreted from the back in figure 21. Here the dots on the grid plan in the lower diagram indicate which pile warps were pulled up on the *front* to make pile. The vertical lines represent the pile warps that were not pulled up, thereby creating the void. The dots on the grid plan of the gold disk shown at the top of figure 21 show which warp pattern steps (each step being a pile warp pair and three non-pile warps) were selected to position pairs of gold wefts to the *back*. The verticals are the warp pattern steps that were not pulled up to position gold wefts on the *front*. The actual gold wefts that should be seen on the back, those that form the hourglass-shaped spaces between gold disks, are not shown because they would cover the dots indicating the warp pattern steps that were lifted.

I was not surprised to find that the contours of disks in other rows of Cooper-Hewitt 1902–1–385 are slightly different from what is shown in figures 11 and 21. If a repeat unit contains a disk or disks for both rows (fig. 25a-e), it is reasonable to anticipate that the two disks will be different. I was surprised, however, that I found variations on other rows as well. Figures 22 and 23 show differences in the upper third of the void. Figure 24 shows a difference in the upper third of a gold disk. This new information suggested that the disks could have been mechanically mirror-imaged on vertical axes as suggested, and that they would not have been mirror-imaged horizontally. Since disks are different in various rows, it seemed that the pattern sheds were not fixed or pre-programmed, but selected freehand. To a considerable degree, this qualifies our perception of what constitutes a repeat unit. Little did I know that I had only begun the recording of the contours of disks, a project that quickly became both time-consuming and challenging.

Since I wanted to record the edges of disks, I had to cope with irregularities that included the chronically loose and often very slack tension of

pile warps, loose tension of non-pile warps, pile seemingly occurring in odd places, and gold wefts extending too far or not far enough into an edge of a disk. Eventually I was able to distinguish random irregularities from those that seemed to repeat. Ordinary random irregularities included pile warps that were inadvertently not raised when perhaps they should have been, or raised when perhaps they should not have been. Some examples of the pattern had more mistakes than others. I hoped that some irregularities that seemed to repeat would provide clues to a repeat system, the size of the repeat unit, and how many disks the unit contained.

Because overhanging pile obscures many of the edges of the disks I studied, I chose to chart contours on the back. Chris Verhecken-Lammens working in Brussels, on the other hand, studied disks from the front, because the edges of gold disks of Brussels TX 464 are separated from the voided area of the velvet by a narrow margin (fig. 3), thereby giving her access to the edges of the void and edges of the gold disk from the front. For the purposes of this section of my study, however, it does not really matter whether the contour of disks was plotted by looking at the front or back of the fabric, since each approach has its limitations.

For convenient recording, rows of disks were numbered consecutively so odd and even rows could be compared by aligning them one above the other. Numbering was, of course, arbitrary. Attempts were made to answer the following questions:

- Can mirror-imaged or straight repeats be proposed and/or confirmed?

- Are disks in the offset odd and even rows the same or different?

- In the case of a straight repeat, do the disks in odd and even rows alternate "a"/"b"?

- Are the two rows of disks—odd/even— that make up a basic repeat unit the same, or are disks in subsequent odd and/or even rows different?

- Can it be determined if pattern lifts were pre-programmed and fixed, or selected by hand?

To present contour diagrams of all the disks I studied would be impractical; three summaries demonstrate how a careful study and recording of contour edges can provide answers to the questions posed (see appendix).

Making A Pattern: Repeat Units and Repeat Systems

Repeats have two fundamental aspects: the threading of warps and the making of pattern sheds. Once a repeat system is programmed by means of threading warps into the loom's repeat system, it is impossible to change unless the loom is rethreaded, a time-consuming task that is generally avoided in traditional manufacturing workshops. Once set into the loom, repeat systems can repeat a unit containing one or motifs

in one of two ways. Units can be mirror-imaged across the width of a warp (fig. 25a–c) or set side by side and in the same position or straight across the warp (fig. 25d, e).

The diagrams in figure 25a–e illustrate how the repeat unit of a pattern with offset rows might be repeated. The options are as follows:

a. Repeat unit with half of a disk from each row mirror-imaged on vertical axes.

b. Repeat unit with a full disk from each row mirror-imaged on vertical axes.

Table II. Variations in the width of disks and the spaces between them, measured in terms of warp pattern steps, and the repeat system of each type.

COLLECTION	WARP PATTERN STEPS DISKS	WARP PATTERN STEPS SPACE
Cooper Hewitt, 1896-1-59	19 & 19	7 & 7
Boston MFA 93.376	19 & 19	7 & 7
Cleveland 1918.30c	20 & 20	6 & 6
Cleveland 1918.30b	20 & 20	6 & 6
Cleveland 1918.30a	20 & 20	6 & 6
MMA 46.156.72	20 & 20	6 & 6
Cleveland 1918.225	20 & 20	6 & 6
Brussels TX 464	20 & 20	8 & 8
Cooper Hewitt 1902-1-385	20 & 20	8 & 8
V&A 545b-1884	20 & 20	8 & 8
Hispanic Society H955 (no.1)	20 & 20	8 & 8
Hispanic Society H955 (no. 2)	20 & 20	8 & 8
Hispanic Society H955 (no. 3)	20 & 20	8 & 8
Brussels TX 465	17 & 17 or 18 & 18	7 & 7 or 8 & 8

controlled by the weaver. In both types of loom, the pattern harness is activated by a second person called the drawboy. An outline of the way these pattern harnesses work is in order.

The pattern harness of the Indian and Iranian loom consists of two sets of cords positioned above the warp. One is a set of horizontal cross cords just above and at right angles to the warp. The other is higher, a vertical set of pattern cords of an equal number, the bottom ends of which are attached to the cross cords. Both are tightly stretched and arranged in a configuration that resembles an inverted T. The horizontal cross cords are secured beyond the sides of the loom at left and right. The set of vertical pattern cords are kept taut, secured to a point far above the loom, their bottom ends attached to an equal number of horizontal cross cords. The drawboy sits above the level of the horizontal cross cords facing the vertical set of pattern cords, which are within easy reach. He also faces the weaver, who is seated at the cloth beam. To make a pattern shed, the drawboy pulls selected vertical pattern cords toward him, which singles out equivalent cross cords that are now slightly raised. The weaver, using a large and carefully balanced leveraging hook suspended above the cross cords, inserts the long pointed fingerlike end under the slightly raised cross cords and leverages them up by pulling down on the handle of the hook. The unique balance of the leveraging hook keeps the pattern shed open so the weaver can insert a pattern weft in the pattern shed that is now held securely open by the balanced hook.

The pattern harness of the Moroccan loom also has two sets of cords, but their configuration represents a proper T and is slightly more complex. The top ends of the vertical set of pattern cords are attached to a horizontal set of an equal number of cords. The drawboy is seated at the side of the loom facing the vertical set of cords, which are within easy reach. The horizontal cords are secured far off to the side of the loom beyond the drawboy and above him, also within easy reach. They are stretched across the top of the sets of warps on the loom where they are held in place until they angle down 45 degrees and are attached to the pattern shafts. To make a pattern shed, the drawboy reaches forward and pulls selected vertical pattern cords toward him. This "draw" singles out and slightly lowers equivalent horizontal cross cords, which he pulls down, thereby lifting corresponding pattern shafts. The drawboy keeps the pattern shed open, leaving the weaver free to insert the pattern weft.

Figure 27 is the lifting plan for the mirror-imaging of a repeat unit as shown in figure 25a. The repeat unit, 28 & 28 warp pattern steps wide, is that of a disk in a velvet at Cooper-Hewitt (1902–1–385; fig. 1). In figure 27, pairs of pile warps and units of three non-pile warps alternate, and each is represented by single alternating verticals. Dots with white centers represent lifts of pile warps only to make the pattern shed for the rod that forms loops. Smaller dots represent the lifts needed to position pairs of gold wefts to front or back.

Because two techniques—velvet and lampas—were used to pattern, a set of shafts or cross cords was no doubt needed for each. The warps for pile were pulled through heddles attached to the appropriate number of shafts or heddles attached to the cross cords of one set. The non-pile warps were pulled through heddles attached to the appropriate number of shafts or heddles attached to the cross cords of the second set. The number of shafts or cross cords in the two sets was determined by the number of pile and non-pile warps in the width of the pattern unit. The order in which heddles were threaded was determined by the repeat system—straight or mirrored—that was set into the warp.

Figure 29 shows only the pattern harness of a loom. To simplify the discussion, I will use the lifting plan shown in figure 28 that is 6 & 6 warp pattern steps wide. There are 6 cross cords or shafts for pile warps at the top of the plan and 6 below that for non-pile warps. The verticals to which they are attached represent the sets of pattern cords that are within reach of the drawboy described earlier. In the Indian loom, the drawboy sits above the warps, the set of pattern cords is equivalent to the stem of the inverted T, the cross cords forming the cross of the inverted T. In the Moroccan loom, the drawboy sits to the side of the loom. The set of pattern cords is equivalent to the stem of the T and the set of horizontal cords to which shafts are attached is the cross of the T. Any number of pattern cords can be pulled at once causing corresponding cross cords or shafts to be raised and with them the heddles through which warps were threaded. This plan shows two sets of vertical pattern cords, one for making pattern sheds for pile rods and the other for making pattern sheds for pairs of gold wefts.

The heddles of the pattern harness are threaded for mirror-imaging with double pointed axes, or along lines that fall between warp pattern steps. Because the axes that extend through the length of the fabric fall in the centers of disks and the spaces between them, they cannot be identified visually. Axes can only be deduced by counting warp pattern steps (as already demonstrated). Pairs of warps that make pile are threaded through heddles of the 6 cross cords or shafts indicated at the top. Non-pile warps are threaded through heddles of the other 6 cross cords or shafts.

For the first weft of the disk shown in figure 29, a pair of gold wefts, the drawboy pulls 4 pattern cords to lift 4 corresponding cross cords or shafts in the pile-warp set and all the pile warps threaded through the heddles attached to them. The drawboy also pulls 4 cords to lift 4 corresponding shafts in the non-pile-warp set and all the warps threaded through heddles attached to them. This creates the shed for the pass consisting of a pair of gold wefts. The next shed is for a pile rod for which the drawboy pulls 4 pattern cords to raise 4 pile shafts or cross cords and all the heddles attached to them. Subsequent pattern sheds for gold and pile are created in a like manner.

Pattern plans such as those shown in figures 27 and 28 could have been within sight of the drawboy or memorized. Reading or following the plan from right to left and making sheds accordingly completes one row of disks. By reading it again, but this time from left to right and making sheds accordingly, the next row of disks will be offset.[12] We can easily imagine that many mistakes can be made while reading the pattern plan in this manner. As pointed out earlier, disks in sequential offset rows are often different.

Was the pattern plan in the mind of the drawboy, or was it in front of him to read? Was the pattern plan read so the pattern could be programmed onto the set of pattern cords and then put aside, or was it referred to during weaving? A pattern is generally programmed by interlacing threads on the pattern cords in the order set out in the pattern plan or the repeat unit with the number of threads equal to the number of pattern sheds indicated on the plan. The repeat unit shown in figure 30 requires 80 lifts or interlaced pattern threads—40 for one row of disks plus another 40 for the offset row. The repeat unit shown in figure 31 requires 40—20 plus 20. If the pattern was programmed and therefore fixed, irregularities such as adding or leaving out pattern sheds can be anticipated. If pattern sheds for disks were selected freehand, pattern cord by pattern cord, all sorts of irregularities in contour could occur.[13]

Figure 30 shows the precise layout of two offset disks of what was earlier called the disk of a basic type, in Cooper-Hewitt 1902–1–385, the pattern plan of which is shown in figure 27. The disks in offset rows are perfectly centered because of mirror-imaging as in figures 25a and 29.

The centering of two disks in a repeat unit to be repeated straight across the width of sets of warps must be discussed in different terms. The number of warp pattern steps in the repeat unit does not modify the system as it did in the mirror-imaging system. The same number of warps per repeat unit is threaded in continuous order, unit by unit, across the full width of the warp. Referring to the 6 pieces with disks that are 20 warp pattern steps wide and have hourglass-shaped spaces that are 6 warp pattern steps wide, there are 52 warp pattern steps in the repeat unit as demonstrated in the sketch of figure 31a. This number, 52, can be divided into 4 equal sections, each having 13 warp pattern steps. Centering lines fall between warp pattern steps 13 and 14, 26 and 27, 39 and 40, 52 and 1, etc. Disks can be centered on these lines in offset rows with 6 warp pattern steps between them in both rows. Even though the middle sections are centered, this does not necessarily mean that the starting and ending horizontals are centered as well. One can expect to find this variability in symmetrical motifs in a straight repeat. The width and pile count of the 5 pieces in this group are within a reasonably close range and could have been woven on the same loom or looms with a similar set-up.

Turning to Brussels TX 465 and the sketch in figure 31b, we can see that 50 warp pattern steps can be divided into two equal sections of 25 warp pattern steps each. Centering lines fall between warp pattern steps 25 and 26, 50 and 1, etc. Disks that are an even number of warp pattern steps wide can be centered on these lines: in this piece the disks in the bottom row are 18 warp pattern steps wide and the spaces between them are 7 warp pattern steps wide. Because 50 cannot be divided into 4 equal parts, or 25 into 2 equal parts, disks in the next or offset row, which are alternately 17 and 18 warp pattern steps wide, must be centered on warp pattern steps 13, 38, etc. Disks that are 17 warp pattern steps wide are perfectly centered, but disks that are 18 warp pattern steps wide are not. The spaces between disks are alternately 7 and 8 warp pattern steps wide.

Variations in the number of warp pattern steps of disks and the spaces between them noted in two pieces in The Textile Gallery,

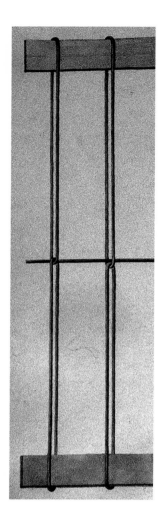

Fig. 32. Detail of a drawing in nineteenth-century weaver's thesis book, showing two types of heddles: (left) two linked looks with a warp threaded through both loops; shafts with heddles threaded in this way can lift or lower warps; (right) two linked loops with a warp threaded through the open space of the top loop; shafts with heddles threaded in this way can only lift warps. Cooper-Hewitt, National Design Museum, Smithsonian Institution, New York, 1957-201-1, Gift of Harvey Smith.

London, suggest that their repeat units might contain more than two disks in each row. Unfortunately, the pieces are not large enough to confirm this possibility.

Statements about repeat systems can be made with a fairly high degree of certainty, but proposals for pattern selection must be offered with extreme caution. The detection of a pattern selection method requires the study of many disks, more than might be available because of the size of a piece, or than can be managed within time constraints. Keep in mind that once a repeat system is set into a warp, it cannot be changed. Pattern selection methods are more flexible, as are all aspects of weaving having to do with wefts, the subject of the next section.

Weaving a Lampas/Velvet

Figure 33 presents a theoretical plan for weaving the lampas/velvet. The previously described pattern harness consists of two sets of cross cords or shafts (shown at the top), and two sets of corresponding vertical pattern cords that, when pulled, raise selected shafts or cross cords (shown at the far right). The structure harness, consisting of two sets of shafts, is shown below the pattern harness.

The structure harness consists of three shafts for the warps of the 3-unit twill[14]—the supplementary weave of the lampas—and three shafts for the pile and non-pile warps, which together make the plain-weave foundation of the lampas. The pile and non-pile warps are threaded through heddles with open tops, such as the top of two linked loops (fig. 32, right). Such heddles are indicated as a V. This type of heddle is required because pile and non-pile warps are lifted not only for the plain weave, but also for the pattern. In order for warps to be lifted by pattern shafts, their movement cannot be restricted by heddles in the structure harness. When lifted by pattern shafts, pile and non-pile warps can be lifted into the upper open part of the heddle loops. Since warps of the twill are not included in the pattern lifts, they are shown threaded through eyes of heddles, or through both loops that are linked to make a heddle (fig. 32, left), on another set of shafts.

The lower half of the pattern plan of figure 28 is what is shown being woven in the weaving plan of figure 33. The first weft is a pile rod for which all pile warps were lifted. This could have been accomplished by pulling all the pattern cords to raise all corresponding pile shafts in the

pattern harness. But I am suggesting that a third shaft for the plain weave in the structure harness could be used to raise all pile warps. All of them must be raised in any case to be included in the plain weave along with non-pile warps for over-one/under-one interlacing. I am proposing a lifting system for these three shafts, each shaft to be raised by depressing one of the attached treadles by means of some sort of leverage system.

Three sheds of plain weave follow a full row of pile. Only one shaft needs to be lifted for the first and third sheds. Lifting two out of the three non-pile warps in each group of three makes these sheds. Two shafts must be lifted for the second weft, and it is this shed that includes all pile warps and one non-pile warp out of each group of three.

Another full row of pile follows and after that the first pattern shed—a shed for a pair of gold wefts to start the disk. For this shed, as demonstrated in figure 29, four pile and four non-pile pattern shafts are lifted, and, in addition, one of the three shafts of the twill in the structure harness. Weaving continues in this manner and can be followed with patient reading of the lifts required of the structure as well as the pattern harness, as indicated on the weaving plan (fig. 33).

The two most obvious features of this lampas/velvet can be seen on the back (fig. 20). First, gold wefts were used only where needed for rows of disks and, therefore, in bands as wide as the height of disks. The narrow bands between rows of disks consisting of full rows of pile did not require pattern lifts for gold wefts and possibly not for pile, as suggested earlier. The number of rows of pile in the unpatterned bands is usually consistent in each piece but sometimes may be off by one. Secondly, the set of warps of the supplementary twill float free of the foundation and over the bands between rows of gold disks. This indicates that the raising of shafts for twill had been temporarily suspended. The floating twill warps were subject to wear because of their length (about 4 mm), and they are often missing.

We will now examine the way in which the twill is attached to the plain weave with pile. It is up to the weaver to determine precisely where the twill warps begin interlacing with wefts of the foundation plain weave. There are three basic choices. First, beginning with the first pair of gold wefts (fig. 34a); second, beginning with one foundation weft before gold wefts (fig. 34b); third, beginning with two foundation wefts before gold wefts (fig. 34c). Variations such as these occur during weaving and have nothing to do with the setting up of warps; more than one variation occurs in the same cloth. The basic possibilities apply no matter where the first pair of gold wefts is placed—whether in the pair of vise-wefts of shed "a" of the plain weave or after the pair of vise-wefts and before the weft of shed "b".

The eccentric interlacing order of the twill warps with the wefts of the plain weave makes sense when we consider it from the point of view of the weaver. Once begun, the anticipation of a shed for a pair of gold wefts could well have been the clue to the weaver that the next twill shed is to be added to the pattern shed.

The effect of reintroducing the warps of the twill is most interesting when studied carefully on both front and back. The interlacing sequence of the warps of the twill with pairs of gold wefts on the front is 1&2 (that of the weft-float face), with the sequence including one or two foundation wefts. Since warps of the twill float over no more than two or three wefts, the pairs of gold wefts are held in horizontal weft-order positions. Such is not the case on the back.

On the back, the interlacing sequence of the supplementary twill is 2&1, over two pairs of gold wefts and under one (that of the warp-float face). The warps of the twill pass over a total of five wefts: two pairs of gold wefts and three foundation wefts. This allows some flexibility in the horizontal weft-order positioning.

Sometimes the first pair of gold wefts or the pair that is the bottom edge of the hourglass shape on the back is curved and sometimes it is horizontal. The same is true for the last pair of gold wefts or the pair that is the top edge of the hourglass. It would be possible for both the bottom and top edges to be curved or for both to be horizontal, or for one to be curved and the other horizontal. These variations were noted in some of the pieces I studied but not always in detail. The models in figure 35a-c show three variations. The first or last pair of gold wefts either curves or is held in a horizontal position whether or not the pair is between the pair of vise-wefts of shed "a" of the plain weave or after the vise and before shed "b" of the plain weave. We will look first at the bottom edge of the hourglass shape.

In the model shown in figure 35a, every third warp of the set of warps of the twill that was floating above the band between the previous row of disks starts the reintroduction of the twill in the next row by interlacing first with a pair of gold wefts and then the second weft of the pair of vise-wefts. In this model, the first gold pair is between vise-wefts of the foundation. The pair of gold wefts curves down for two reasons: first, because the one out of three warps of the twill that starts the twill interlacing sequence places the pair of gold wefts over these warps; second, because the other warps, not having begun their interlacing, are seamless continuations of the warps that had been floating across the back of the band that separates the rows of disks. Thus, nothing holds the pair of gold wefts in place, and it is free to curve down unchecked, assuming its natural position. The curve is held in check by the degree of flexibility of the gold wefts themselves and the tension exerted on them by having been placed in the pattern shed and their being positioned alternately to the front or to the back to create the pattern.

In the model shown in figure 35b, the first pair of gold wefts is held in a horizontal position because every third warp of the twill that starts the interlacing sequence does so by first going under two foundation wefts. The gold pair is between the pair of vise-wefts of the foundation. Similarly, in figure 35c, every third warp of the twill goes under one foundation weft before the first pair of gold wefts. In this model, the first gold pair is after the vise-wefts in shed "a" of the foundation and is not free to curve down.

The last pair of gold wefts or the pair that is the top edge of the hourglass shape curves up in the model shown in figure 35a for the same reasons as the pair at the bottom edge. Every third warp of the set of warps of the twill that ends the twill interlacing sequence passes under the last pair of gold wefts and continues under two foundation wefts, thereby placing the pair of gold wefts over these warps. The other warps are seamless continuations of the warps that will float across the back of the band that separates this just-completed row of disks from the next. The pair of gold wefts is free to curve up into its natural position.

The pair of gold wefts that is the top edge of the hourglass in the models in figure 35b, c is held in a horizontal position for the same reason as the first pair at the bottom edge of these models. The one out of three warps of the twill that ends the twill interlacing sequence continues to interlace with one foundation weft in figure 35b and with two foundation wefts in figure 35c.

In the last phase of this research, the variations in precisely how the warps of the twill are made to start and stop the 1&2 twill interlacing sequence, which includes foundation wefts, came into focus. I was able to document variations in only a few pieces, including those that follow, and

I would expect there to be more variations than those presented in the following three examples.

In figure 36a, the pair of gold wefts that is the bottom edge of the hourglass on the back of Cooper-Hewitt 1902–1–385 is between the pair of vise-wefts and horizontal as demonstrated in figure 35b. The pair of gold wefts that is the top of the hourglass follows the pair of vise-wefts and curves up as in figure 35a.

In figure 36b, the pair of gold wefts that forms the bottom edge of the hourglass on the back of Cooper-Hewitt 1896–1–59 is between a pair of vise-wefts and curves down, similar to what is shown in figure 35a. Instead of going under the second foundation weft of the vise, it goes under both foundation wefts of the pair of vise-wefts. The pair of gold wefts that forms the top edge is after the pair of vise-wefts and curves up as in the model in figure 35a, although not as dramatically as at the bottom.

In figure 36c, a piece in the collection of The Textile Gallery, London, the first pair of gold wefts at the bottom of the hourglass shape is between the pair of vise-wefts and curves down, as in figure 35a. The weft that is the top is between the pair of vise-wefts and is horizontal, as in figure 35c.

An interesting variation is noted in Cooper-Hewitt 1896–1–59, in the fifth row of disks from the bottom. In this row, the pair of gold wefts forming the bottom edge is also between the pair of vise-wefts and is horizontal. Every third warp of the twill starts the interlacing sequence similar to what is shown in figure 38b, but instead of first going under two foundation wefts, it goes under only the first vise-weft of the pair. In addition, the first float span of every third warp is not over two pairs of gold wefts, but over one pair. Once the interlacing sequence was started, it continued in the manner already diagrammed.

As fascinating or as tedious as the variations that concern the twill might be to record and sort out, it is variations such as these that make individual pieces distinct, especially when several occur in one piece. They provide a significant insight into how the weavers actually threaded looms and wove these lampas/velvets. I am referring again to slight differences in the setting up of looms and making sheds for structure and pattern. What at first glance appears to be a uniformly woven piece might not, when studied carefully, have been woven according to rigid modern standards. What might appear to be a closely related group of pieces might, in fact, include pieces that are different from one another yet not sufficiently distinct to define another group.

Fig. 36. Hourglass shapes between disks on the back of three pieces: (a) Cooper-Hewitt 1902–1–385: the pair of gold wefts that is the bottom edge is horizontal; the pair that is the top edge curves up (see also figures 1, 2, and 20); (b) Cooper-Hewitt 1986–1–59: the bottom edge curves down; the top edge curves up; (c) The Textile Gallery, London, no. 1: the bottom edge curves down; the top edge is horizontal. Photos by Sandra Sardjono.

a

b

c

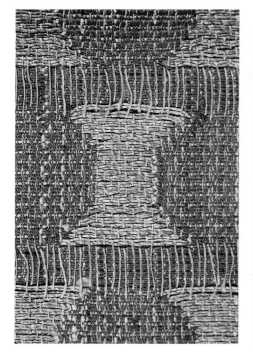
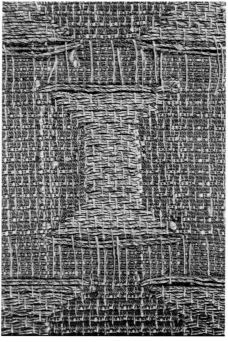
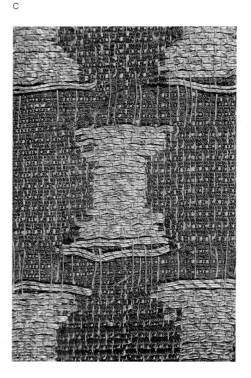

Width and Side Finishes

Of the five pieces that make up Bargello F127, one claims attention because of its length—it is 234 cm long—and its full selvedge-to-selvedge width of 68 cm. There are 35 complete disks in one row and 34 in the offset row, plus a half-disk at left and right. If the number of disks in a row is an indication of the full width of this group of lampas/velvets, two of the four pieces sewn together with edges turned under that make up the example in the Stibbert Museum in Florence, the back of which is not accessible, may also be full widths of about 68 cm, also with 35/34 disks per row.

The side finishes of this group of lampas/velvets can easily be identified by an approximately 5-mm wide stripe devoid of pile between the actual selvedge, or the point at which foundation gold wefts turn, and the vertical line along which pattern begins.[15] I have seen complete side finishes in six collections, but considering how many pieces exist, undoubtedly there are more. Time and conditions did not allow me to thoroughly analyze all the side finishes; I can present descriptions and a thorough analysis of one side finish that I did and one by Chris Verhecken-Lammens. It seems that in all examples, the side stripes begin—or end—on a vertical line that more or less divides disks in half.

The side finishes fall into two identifiable groups, which share common features: the warps of the stripe are various shades of blue, blue-green, or white. The warps of the stripe interlace in plain weave as in the patterned section between left and right stripes with one important modification: the elimination of warps that produce pile. The diagram in figure 5 shows how, as a result of removing pile warps, warps alternate single and paired, the pair being the foundation warps to left and right of the removed warps that would have produced pile. In addition, the warps of the stripe are doubled or tripled, somewhat disguising the fact that their number is the result of removing every fourth pile warp from the plain weave. What structurally could be said to be an alternation of single warp and a pair of warps, is now literally an alternation of a pair of warps and a group of four warps. However, some warps could be tripled. The last two warps of the plain weave are each a group of four or more. All foundation wefts and the pairs of gold wefts extend the full width of the warp and turn around the last warp at left and right. A particularly interesting feature of the foundation plain weave, however, is that two shuttles were used to carry foundation wefts (fig. 37).

Referring to figure 37a, if a single shuttle is used for a plain weave that is to have a single weft in one shed alternating with a pair of wefts in the next, every third weft-turn will be able to slip into the shed with paired wefts on its return across the width of the warp. This can occur at the left and right sides. When two shuttles are used, all weft-turns are held in place as demonstrated by the models in figure 37b-c. The difference between the two models is simply how the two wefts cross each other as a result of how the weaver put down and picked up the two shuttles one after the other. That the two sides are different in both variations is highlighted by using two colors to identify which weft was carried by which of the two shuttles. On one side, one weft-turn encloses another. On the other, the weft-turns overlap. It seemed to me that on one selvedge I saw in London, both turnings occurred on one side. I could not confirm this because of lack of time, but the model in figure 37d demonstrates how easily it could be done. Considering how many variations can and do occur in one fabric as a result of a weaver's decisions or actions, it stands to reason that what is demonstrated in figure 37d might occur in pieces of this group of lampas/velvets not yet examined.

Chris Verhecken-Lammens suggests that

Fig. 38. Detail of Brussels TX 465 showing the side finish, approximately 6 mm wide, a stripe of white warps covered with the pairs of gold wefts of the 1&2 twill (fig. 3). Photo by Chris Verhecken-Lammens, courtesy of the Koninklijke Musea voor Kunst en Geschiedenis, Brussels.

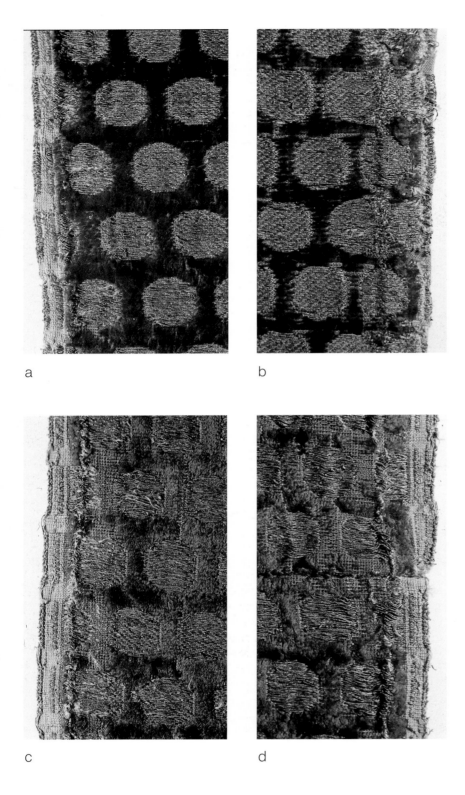

a

b

c

d

Fig. 39. Details of Bargello F127, showing side finishes, approximately 5 mm wide. Photo by Teodoro Seliantis, courtesy of the Museo Nazionale del Bargello, Florence.

"gold threads were already paired in the weft device. Of course two shuttles with gold threads can be introduced one after the other, but I doubt this was used here because you have to control two separate threads in one open shed. I rather think that the pair of gold wefts was wound around the length of a stick or flat wooden slat. You only have to unwind a sufficient length for one shed and put the stick through the shed, leaving the paired gold wefts in the shed" (personal communication).

All pairs of gold wefts turn around the last warp at left and right edges, but how they cross the side stripes accounts for two easily discernible variations. In the first variation, the pairs of gold wefts are on top of the warps of the side stripe and are bound by warps of the twill as they are in the pattern section between left and right side stripes (fig. 38). Three examples can be cited. In Hispanic Society H954, there is a short length of this selvedge on the left of one piece (no. 7). The warps of the stripe are white silk, the gold wefts of disks are bound in the z direction, and gold wefts on the stripe are also bound z. In Cleveland 1918.225, a tiny section in poor condition survives on the left. The warps of the stripe are blue silk, the pairs of gold wefts of the disks are bound z, and it appears as if the pairs of gold wefts on the stripe are bound z as well. In a third example, Brussels TX 465 (fig. 38), there is a section on the right of one of the three pieces sewn together. The warps of the 6-mm wide stripe are white silk, the pairs of gold wefts of disks are bound z, but on the stripe they are bound s. The piece in Krefeld is described as if it is of this type with a stripe of white silk warps (Gasthaus 1979, no. 10).

In the second variation, pairs of gold wefts float on the front for short spans to form a narrow stripe, no doubt achieved by raising warps to position them on the front of the stripe. Each warp pattern step in the stripe includes only non-pile warps, the warps for pile having been removed. The patterning of the stripe eliminates the need for warps of the twill; therefore, they are not included in the stripe. It is this variation of the side finish that Chris Verhecken-Lammens and I were able to examine in detail: Brussels TX 464 and one example in the collection of The Textile Gallery, London, respectively. They are very like those shown in figure 39a–c.

In Brussels TX 464, the 5-mm wide side finish is on the left of the full length of the 34-cm long piece (fig. 3, right). The warps of the stripe are blue silk, and there is one column of gold vertical dashes that is not centered within the width of the stripe. Five warp pattern steps were lifted to make the stripe created by gold weft floats, but there are errors. Chris Verhecken-Lammens notes that foundation wefts turn with one enclosing another (fig. 37b, selvedge on the left). The piece in The Textile Gallery, London, has a short section of this side finish on the right, the condition of which did not allow accurate warp by warp analysis. The warps of the stripe are blue silk, and there is one column of gold vertical dashes fairly well centered within the width of the stripe for which possibly two warp pattern steps were lifted. Foundation wefts turn with one enclosing another. The issue that caused much discussion and required precise analysis concerned the turning of the pairs of gold wefts. Chris Verhecken-Lammens and I conclude that gold wefts turn around the last warp only. I am not willing to speculate upon how this was managed, but Verhecken-Lammens suggests that the turn might have been accomplished by the weaver lifting the last warp thread by hand. She adds that "it seems very primitive but so is the loom" (personal communication). These are the only end finishes that were studied in detail in preparation for this paper.

Since pairs of gold wefts were used in bands as needed for rows of disks (fig. 2), the floats of gold wefts do not form a continuous stripe, but instead make short vertical dashes that are as high as the height of the disks in each row. Due to the combined thickness of the gold wefts that are paired in each shed of the twill, their turns at the outer edges are bulky and appear as another stripe—a stripe that is not the result of a pattern lift. Verticals in the side finishes are more easily read as narrow stripes that are the warps of the side finish.

Another side finish in the collection of The Textile Gallery, London, is the variation just described; it has a stripe with blue warps on the left side, but it is not easily accessible, having been turned under and stitched to adjoining fragments.

The most interesting side finishes are seen in Bargello F127 (fig. 39a-d), which is made up of five pieces sewn together. The side finishes with their selvedges are well preserved because they were never turned under and sewn into a seam. Except for one, they are flat, easy to see, and evenly straight-edged as compared to those that are so often crimped as a result of wefts having drawn warps tightly together when they turn in their passages to and fro. Four of the pieces have a total of five side finishes (fig. 39a-d); the largest

piece is 234 cm in length with 5-6 mm wide selvedges on both sides (fig. 39a, b) with light blue warp stripes. The length seems to have been tacked to a flat surface, as evidenced by small holes regularly spaced on both sides. The second piece (fig. 39c) has a similar side finish on the left, 27 cm long, and may be from the same length of cloth. The third piece (fig. 39d, lower), from a different length of cloth, has a side finish 4-5 mm wide on the left, 35.5 cm long. The fourth piece (fig. 39d, upper) has a side finish 7 mm wide on the left, 16.5 cm long, but the warps of the stripe are green, and there is a pair of stripes created by floats of the gold wefts.

Four blue warps remain along a short section on the left side of Cooper-Hewitt 1896–1–59, but color alone does not indicate its side finish.

Discussion

Features that are common within limited range to all of the velvets in this survey include the following:

- gold disks are small, approximately of equal size;
- pile and non-pile warps are firmly twisted Z;
- dyes were probably cochineal for pile warps and madder for non-pile warps;
- warp and weft counts are approximately the same;
- lampas technique, with pile in the plain weave of the foundation and pairs of gold wefts in the supplementary 1&2 twill;
- gold wefts are paired in each shed of the twill;
- gold wefts are comprised of narrow strips of gilded animal material (parchment, membrane, or leather) wound in the Z-direction around a yellow (possibly also pale rose, tan, or orange) silk that has a Z-twist, with the gilded strips almost completely covering the silk.

We know that once warps are threaded on a loom, they cannot be changed without rethreading or by tying on new warps. By reconstructing the threading plan, certain features are revealed that can be used to identify different warp setups. They include the following:

- warp order;
- number of warps per unit of measure;
- repeat system;

- width of repeat units or the number of warp pattern steps within the unit;
- mistakes associated with warping and threading heddles.

These features can be changed only if the warps are completely rethreaded through the various heddles of a loom. Color is one feature, however, that can be changed without rethreading by tying new warps on to those already threaded and pulling them through the heddles. Similarly, by tying on, the same warp set-up can be used over and over again.

Several features that vary have nothing to do with the threading of warps and reflect instead differences in the pattern plan or the opening of sheds as controlled by the weaver. The following can be included:

- twill direction;
- the number of full rows of pile that are the bands between rows of disks;
- differences in the contour of disks and the likelihood of a fixed or a freehand pattern draw;
- the starting and stopping of the interlaced connection of the warps of the twill with the plain-weave foundation;
- mistakes associated with weaving and reading the pattern plan.

The existence of so many variations could lead to a possible but not necessary conclusion that these textiles represent a wide geographic and chronological range of production. Specific features of the variations, when considered within the three contexts just outlined—the context of the group as a whole, the context of cloths from different looms, and the context that is limited to a specific length of cloth—point to a closely defined group of cloths that are basically the same despite minor variations. A single workshop might have had many looms, some warped for straight repeats and others for mirror-imaging, each with a varying number of warps per repeat unit. Alternatively, there might have been independent workshops, each with several looms to supply a single overseer, dealer, or wholesaler with multiple lengths of a required pattern. Looms within a single workshop might have been set up slightly differently and, more likely, the set-up of the looms might have varied from workshop to workshop.

As for textiles that share technical features regardless of pattern, it is important to consider that it is much easier to re-program a pattern than it is to re-thread a loom. While such a practical approach to production may facilitate the identification of weaving centers, the practice itself makes it difficult to determine how long a specific pattern might have been woven in a certain center or specific workshop.

If we judge solely from the number of surviving textiles with gold disks in offset rows, it appears that within a particular period, this pattern was highly favored. Wardwell lists seven inventory entries that describe patterns with disks: four for Boniface VIII of 1295; one for Clement V of 1311; one in Assisi of 1341; and one in Canterbury Cathedral of 1315 (Wardwell 1988–89, p. 139, nos. 49–54 and p. 144, no. 109). One of them, no. 51 of Boniface VIII, is a red Tartar velvet with gold disks: *Item, unum pannum tartaricum pilosum rubeum ad madelias aureas.* Pope Boniface VIII consecrated Louis of Anjou as bishop of Toulouse in 1296. Louis died in 1297 and was canonized in 1317, the year of Simone Martini's altarpiece (Monnas 1993).

That Mongol silks were popular in the West is well established (Wardwell 1988–89) and vividly expressed by Lisa Monnas (1993, p. 169). In describing the fabrics worn by St. Louis and Robert of Anjou, Monnas writes:

> Both brothers are wearing "tartar silks" which were greatly in vogue among rulers of Europe during the late thirteenth and early fourteenth centuries. Thanks to the re-opening of the Silk Road under the Mongols, Oriental silks were pouring into Europe, imported by intrepid Italian merchants. Cloth also came as diplomatic gifts from the Mongols themselves.

> In an age when the richness of a silken cloth proclaimed the estate of the wearer, and at a time when such matters were treated with the utmost seriousness, costly tartar fabrics became an essential part of formal dress in both Oriental and Western courts. In 1332 John of Maundeville went so far as to state in his *Travels* that no foreign envoy was admitted to the presence of the Sultan of Babylon unless he were dressed in cloth of gold, or camocas, or tartar [cloth]… These materials were worn at the Angevin court of France, reaching England and Northern Europe… The depiction of tartar silks in the St. Louis panel, following the dictates of contemporary fashion, evidently constituted a display of recognizable status symbols.

The Mongols' love of cloth saturated with gold was demonstrated by the exhibition and catalogue *When Silk Was Gold* (Watt and Wardwell 1997). The large amount of gold may have been what made Mongol silks so popular in the West. The gold disks of the pattern scrutinized here may allude to small gold coins or commemorative medallions attached to a rich red cloth (Davanzo Poli 1995, p. 101, no. 83), possibly a bright insect-red plain velvet. Wardwell in "'Panni Tartarici'" writes, "The design of gold disks is very ancient in the Middle East and occurs in other media as well. But in the context of textiles, it may relate to embroideries of the 8th and 9th centuries that were known as mudannar or mufallas, because they were ornamented with gold or copper coins…" (1988–89, p. 111). However, if the pattern is thought to have been woven in Venice, the disks can be said to represent Venetian coins (Davanzo Poli 1995, p. 101, no. 83). The painting in the Uffizi mentioned earlier is a triptych, the center panel of which is filled by the standing figure of St. Matthew wearing an unpatterned red garment. It is in the flanking panels that the pattern of offset rows of gold disks is clearly depicted in two small roundels set on either side of the pointed arch of each frame (Sangiorgi 1920, p. 117). The painting was commissioned in about 1367 by the Arte del Cambio (the guild of money changers who represented the powerful Florentine banking houses), to be hung on a pillar of Orsanmichele, the church of their patron saint. The coat of arms of the guild was gold coins set on a red ground.[16]

When seen from a distance, the reflective qualities of the long lustrous red silk pile and the vibrant sparkle of tightly packed gold coins or disks must have had an effect not unlike a shimmering mirage, whether the sparkle came from real gold coins or the considerably cheaper woven gold. In spite of its sumptuous surface effect, when studied closely, the pattern of this lampas/velvet lacks finesse, as do the patterns of many Mongol lampas-type silks dominated by gold wefts. The disks of this pattern are awkwardly shaped, even when accounting for their small size. The plain weave with pile is well thought out, but as a foundation for lampas it has a number of drawbacks. The edges of disks are not smooth and weaving is complicated. The disks of a straightforward lampas without pile would have been more cleanly shaped. With pile, left and right edges are slightly different (as shown earlier), and the tops of disks have a shaggy look because of overhanging pile. While it is true that these details have little effect when seen from afar, there is, nevertheless, a certain tension between the gold and the pile.

International connections are essential to any discussion of textile motifs, techniques, or use. For example, Chinese silk threads, fabrics, and garments seem to have been imported into the Mediterranean area in the first century B.C. (Forbes 1964, p. 54), and one need hardly mention the caravan routes across Central Asia. Of particular importance to this study is the protection and relocation of textile artisans over vast distances by the Mongols in the thirteenth and fourteenth centuries. This situation no doubt would have had an impact upon the possibility that these lampas/velvets were woven within this period, and not in Spain or Italy. It is therefore important to evaluate the specific aspects of a wide range of compound silks in order to develop a broad geographic and chronological framework for this placement (Allsen 1997; Wardwell 1988–89; Watt and Wardwell 1997; Monnas 1986).

While a survey of dyes is beyond the subject of this paper and my expertise, a suggestion of geographic and chronological use of insect and madder reds up to the fifteenth century is in order. In the West, silks of thirteenth-century Spain come to mind immediately, and the use of two reds remains a distinct Spanish feature into the fifteenth century and probably later. The brightness and clarity of one of the two reds in Spanish silks suggest that the brighter red is cochineal and the duller red madder, as in three pieces of these lampas/velvets. Two reds were used in Italy in the fourteenth century, but the reds are generally not as bright and clear as the reds in textiles from Spain. Little is known about dyes used in areas dominated by the Mongols, especially during the critical period of the thirteenth century, when textile craftsmen and their expertise were relocated over a vast area including the eastern Iranian world and China (Watt and Wardwell 1997, p. 127). In the Far East, it has been noted that red dye possibilities of the Northern Song Dynasty in China (A.D. 960–1127) include madder and cochineal (Taylor 1991). Since insect reds were more expensive than madder reds, it is important to note how the two were used. In compound weave, was madder red used for a hidden set of warps, or wefts, and an insect red for those that are visible, as is the case in this group of velvets?[17]

Wardwell admits that very few silks survive on which to build definitive conclusions; nevertheless, the features she observed and worked with over a long period of time were consistent enough to construct a general outline (personal communication). One feature in particular applies to these lampas/velvets: her discussion of side finishes as well as their possible origin. The side finishes in all the silks included in Appendix I of her article "'Panni Tartarici'" (Wardwell 1988–89, p. 133; see corrected appendix inserted after publication), are described as having "borders." She points out that three of her eight categories have side finishes with stripes—categories II, IV, and V, which she attributes to Central Asia. She offers a description of a side finish that appears to be similar to the ones of the lampas/velvets described earlier: "the selvage border has paired, sky-blue main warps; in the areas where the gold wefts occur, the lines of blue warps form two stripes against the gold wefts predominating on the face. The outer selvage is completed by two bundles of warps around which all wefts turn" (Wardwell 1988–89, p. 103). Silks in category II are attributed to Central Asia. She offers a similar description of a silk in category IV, also attributed to Central Asia: "On the face of each selvage border are pattern wefts interrupted by three thin stripes of main warps. These are the same color as the rest of the main warps but are paired. Each outer edge is completed by two bundles of warps around which both ground and pattern wefts turn" (p. 105). Side finishes of silks of category V (Wardwell 1988–89, pp. 107, 108) are also striped. Stripes in the side finish of a silk in her category IV are clear in the detail photo (her figure 30A, p. 156), as are the stripes in a silk in category V (her figure 36, p. 158).

In another lampas described as Eastern Islamic, dated to the second half of the thirteenth century or the fourteenth century, the side finish on the right side has no warps of the supplementary weave.[18] It is patterned by three narrow stripes that are blue warps of the foundation weave and/or three stripes that are vertically aligned floats of metallic wefts of the supplementary weave (the number of metallic stripes includes the point at which they turn at the outer edge, or selvedge). Assuming the lampas was woven back-side up, the stripes that on the front are vertically aligned floats of gold wefts, were created by lifting warps of the foundation weave by means of the pattern harness. The same was true with the lampas/velvets, but these were woven front-side up. At the edge there are two bundles of warps that were most likely threaded through heddles of shafts of the structure

harness so they interlace 1:1 with the set of wefts of the foundation weave, a 4-unit twill. However, the two bundles of warps at the edge do not seem to have been raised for the 1:1 interlacing with the set of metallic wefts of the supplementary weave, a 3-unit twill. Instead, interlacing was achieved by the weaver's hand manipulation, as noted in the lampas/velvets.[19]

Anne Wardwell is firm in her conclusion that silks with striped side finishes are not Italian or Spanish. She writes: "The selvage edges of Italian drawloom silks from this period are completed by linen cords; those of Spanish silks are also reinforced cords that are usually linen or occasionally silk. In the textiles attributed to Central Asia, on the other hand, as well as some attributed to the Middle East, the selvage edges are reinforced by bundles of silk warps, but never linen cords" (1988–89, p. 96). On the same page and in conversations with me, she emphasizes the importance of the materials of gold threads. In summary, silks woven with gold wefts used in pairs, the surface of which is gold (Indictor 1988, Table 4, p. 15 and Table 5, p. 16) and the animal substrate of which is coarse and thick, are eastern in origin. The silks in Wardwell's category VI are attributed to northeastern Iran and include a lampas/velvet patterned with offset rows of gold disks in the Cleveland Museum of Art (her figure 57, p. 165). Since Wardwell was not aware that these lampas/velvets have side finishes with stripes, this feature can be added to her category VI.

Wardwell offers various reasons why this group of velvets patterned with offset rows of gold disks is neither Italian nor Spanish. It is worth reviewing her arguments regarding their origin. She points out that a few thirteenth- and fourteenth-century travelers saw velvet in Central Asia, Iran, and Iraq. Velvet is mentioned by Rashīd al-Dīn, and a velvet is the only cloth mentioned by Ibn Battūta (p. 96). Moreover, "Ibn Battūta refers to the cloth as *kamkhā*… a Persian word shortened from *kamkhwāb*, meaning "having a little nap, or pile" (Wardwell 1988–89, note 6, p. 122). It must be said, however, that fabrics other than velvet can be described using the same terms. Wardwell attributes them to Tabriz because:

> that city not only produced luxury textiles before the arrival of the Mongols in the mid-thirteenth century, but… it was relatively undisturbed by the concomitant social and economic upheavals suffered elsewhere. Finally, this center must have

produced a variety of luxury textiles including velvet as well as lampas weaves. The only city that fits these qualifications is Tabriz. Not only was it spared by the Mongols, but it served as the Ilkhanid capital until Sultaniya was built. Yāqūt, who traveled to Tabriz in 610 H./A.D. 1213, wrote of luxury fabrics produced there, and evidence from Bar Hebraeus, 'Umari, and Bidlīsī strongly support the existence of a *tiraz* factory or workshop in Tabriz during the Ilkhanid period [1256–1349, established by Hulagu, the grandson of Jenghiz Khan]. According to Marco Polo, Rashīd al-Dīn, and Ibn Battūta, a variety of sumptuous textiles were woven there, including silk and gold fabrics and velvet (Wardwell 1988–89, p. 111).

Within the context of international contacts, Wardwell offers:

It is interesting that Tabriz is identified in the 1295 inventory of Boniface VIII as the place of manufacture for four textiles... At that time, of course, a colony of Italian merchants was in residence there, and quantities of luxury textiles woven in Tabriz must have been imported into Europe. What is particularly interesting, though, is that they could be distinguished —at least to the eye of the compiler of the inventory—as textiles woven elsewhere (Wardwell 1988–89, n. 156, p. 129).

While thirteenth-century Mongol Iranian velvets are documented, it does not mean that velvet weaving originated in Iran. The two techniques that were combined to weave the pattern of this group—plain weave with pile and the lampas-type use of the gold twill—may provide a useful basis for piecing together a history of velvet techniques.

Plain weave is the foundation of this lampas/velvet. The earliest Western velvets known that are a plain weave with pile date from the Late Antique period of about the fourth or fifth century A.D. (Bellinger 1955, figs. 25–27; Kendrick 1921, nos. 301, 302, 303 on pp. 10–11, and pl. I), as shown in figure 40 (note that Kendrick does not identify these as velvet). The pile of these velvets is uncut loops of linen warps that are supplementary to the linen plain-weave foundation. They survive, not necessarily because they are velvet, but because of the purple wool and linen tapestry that is surrounded by the pile. It may be that the weaving of velvet had continuous

traditions in a number of areas from as early as the Late Antique period, as evidenced by the linen velvets just mentioned. Perhaps the work of scholars of Byzantine art and history, for example, will some day link the velvets of the fifth century A.D. to other areas prior to the thirteenth century.

Unfortunately, the conventions used by early painters for plain surfaces do not allow us to be specific about the textiles they are trying to represent. Plain velvet might be what is shown in fourteenth-century Italian paintings as the fabric for garments of the Virgin and upper level clergy. What might be interpreted as the sheen of silk might just as well represent the play of light on changing directions of silk pile. If a garment worn by an important figure, however, is embroidered in what is clearly indicated as gold, it is possible that it represents an embroidered plain velvet, especially considering the later long and important tradition of embroidery on velvet—a combination of two precious materials.

There are velvets with plain-weave foundations woven within the fourteenth and fifteenth centuries (Monnas 1986; Desrosiers 1993), but this paper is not the forum for a general discussion that includes such velvets and certainly not detailed analyses of their structures and techniques.

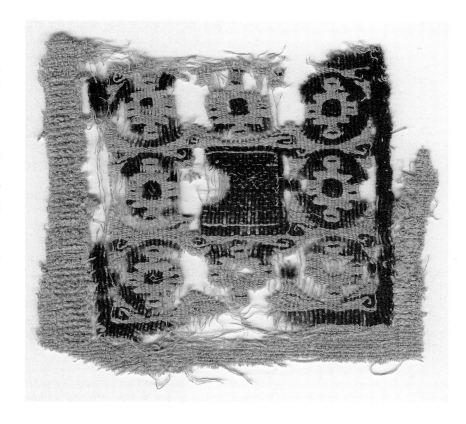

Fig. 40. Velvet, fourth or fifth century A.D., found in Egypt: loops of a set of linen supplementary pile warps set into linen plain weave surround a tapestry-woven square with purple wool and linen wefts. The Textile Museum 71.135, acquired by George Hewitt Myers in 1955.

I interpret this velvet as a lampas to which pile was added. Lampas as a patterning technique was well established before the thirteenth century. Using the lampas technique with continuous gold wefts offered a cheaper and faster method to produce this pattern than brocading each gold disk. A significant amount of gold was saved by not using it in the bands between rows of disks. Weaving this lampas/velvet with its complicated treadlings was made a bit faster by not having the set of warps of the twill interlace with the set of wefts of the foundation between rows of disks. It is possible that techniques for patterning plain velvet during weaving by means of voiding pile and filling voided areas with metallic or silk wefts were being explored in a number of regions and cultures. It may be no coincidence that the tapestry sections of the Late Antique velvets and the gold disks of the lampas/velvets under discussion (possibly of the thirteenth century) are set in areas voided of pile, despite the differences in technique.

The use of gold wefts in velvet raises a fascinating issue. It is important to note which velvets might have had pattern lifts for metallic or silk wefts—for example, the lampas technique discussed in this paper—and which did not. In this context, I, and possibly others, have documented fifteenth-century velvets in which gold wefts were used by means that could be described as related to the lampas technique. In the future, information about how gold wefts were handled must be gleaned from careful studies of velvet, current published sources being sparse. I will summarize two examples.

Cooper-Hewitt 1902–1– 876 is patterned by a bold vine curving on the Z-diagonal bearing bold flowers, of which some use wefts wrapped with foil, and others have green cut-pile with gold centers (Cox 1900, pl. XXII, fig. 7). The textile is most likely Italian and dated to the first quarter of the fifteenth century. The foundation is a green silk 4&1 satin and the gold areas are a 1&2 Z-twill with its own set of warps. The gold wefts are composed of narrow strips of foil wrapped S around yellow silk that has an S-twist. They are used singly and are not continuous across the full width of the velvet, but are brocaded in areas where required by pattern. The set of warps that binds them are set in stripes about 8 cm separated by a space 2 cm wide. The set of twill warps is attached to the foundation in a way that is completely different from that described in this paper. Foundation warps no doubt would have been lifted to position gold wefts for pattern. In this case, however, the pattern lift would not

have had to include pile warps, not because gold-brocaded details are superimposed on a surface voided of pile, as one would expect, but because they are surrounded by areas voided of pile, in some cases by a wide margin.

In an article dedicated to Gabriel Vial (Sonday 1992) about a late fifteenth-or early sixteenth-century velvet, I combined the terms velvet and lampas. The supplementary weave of Cooper-Hewitt 1983–4–2 is also a 1&2 Z-twill. The yellow silk wefts of the twill continue across the full width of the velvet and remain always on the front, not on both front and back. They are hidden in areas of pile and exposed in the areas voided of pile. This combination of foundation weave and supplementary weave could fall within a definition of lampas, except that wefts of the supplementary weave act as a facing that did not require pattern lifts.

The velvets, Cooper-Hewitt 1902–1–876, Cooper-Hewitt 1983–4–2, and those discussed here, can be described as having supplementary wefts bound by a set of warps used specifically to attach the supplementary wefts to the foundation. This description could be the basis for a description of lampas. However, it does not specify that two weaves can be identified, which, to me, is one of the key features of the lampas technique. Without this feature, a set of supplementary "binding" warps can be used in other techniques. Two weaves, each with its own set of warps and set of wefts, can be identified in the velvets just mentioned—one a foundation and the other added to it, or supplementary. In the group patterned with disks, the foundation weave has warps that make pile, the 1&2 twill with gold wefts (the supplementary weave) is attached to the foundation, and the gold wefts of the twill pattern by means of pattern lifts, but in bands for each row of disks. In Cooper-Hewitt 1902–1–876, the foundation satin weave has a set of pile warps added to it, the supplementary 1&2 twill with gold wefts is attached to the foundation, and gold wefts pattern by means of pattern lifts. In this example, however, the set of warps of the supplementary twill is a series of separated stripes and the gold wefts of the twill are discontinuous or brocaded in widely separated bands as determined by the pattern. In Cooper-Hewitt 1983–4–2, the foundation has pile warps, and the 1&2 twill with yellow silk wefts is attached to the foundation. In this example, the silk wefts of the twill are continuous and used throughout the length of the cloth; because they remain always on the front, they do not require pattern lifts.

Therefore, I suggest that the term lampas is often subjective and not always definitive. An author's definition should be stated if it is not implied, as it often is, by means of the context of the fabrics discussed. I use it in this presentation for clarification, to provoke discussion, and to stimulate much-needed research on early velvets.

Summary

The technical report I offer here neither confirms nor refutes where and when the velvets patterned with offset rows of disks were woven. But these velvets may represent one of the earliest uses of the lampas technique to pattern velvet. Visual evidence that the pattern with offset rows of gold disks was used in the West in the thirteenth and fourteenth centuries has been demonstrated. References in Italian inventories of the period confirm the use of fabrics with the pattern of offset rows of disks. Judging from the number of pieces extant, this pattern was favored. Moreover, the fact that in an inventory dated 1295 one cloth is described as a Tartar velvet is backed by references to the weaving of velvet far to the east of Italy—specifically in or around the city of Tabriz. The proposal that the velvets of this group were woven in the east, in the area of Tabriz as Anne Wardwell suggests, must be accepted for now. Meanwhile, one hopes that another scholar or a team of specialists attempts the daunting task of analyzing the myriad aspects of a significant number of compound woven silks of the thirteenth and fourteenth centuries and organizes them in categories spanning the wide geographic span from Spain to China. It is in this context that I offer my detailed discussions.

Acknowledgments

I wish to thank the following individuals for making fabrics available for study, for fruitful discussions, or for photographs: Louise Mackie, Cleveland Museum of Art; Anne Wardwell, Cleveland; Constancio del Alamo, The Hispanic Society, New York; Thomas Campbell and staff of the Ratti Center, The Metropolitan Museum of Art, New York; Ann Coleman, Museum of Fine Arts, Boston; Linda Woolley, Victoria and Albert Museum, London; Lisa Monnas, London; The Textile Gallery, London; Dr. Angela Völker, Österreichisches Museum fur Angewandte Kunst, Vienna; Hans Koenig and Regula Schorta, Switzerland; Dr. Werner Adriaenssens, Koninklijke Musea voor Kunst en Geschiedenis, Brussels; Dr. Kirsten Aschengreen Piacenti, Stibbert Museum, Florence; Dr. Giovanna Gaeta Bertela and staff of the Museo Nazionale del Bargello, Florence. Working with me and Lucy Commoner, Textile Conservator, Sandra Sardjono provided charts and close-up photographs of pieces in Cooper-Hewitt. Roberta Orsi Landini, Director of the Fondazione Arte della Seta Lisio in Florence, arranged for photographs to be taken of side finishes of the textiles in the Bargello in Florence. Joyce Denney in the Department of Asian Art at The Metropolitan Museum of Art offered sensible advice on various sections of my discussion. Special appreciation is given to the editors and curators of The Textile Museum, especially Carol Bier and Mattiebelle Gittinger, for their generous support, valuable suggestions, and patience. Much of my discussion would not have been possible without the support of Anne Wardwell, who generously summarized aspects of her work for this publication.

About the Author

Milton Sonday received his early training in the field of historic textiles at The Textile Museum before becoming Curator of Textiles at Cooper-Hewitt, National Design Museum, Smithsonian Institution, in New York. He now holds the post of Senior Researcher, Textiles. At The Textile Museum, Sonday began to apply his artistic talents to the illustration of textile structures; over the years the graphic style of his diagrams has evolved. His research focuses on a broad spectrum of historic weaving techniques.

A member of the advisory council of CIETA (Centre International d'Etudes des Textiles Anciens), Sonday is also a founder of the Textile Society of America and past president.

Notes

1. An early version of this study was read at the General Assembly of CIETA in Bern, Switzerland, in September 1999.

2. For example: Cox 1900 (Venice, beginning of the 15th century); Sangiorgi 1920, p. 117 (Italy, 14th century); Errera 1927, nos. 99–100 (Italy, 14th/15th century); May 1957, figs. 146–47 (Spain, first half 15th century); Mayer-Thurman 1975, no. 44 (Spain, 15th century); Gasthaus 1979, no. 10 (Ostasien, 15th/16th century); Buss 1983, pp. 130–31 (Italy or Spain, 14th/15th century); Davanzo Poli 1995, no. 83 (Venice? 14th/15th century). A note on a catalogue card in the Cleveland Museum of Art indicates Miss Underhill changed the attribution from Turkey to Italy in 1943.

3. As of the date of this publication, examples can be found in seven museums in the United States, one museum and two private collections in London, two museums in Paris, two museums in Florence, one in a private collection in Switzerland, and one in a museum in each of these cities—Lyon, Strasbourg, Brussels, Milan, Venice, Turin, Prato, Geneva, Tarassa, Barcelona, Krefeld, Cologne, Vienna, Copenhagen, and Toronto.

4. Chris Verhecken-Lammens works with textiles in the collection of the Koninklijke Musea voor Kunst en Geschiedenis in Brussels. She and I worked together on these pieces with joyful intensity, so it is with humble thanks that I acknowledge her contributions throughout this paper.

5. Cooper-Hewitt Museum 1896–1–59, one piece; 1902–1–385, one piece; Hispanic Society H954, fifteen pieces of various sizes sewn together, some of them small, numbered by M.S. 1–15; H955, four pieces of various sizes sewn together, one tiny and one large patched with two small pieces, numbered by M.S. 1–4; The Metropolitan Museum of Art 46.156.72, one piece; Cleveland Museum of Art 1918.30a, one piece; 1918.30b, two pieces sewn together, one tiny, numbered by M.S. 1–2; 1918.225, one piece; Museum of Fine Arts, Boston 93.376, one piece; Victoria and Albert Museum 545a-1884, one piece; 545b-1884, two pieces sewn together, one tiny; The Textile Gallery, London, no number, one piece; no number, one piece; no number, 4 pieces sewn together, one much larger than the others; private collection, London, no number, one piece; Brussels TX 464, one piece; TX 465, three pieces sewn together, one much larger than the others; Bargello, Franchetti Collection (F127), five

pieces of various sizes sewn together, one of them 234 cm (selvedge to selvedge), and one of them tiny; Stibbert Museum no. 16110, five pieces, each about the same size, sewn together.

6. The Italian analysis is presented as a grid of coded squares. Two velvets are illustrated, one in Museo del Bargello, Florence; the other in Civiche Raccolte d'Arte Applicata, Milan. The pile of both is red.

7. The first test was conducted by Denyse Montaguet of the Fashion Institute of Technology, New York; she used the Schweppe technique for one piece in the collection of the Cooper-Hewitt. More advanced tests of the two Cooper-Hewitt pieces were carried out by Witold Nowik at the Laboratorie de Recherche des Monuments Historiques, Paris, in cooperation with Dominique Cardon in France. Nowik's identification was based on a qualitative and quantitative investigation of the dyestuff's composition by high performance liquid chromatography separation and photodi-ode array detection (HPLC-PAD). He found the red or non-pile warps to have been "colored with madder (*Rubia tinctoria*) root extract. Moreover, the composition of dye in both samples is qualitatively identical and has only slightly different relative quantity of characteristic compounds." He says the red of the pile warps was "dyed with extract of carminic acid containing cochineal." Dr. Jan Wouters, head of the laboratory for materials and techniques at the Koninklijk Institut voor Het Kunstpatrimonium, Brussels, tested one piece in the Cleveland Museum of Art. He identified mad-der, very probably *Rubia tinctorum*, as well as Polish cochineal (*Porphyrophora polonica*) using the same technique. The cooperation of the Cleveland Museum of Art is greatly appreciated, in particular that of Louise Mackie, Curator of Textiles and Islamic Art, D. Bruce Christman, Chief Conservator, and Robin Hanson, Textile Conservator. For an insightful discussion of the current state of dye analysis, see Wouters 1993. Wouters refers to the detailed results gained from high performance liquid chromatography (HPLC) and points out that it is useful "in establishing relationships between fragments supposedly from the same textile." By extension, HPLC could help us place fabrics into groups, each dyed with like or similar materials. Based on his analysis of the two velvets in Cooper-Hewitt, Nowik says, "These velvets are probably dyed and made in either the same conditions (according to tradition) or even in the same work-shop by living people. The [two] fragments could also [have] been original from one piece." While my analysis shows they are not from the same

piece, Nowik confirms they are closely related. This paper would have been greatly enriched had it been possible to analyze the dyes (not to mention the gilded animal substrate) of more of these velvets grouped by technique.

8. If the warps that produce pile are considered a separate set, then the interpretation and description of the structure of non-pile warps must be modified to indicate a pairing of non-pile warps. I am not offering this interpretation because of the many velvets in which warps that make pile are clearly a separate set, with the non-pile warps being unaffected by their one-warp-at-a-time interlacing sequence, be it plain weave, twill, or satin.

9. If warps of the supplementary weave do not interlace with wefts of the foundation weave, it is the wefts of the supplementary weave that are positioned in their paths to either front or back in their passage from selvedge to selvedge that hold the two weaves together. It must be noted that the two weaves are on separable layers in some areas. I have been describing this lampas variation as one with no interlaced connection—one that has a venerable history, a detailed discussion of which is not appropriate for this presentation. Unfortunately, there is, as of this date, no single reference that carefully illustrates and explains the two lampas variations—those with and those without an interlaced connection—nor are they generally described as such. I should also point out that not everyone applies the term lampas as strictly.

10. A line along which a motif can be divided is simply a line. An axis of mirror-imaging, by contrast, is the hinge on which repeat units fold, flip, or turn from one side to the other. I prefer to reserve use of the term "axis" for mirror-imaging resulting from mechanical or technical means built into the pattern harness.

11. To understand the Indian loom, see DuBois 1983, p. 224 (diagram), and p. 225 (photograph); see also Wulff 1966, pp. 205–10 and Becker 1987, p. 252 (color photo) and p. 259 (diagram). For good illustrations of the Moroccan loom, see Vial 1980, figs. 5, 6; for a video of a Moroccan loom in action, see Mackie 1996.

12. Reading a pattern plan for a repeat unit first from left to right and then from right to left is probably an ancient practice. By reading a pattern plan in this manner, a vertical axis is created that divides the two repeat units, now one on top of the other, in half. The two units are mirror images of each other, but their axes, instead of falling on the sides of the units, are in the middle. This axis is not mechanical as for mirror-imaging as described in n. 10. This type of mirror-imaging can be described as pivoted. For an illustration see Sonday 1987, pp. 62, 63. A pattern plan can be read in this way and repeated in the straight manner as well as mirror-imaged.

13. Rahul Jain (1995, p. 56) discusses the pattern harness and the pattern cords or "drawcords." He notes, "One variant, for example, has no drawcords and the pattern selection is made directly on the crosscords." He adds that in this example, the drawboy and the set of pattern cords onto which the patterns would have been fixed are eliminated.

14. I am suggesting three shafts for the plain weave to show that it would be possible, and for a bit of fun. It also visually emphasizes warp order—one pair of pile warps between a pair of non-pile warps—with the pile warps threaded through heddles on shaft no. 3 and the non-pile warps to left and right threaded through heddles on shaft no. 2. The foundation plain weave could just as easily have been threaded on four shafts in continuous order—1, 2, 3, 4, etc.—with non-pile warps threaded through heddles on shaft nos. 1, 2, and 3 and pile warps through heddles on no. 4. With shaft no. 4 lifting warps for pile, it would be this shaft along with shaft no. 2 that would be lifted for shed "b" of the plain weave, or alone for full rows of pile between rows of disks. Shaft nos. 1 and 3 would be lifted for shed "a" of the plain weave. Chris Verhecken-Lammens prefers the plan with four shafts, and indeed it may be more practical. In both cases, only two treadles are needed for the plain weave. The third treadle is optional for full or non-voided rows of pile if all pattern cords for pile were not used for this purpose.

15. I define *selvedge* as the point at the side edge of a fabric at which wefts turn around in their passage from left to right and right to left. A pattern may or may not continue up to the last warp, the warp at the turnaround. The term *side finish* signifies that other features were introduced. One or more warps at the edge might be thicker and/or of another fiber and make-up, outstandingly different from those of the patterned section of the fabric. There might be a stripe between the line on which the pattern ends and the weft turns around the last warp: the selvedge. The color of the warps of the stripe may be different from those of the patterned section. The stripe itself might be patterned by wefts, or striped by warps of different colors.

It must be noted that what I might describe as features of a side finish, other authors might describe as features having to do with the selvedge, as Wardwell does in the quotes taken from her work in my discussion section.

16. I am grateful for the help of two staff members of the Department of European Sculpture and Decorative Art, The Metropolitan Museum of Art: Melinda Watt provided the initial reference, and Robert Kaufman updated the information on the painting using the Uffizi's web site. I also wish to acknowledge Sharon Herson for providing a more detailed description.

17. A set of warps or wefts can be hidden in simple and compound weaves. A simple weave is defined as having one set of warps and one set of wefts. If threads of a set of warps are placed very close together, the set of wefts is hidden, as is often the case in satins. If warp threads are spaced wide apart, wefts can be made to cover the set of warps, as in the standard tapestry technique. A compound weave is defined as having more than one set of warps or wefts. For example, in techniques such as *taqueté, samit, lampas,* and *velvet,* a set of warps or wefts is more or less hidden. *Taqueté* is a term used by CIETA (Centre International d'Étude des Textiles Anciens, Lyon, France) that for about four decades centered in the twentieth century was called *weft-faced compound tabby,* or plain weave, and in the second half of the 20th century, *plain weave with complementary wefts and inner warps.* *Samit* is a term used by CIETA that was called in the same periods *weft-faced compound twill* and *twill with complementary wefts and inner warps.* In a *taqueté* and a *samit,* there are two sets of warps: the set of inner warps (the warps that are lifted to make pattern) is hidden, and the set of structure or binding warps is minimally exposed. In these techniques it is the wefts that dominate (Burnham 1980, pp. 172, 180). In a *lampas,* the wefts of the foundation weave are often not visible, and, to a lesser extent, neither is the set of warps of the supplementary weave. It is the set of warps of the foundation weave and the set of wefts of the supplementary weave that dominate. In *velvet,* the foundation weave—its warps and wefts included—is hidden by obviously dominant pile. Areas of the foundation voided of pile are not hidden, unless covered by a set of covering or facing wefts.

18. Clearly illustrated in color, this piece (1996.286) has a striped finish of the type described earlier (Metropolitan Museum 1997, p. 19). Daniel Walker, Curator of Islamic Art, The Metropolitan Museum of Art, graciously made the silk available. The foundation weave of the lampas is a 3&1 S-twill; the supplementary weave with metallic wefts is a 1&2 Z-twill; there is an interlaced connection; the warps of the foundation weave are single; the metallic wefts of the supplementary weave are used singly. One other feature is consistent with lampas I have noted to be "Eastern": the four foundation warps between warps of the twill are the warps that form warp pattern steps.

19. This raises the general issue of how the wefts of the supplementary weave of a lampas turn at the selvedges. Variations in how they turn are important in discussions by Wardwell (1988–89). Nevertheless, the specifics of how the wefts in the supplementary weaves of lampas turn, in terms of the mechanics of looms covering wide geographic and time spans, have yet to be outlined.

References

Allsen, Thomas T.
1997   *Commodity and Exchange in the Mongol Empire: A Cultural History of Islamic Textiles.* University Press, Cambridge.

Becker, John
1987   *Pattern and Loom.* Rhodos, Copenhagen.

Bellinger, Louisa
1955   *Textile Analysis: Pile Techniques in Egypt and the Near East.* Workshop Notes, Paper no. 12, December. The Textile Museum, Washington.

Burnham, Dorothy
1980   *Warp and Weft: A Textile Terminology.* Royal Ontario Museum, Toronto.

Buss, Chiara, Marina Molinelli, and others
1983   *Tessuti serici italiani 1450–1530.* Electa, Milan.

Cox, Raymond
1900   *L'art de décorer les tissus.* P. Mouillot, Paris.

Davanzo Poli, Doretta, Grazietta Butazzi, and others

1995   *I mestieri della moda a Venezia Serenissima: The Arts of Fashion in Venice from the 13th to the 18th Century.* Revised edition. The Equitable Gallery, New York.

Desrosiers, Sophie

1993   Trois representations d'un métier a la tire florentin du XVe siècle, *Bulletin de Liaison du CIETA*, no. 71, pp. 37–47. Centre International d'Etude des Textiles Anciens, Lyon.

DuBois, Emily

1983   Banares Brocade, *Ars Textrina*, vol. 1, pp. 209–27. Winnipeg

Errera, Isabelle

1927   *Catalogue d'étoffes anciennes et modernes.* Third edition. Musées Royaux du Cinquantenaire, Brussels.

Forbes, Robert James

1964   *Studies in Ancient Technology*, vol. 4. Second revised edition. E. J. Brill, Leiden.

Gasthaus, Ruth, Brigitta Schmedding, and Carl-Wolfgang Schümann

1979   *Samte, Velvets, Velours.* Girmes-Werke Aktiengesellschaft, Oedt.

Indictor, Norman, Robert J. Koestler, Sheila C. Blair, and Anne E. Wardwell

1988   The Evolution of Metal Wrappings from Medieval Textiles Using Scanning Electron Microscopy-Energy Dispersive X-Ray Spectrometry, *Textile History*, vol. 19, no. 1, pp. 3–22. Maney Publishing on behalf of Pasold Research Fund, Leeds.

Jain, Rahul

1995   The Indian Drawloom and its Products, *The Textile Museum Journal 1993–94*, vols. 32 and 33, pp. 50–84. The Textile Museum, Washington.

Kendrick, Albert F.

1921   *Catalogue of Textiles from Burying Grounds in Egypt, vol. 2, Period of Transition and of Christian Emblems.* Victoria and Albert Museum, London.

Mackie, Louise

1996   *Threads of Time, Handmade Textiles for Weddings in Fez, Morocco,* video. Royal Ontario Museum, Toronto.

May, Florence Lewis

1957   *Silk Textiles of Spain, Eighth to Fifteenth Century.* The Hispanic Society of America, New York.

Mayer-Thurman, Christa

1975   *Raiment for the Lord's Service.* The Art Institute of Chicago, Chicago.

Metropolitan Museum

1997   *Recent Acquisitions, A Selection: 1996–1997.* The Metropolitan Museum of Art, New York.

Monnas, Lisa

1986   Developments in Figured Velvet Weaving in Italy during the 14th Century, *Bulletin de Liaison du CIETA*, no. 63–64, pp. 63–100. Centre International d'Etude des Textiles Anciens, Lyon.

1993   Dress and Textiles in the St. Louis Altarpiece: New Light on Simone Martini's Working Practice, *Apollo*, March, pp. 167–74. London.

Sangiorgi, Giorgio

1920   *Contributi allo studio dell'arte tessile.* Casa Editrice d'Arte Bestetti & Tuminelli, Rome and Milan.

Sonday, Milton

1987   Pattern and Weaves: Safavid Lampas and Velvet, *Woven from the Soul, Spun from the Heart: Textile Arts of Safavid and Qajar Iran (16th–19th Centuries)*, pp. 57–83. Edited by Carol Bier. The Textile Museum, Washington.

1992   Notes on the Renaissance Silk Velvet with Phoenix and Inscription 'NORS VIVE', *Bulletin du CIETA*, no. 70, pp. 139–46. Centre International d'Etude des Textiles Anciens, Lyon.

Taylor, George

1991   Official Colours: Dyes on Chinese Textiles of the Northern Song Dynasty, *HALI*, no. 58, August, pp. 81–83. London.

Vial, Gabriel

1980   *Treize ceintures de femme marocaines du XVIe au XIXe siècle.* Foundation Abegg, Berne.

Wardwell, Anne E.

1988–89 'Panni Tartarici': Eastern Islamic Silks Woven with Gold and Silver (13th and 14th centuries), *Islamic Art III*, pp. 77–173. The Islamic Art Foundation, New York.

Watt, James, and Anne E. Wardwell

1997   *When Silk Was Gold: Central Asian and Chinese Textiles.* The Metropolitan Museum of Art, New York.

Wouters, Jan

1993   Dye Analysis of Coptic Textiles, *Coptic Textiles from Flemish Private Collections,* pp. 53–64. Edited by A. de Moor. Provinciaal Archeologisch Museum van Zuid-oost-Vlaanderen, Zottegem.

Wulff, Hans

1966   *The Traditional Crafts of Persia.* The M.I.T. Press, Cambridge and London.

Appendix

Thread Counts

It was not possible to note the technical features of the warps and wefts for all the pieces mentioned in this study. In general, warp and weft counts per centimeter vary within a narrow margin, as exemplified by textiles in Cooper-Hewitt:

	1896–1–59	1902–1–385
non-pile warps	42	45
pile warps	14	15
sheds of plain weave	17	19
pairs of gold wefts	17	19
pile rods	9	10

Thread Make-up

Lampas/velvets in this study which were examined sufficiently to determine technical features shared the following:

- Foundation warps have a firm z-twist; those for pile are paired.
- Warps of the twill have a firm z-twist and are slightly thinner than foundation warps.
- Foundation wefts have no apparent twist.
- The gold wefts, used in pairs, are made up of narrow strips of gilded animal material wound z around a silk thread with a z-twist, with the strips almost completely covering the silk thread.

Contour Edges of Disks

The diagrams that accompany each summary can be interpreted as follows. Each octagon is outlined. Top and bottom horizontal edges are highlighted, and their width is noted in terms of warp pattern steps. Horizontal lines to left and right of an octagon indicate its three sections with the number of weft pattern steps of the void indicated on the left and those of the gold disk indicated on the right. If a pattern shed for gold or a voided pile row starts the disk, it is so noted. It is understood that a voided pile row always ends the disk at the top and therefore is not noted. Disks that are mirror-imaged are identified by a solid vertical in the center of the octagon flanked by z-and s-diagonals. Those disks that are repeated in the straight manner are indicated by a z-diagonal in the center of the octagon. If a disk can be divided in half horizontally and if it might have had a fixed or hand-selected pattern, it is so noted at the left of the abstract octagon. The diagrams indicate the generally uniform height of disks of the pieces they represent with height measured in terms of weft pattern steps.

The following summaries include information that is necessary for a discussion of repeat units and repeat systems. This includes what the repeat system might have been, where axes of mechanical mirror-imaging fall, and whether or not pattern selection might have been fixed. Unfortunately, the abstract octagons do not show differences in the contour of voids and gold disks. The importance of contour in determining repeat units and repeat systems is explained in the summary of the second example, Cooper-Hewitt 1902–1–385.

Cooper-Hewitt 1896–1–59

Seven rows studied: two odd, five even. All voids and gold disks have the same number of weft pattern steps and no major differences in disks were found. A mirror-imaging system can be proposed. Axes fall on a warp pattern step. Pattern sheds might have been fixed. If disks can be divided in half horizontally, the fixed pattern sheds could have been used in reverse order with some flexibility: the lower and upper thirds are not exactly the same, no doubt to make sure that the top edge of the disk is a voided row and that the resulting gap is covered by the over-hanging pile of the next non-voided row or first full row of pile of the narrow horizontal band between rows of disks (fig. 19).

Cooper-Hewitt 1902–1–385 (fig. 1)

Six rows studied: three odd, three even. All the voids and gold disks have the same number of weft pattern steps as indicated in the accompanying diagram. Contours of voids and disks are the same in two odd and three even rows—the basic disk shown in figure 21. Disks in two odd rows are different. In one, the upper third of the void is different (fig. 22). In another, the top of the void is yet again different (fig. 23), and the top third of the gold disk is different (fig. 24). A mirror-imaging system can be proposed. Axes fall between warp pattern steps. Pattern sheds were probably selected freehand.

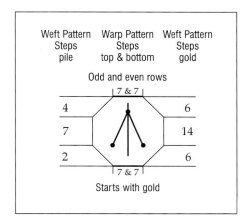

Cooper-Hewitt 1896–1–59

Mirror imaged
Axes on a warp pattern step
Horizontal center line?
Fixed pattern tie-up?

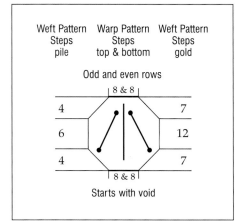

Cooper-Hewitt 1902-1-385

Mirror imaged
Axes between warp pattern steps
No horizontal center line
Free-hand pattern selection

Cleveland Museum of Art 1918.30a

Seven rows were studied: four odd, three even. Disks in all rows alternate "a"/"b". Three odd rows are different and the fourth appears to be a duplicate of another but lacks one pile and two gold pattern sheds. Two even rows appear to be the same and one is different. A straight repeat can be proposed. In even rows the lower and upper horizontals are off-center but the 20 warp-pattern-step wide middle section is centered. Despite the variation from disk to disk in the number of weft pattern steps in three sections of the disk, the total number is fairly uniform. This is a good example of the minor differences one can expect in a straight repeat. The pattern was undoubtedly selected freehand.

Cleveland Museum of Art 1918.30a

Straight repeat
No horizontal center line
Free-hand pattern

Weft Pattern Steps pile	Warp Pattern Steps top & bottom	Weft Pattern Steps gold		Weft Pattern Steps pile	Warp Pattern Steps top & bottom	Weft Pattern Steps gold

An odd row, disks "a"

|12 & 12|
2/3 — 4
4 — 8
2 — 8
|12 & 12|

Starts with gold
No vertical center line

An odd row, disks "b"

|12 & 12|
3 — 4
4 — 8
2 — 8
|12 & 12|

Starts with gold
No vertical center line

An odd row, disks "a"

|12 & 12|
2 — 5
4 — 9
3 — 6
|12 & 12|

Starts with gold
No vertical center line

An odd row, disk "b"

|12 & 12|
2 — 5
4 — 9
3 — 6
|12 & 12|

Starts with gold
No vertical center line

An odd row, disks "a"

|12 & 12|
2 — 4
4 — 10
3 — 6
|12 & 12|

Starts with gold
No vertical center line

An odd row, disk "b"

|12 & 12|
2 — 4
4 — 10
3 — 6
|12 & 12|

Starts with gold
No vertical center line

An odd row, disks "a" and "b"

|12 & 12|
2 — 5
3 — 7
3 — 6
|12 & 12|

Starts with gold
Vertical center line

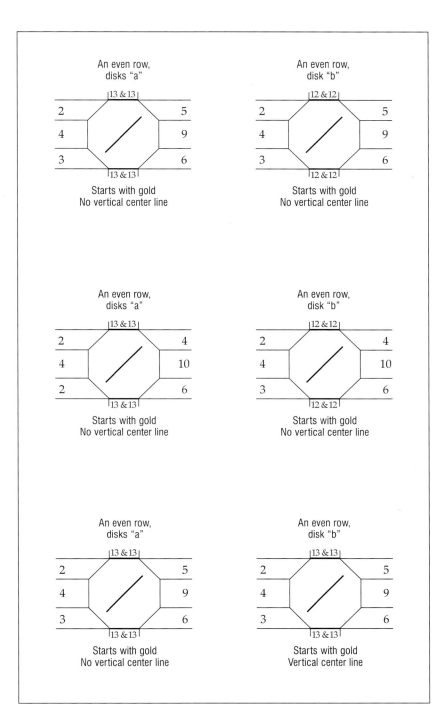

An even row,
disks "a"

|13 & 13|

2   5

4   9

3   6

|13 & 13|

Starts with gold
No vertical center line

An even row,
disk "b"

|12 & 12|

2   5

4   9

3   6

|12 & 12|

Starts with gold
No vertical center line

An even row,
disks "a"

|13 & 13|

2   4

4   10

2   6

|13 & 13|

Starts with gold
No vertical center line

An even row,
disk "b"

|12 & 12|

2   4

4   10

3   6

|12 & 12|

Starts with gold
No vertical center line

An even row,
disks "a"

|13 & 13|

2   5

4   9

3   6

|13 & 13|

Starts with gold
No vertical center line

An even row,
disk "b"

|13 & 13|

2   5

4   9

3   6

|13 & 13|

Starts with gold
Vertical center line